WITHDRAWN
UTSA Libraries

**Models
of Urban
Structure**

Models of Urban Structure

Edited by
David C. Sweet
Ohio Department
of Development

Lexington Books
D.C. Heath and Company
Lexington, Massachusetts
Toronto   London

Copyright © 1972 by D.C. Heath and Company.

All rights reserved. No part of this publication may be reproduced or transmitted in any form or by any means, electronic or mechanical, including photocopy, recording, or any information storage or retrieval system, without permission in writing from the publisher.

Published simultaneously in Canada.

Printed in the United States of America.

International Standard Book Number: 0-669-61366-5

Library of Congress Catalog Card Number: 79-139081

Table of Contents

List of Figures	vii
List of Tables	ix
Introduction	xi

Part I.   Application of Urban-Structure Models — 1

Chapter 1. Models of Urban Land-Use Development — 3
  Leslie J. King — Department of Geography, McMaster University

Chapter 2. The Role of Urban Development Models in Metropolitan Plan Making — 27
  David E. Boyce — Department of Regional Science University of Pennsylvania

Chapter 3. A Model for the Distribution of Residential Activity in Urban Areas — 37
  John Herbert — PADCO, Washington, D.C.
  Benjamin Stevens — Department of Regional Science University of Pennsylvania

Chapter 4. A Land Use Plan Design Model — 53
  Kenneth J. Schlager — Consultant to Southeastern Wisconsin Regional Planning Commission

Chapter 5. Techniques for Relating Transportation Improvements and Urban Development Patterns — 69
  Dan Brand — Department of Planning, Harvard University
  Brian Barber — Amerkan Yugoslav Project
  Michael Jacobs — Peat, Marwick, Livingston and Company

Chapter 6. Application of a Land Use Allocation Model for Franklin County, Ohio — 91
  William C. Habig — Midohio Regional Planning Commission

Part II.   New Concepts in Urban-Structure Models — 107

Chapter 7. Decision Agent Models: An Alternative Modeling Approach for Urban Residential Growth — 109
  Edward J. Kaiser — Department of City and Regional Planning, University of North Carolina

Chapter 8. On the Derivation of Spatial Equilibrium Urban Land
Value Functions 123
Emilio Casetti – Department of Geography,
Ohio State University

Chapter 9. Analytical Convergence in Ecological Research:
Factorial Analysis, Gradient, and Sector Models 135
Kent P. Schwirian – Department of Sociology,
Ohio State University

Chapter 10. The Neighborhood Effect in Urban Voting
Response Surfaces 159
Kevin R. Cox – Department of Geography,
Ohio State University

Chapter 11. The Effect of Metropolitan Political Fragmentation
on Central City Budgets 177
John C. Weicher – Department of Economics,
Ohio State University

Chapter 12. Computer Mapping of Urban Structure 205
Harold L. Goldstein – Department of Civil Engineering
Northwestern University

Appendix A
Models of Urban Structure – Annotated Bibliography 227

Appendix B
**Computer Utilization and Model Development in Urban
Planning Program – Survey Results** 243

List of Figures

1-1	Land-Use Modeling Process	5
1-2	Spectrum of Systems Analysis	6
4-1	Land-Use, Transportation Study Planning System Diagram	55
5-1	The Eastern Massachusetts Region	73
5-2	Southeastern Massachusetts Planning Region	74
6-1	The Model's Place Within RPC's Planning Function	92
6-2	General Structure of the Model	94
7-1	The Residential Land Conversion Process	111
7-2	Linking Together Several Decision Agent Models	113
7-3	Elements in The Developer's Residential Subdivision Location Decision	114
7-4	Illustration of Use of Graphic Processing System	120
10-1	Transition Probability Matrix for Party Preference	167
10-2	Transition Probability Matrix for Party Preference 1960-64 in the Columbus Metropolitan Area	169
10-3	RESIDUALS $Dev.i_{t_2} - Dev.i_{t_2}$	170
10-4	Transition Probability Matrices by Race	171
10-5	Scatter Diagram and Regression Line Predicted on Basis of Citywide Transition Probabilities, City of Paris	172
10-6	Scatter Diagram and Regression Line Predicted on the Basis of Citywide Transition Probabilities, City of Columbus	173
10-7	Transition Probability Matrices for Columbus and Paris Based on Survey of Ecological Regression Estimates	173
12-1	Map Generated Using SYMAP (Contour Option)	212
12-2	Map Generated Using SYMAP (Conformant Option)	213
12-3	Map Generated Using SYMAP	214
12-4	Map Generated by Special Polk Program	215
12-5	Map Generated Using Map 01	216
12-6	Map Generated Using Map 01	217
12-7	Map Generated on a Calcomp Plotter	218
12-8	Plot Generated on a Benson-Lehner Electroplotter	219
21-9	Map Generated on a Stromberg Carlson SC-4020 CRT	220
12-10	Map Generated on a Geo Space Plotter, First Type	221
12-11	Map Generated on a Geo Space Plotter, Second Type	222

List of Tables

2-1	Comparison of Change in Population in Boston From 1963 to 1990 With the Extreme Differences Among the 1990 Alternatives	31
2-2	Comparison of Change in Population in Baltimore From 1965 to 1985 With the Extreme Differences Among the 1985 Alternatives	32
5-1	Statistical Summaries Observed vs. Calculated Population and Employment Levels	77
5-2	Future Regional Control Totals	83
6-1	Available Data Files	96
6-2	Additional Data Files Developed by RPC	96
6-3	Additional Data Files Developed by CONSAD	97
6-4	Dependent Variable: Net Change in Income Group 1	98
6-5	Dependent Variable: Net Change in Income Group 2	99
6-6	Dependent Variable: Net Change in Income Group 3	100
6-7	Dependent Variable: Net Change in Income Group 4	100
6-8	Dependent Variable: Net Change in Income Group 5	101
6-9	Dependent Variable: Net Change in Income Group 6	101
6-10	Dependent Variable: Net Change in Income Group 7	102
6-11	Dependent Variable: Net Change in Total Dwelling Units	102
6-12	Dependent Variable: Net Change in Industrial (Manufacturing and Nonmanufacturing) Employment	103
6-13	Dependent Variable: Net Change in Commercial Employment	103
6-14	Dependent Variable: Net Change in Local Public Employment	104
6-15	Dependent Variable: Net Change in Total Employment	104
7-1	Comparison of Percentage of Sample Cells Classified Correctly by Discriminant Analysis as Opposed to the Operational Discriminant Model	117
9-1	Results of the Factor Analyses of the 11 Principal Canadian Cities	146-148
9-2	Percent of the Total Sum of Squares of Social Area Variables Explained by Sectors and by Distance for 11 Canadian Cities	151
9-3	Results of Factor Analysis of Puerto Rican Cities Data	154
11-1	Regression Analysis of Selected Municipal Expenditure Categories	192
B-1	Population Served by Responding Agencies	244
B-2	Data Collected by Planning Agencies	245

Introduction

Models of Urban Structure is a collection of papers which discusses various aspects of urban structure. Much of the modeling work that has been completed on urban structure has focused on land use development. However, urban structure can be examined from other perspectives, such as fiscal structure or political structure or social organization. In an attempt to explore these aspects, as viewed by various disciplines, a conference sponsored jointly by Battelle Memorial Institute-Columbus Laboratories and The Ohio State University - College of Social and Behavioral Sciences was held. A small group of social scientists and planners were invited to present and discuss papers with the theme, "Models of Urban Structure." One objective was to develop an appreciation among the various social science disciplines of the perspective of the geographer, economist, sociologist, political scientist, psychologist, planner, and regional scientist as they viewed the processes which lead to the development of the structure of an urban area.

One problem associated with multi-disciplinary efforts of this type is developing a common vocabulary by which to communicate with representatives of the other disciplines. Another problem is to develop the communication links between the practitioner and the researcher. The results of the conference indicated that this type of understanding and communication is possible; however, it requires considerable discussion on the part of all participants to achieve any kind of meaningful dialogue.

Models of Urban Structure includes most of the papers presented at the conference; however the papers were rewritten to incorporate comments made during the discussions. Also, several additional papers have been reprinted to provide a better perspective of the state-of-the-art in modeling of urban structure. Part I contains a set of papers which review this state-of-the-art as well as specifically discusses models which have been utilized in urban planning programs.

Part II discusses new frontiers in developing models of urban structure. This includes improved efforts in land development models, as well as other concepts which have not yet been introduced into urban planning programs. Two appendixes are included in this volume. The first is an annotated bibliography on urban models, and the second is a discussion of the results of a survey on model usage by urban planning agencies.

Part I
Application
of Urban Structure
Models

The papers contained in Part I discuss urban model development and application. Urban structure is primarily analyzed in terms of land-use patterns and activity patterns. King provides an overview of models which have been reported in the literature and by various planning agencies. His paper is supplemented in Appendix A with an annotated bibliography. Boyce discusses model usage in major urban planning programs. His analysis is supplemented by a survey of model usage in urban planning agencies reported in Appendix B. The remaining four papers discuss specific models developed for various planning programs. The Herbert-Stevens model was utilized in the Penn-Jersey study. The model discussed by Schlager was developed for the Southeast Wisconsin Planning Program; the EMPIRIC model described by Brand, Barber and Jacobs was for the Boston region; and the Habig paper discusses a model utilized in planning for Central Ohio.

1 Models of Urban Land-Use Development

Leslie J. King

This paper reviews the general problem of constructing models for the forecasting of urban land-use development. In particular, the different analytical approaches adopted in constructing such models are discussed and the extent to which computer facilities were utilized is noted. This general review brings into focus several of the basic issues involved in modeling complex urban systems and prompts some questions as to the overall utility of social planning and engineering.

Particular emphasis is placed on those land-use studies and models that are essentially positive in their approach — that is, those that deal mainly with explanations of what has happened in urban land-use patterns and with the prediction of future developments consistent with these explanations or understandings. But some more challenging and provocative normative analyses — that is, studies of what land-use patterns should or could be consistent with certain objectives, constraints, and standards — have been proposed, for example, in the work on land-use design being pursued by the Southeastern Wisconsin Regional Planning Commission. (Southeastern Wisconsin Regional Planning Commission, 1968). Much of this work is still only in the development phase, but again, it prompts an interesting set of questions concerning the philosophy and strategy of social planning. Some of these questions, for example, concerning the nature of the objective functions to be optimized and the value system implied, will be considered at a later point in this paper.

Land-Use Forecasting

The past efforts at forecasting urban land-use development appear to have been prompted by at least two major considerations:

(1) It has been established analytically in some contexts (for example, trip-generation studies and financial analyses) and suspected for many others (for example, the overall level of social welfare in the city) that the pattern and nature of land uses are significant predictor variables.

(2) The recognition that land-use patterns in any urban area are influenced, in turn, by many complex and interacting forces that are dynamic both over

time and space. Within the city, for example, particular areas are specialized in certain land-use activities, but these functions may change over time as competing land uses wax and wane in their fortunes.

Given these considerations, it is perhaps not surprising to find that most of the major urban land-use studies have been set within the context of transportation planning programs. It is really only in these types of programs that serious consideration has been given in the past to systems analysis of the urban complex. This emphasis upon land-use and transportation systems will undoubtedly continue, but it is also possible that land-use forecasting will assume additional future importance in the context of planning and shaping the form of the city (the relevance to zoning controls is obvious) and in predicting future requirement levels for municipal and other services.

The "typical" approach in land-use modeling is to assume first that certain factors or values are given (these are the so-called exogenous factors in some of the models); the model then generates certain levels of employment, and/or economic activity, and/or population by use of mathematical functions or statistical estimators. These derived levels are then allocated spatially to different areas of the city, again by the use of particular allocation functions; and finally, the future land uses in each area are derived by the use of land-requirement functions for the different allocated variables.

In very crude form then, the problem involves the three components shown in Figure 1-1. There are the data inputs which involve the exogenously determined values and the data to be used in estimating the different parameters of the model. (This latter phase is often referred to as the calibration of the model.) Then there is the model which performs the generation and allocation of the variables of interest. As discussed later, this model may be of many different forms, perhaps a set of rules and procedures for a game simulation on the one hand, or a set of complex mathematical functions on the other. Finally, there are the outputs which are the predicted levels of development for each land-use activity and each subregion of the city.

Obviously, the above comments grossly oversimplify both the modelling process and the nature of the land-use development models. The published literature, in fact, provides ample evidence of different ways of viewing these components. Britton Harris (1968), for example, on the basis of extensive experience in this field of research, emphasizes the following six major dimensions of land-use modelling:

(1) *descriptive* or empirically based statements versus *analytic* or deductive formulations;
(2) *holistic* approaches which attempt to deal with the total urban environment versus *partial* analyses focusing on certain selected aspects of the urban complex;

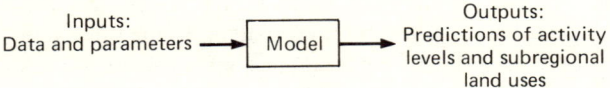

Figure 1-1. Land-Use Modeling Process.

(3) *macro* or aggregative models versus *micro* and behavioral models;
(4) *static* versus *dynamic* formulations;
(5) *deterministic* models which do not allow for chance elements in the land-use process, versus *probabilistic* models which attempt to deal with such elements; and
(6) *simultaneous* versus *sequential* solutions.

Harris presents an excellent review of the different models of commercial, residential, and industrial land uses within the framework of his discussion of the dimensions of modeling.

Kilbridge, et al. (1969) have also recently examined the dimensions of urban planning models. Their review is more general than that of Harris, and they stress (1) the *subject* of the model, (2) its *function*, (3) the *theory* on which the model is based, and (4) the *method* by which the model uses the theory.

Again, Wilson (1968), in discussing models of urban planning, constructs a "hierarchical relevance tree" setting out the tasks of such models and their interrelationships. He recognizes three broad levels of policy, design, and understanding. Within these categories, the following eight tasks are identified:

Policy:	(1) Action, (2) Goals, (3) Evaluation
Design:	(4) Plan formulation, (5) Design techniques, (6) Problem formulation
Understanding:	(7) System models, (8) Techniques.

Lowry (1968), in discussing seven of the more highly developed land-use models, deals with a broader theoretical question, namely, the extent to which the different models relate to a generally accepted theory of the market mechanism for urban land. Lowry's contention is that "the market processes of transactions between willing buyers and willing sellers determine the spatial organization of urban activities." He defines an investment function by means of which owners appraise the merits of site improvements, and an evaluation function relating to the price a particular establishment will be willing to pay for a certain site.

Lowry's subsequent review of the seven models considers the extent to which these functions are treated — either implicitly or explicitly — in the models. Lee (1969) outlines an excellent discussion of the conceptual frameworks, the techniques, the model constructions, and the particular applications which have characterized urban land-use analyses to date. In the same vein, Lamb (1967) has reviewed some 10 different land use models with emphasis upon the analytical frameworks employed in them.

The reviews by the authors mentioned above are illuminating and provocative. But, with the exception of the ones by Lee and Lamb, they deal essentially with broader issues than those concerning this paper. The concern here is mainly with the methods and forms of land-use modeling, with some related features of computer utilization, and with selected problems associated with these approaches.

The discussion in this paper is strongly influenced by the comments of Geisler, et al. (1962) on the continuum of systems-analysis techniques. They note that increasing abstraction in analysis involves moving from left to right along the scale shown in Figure 1-2.

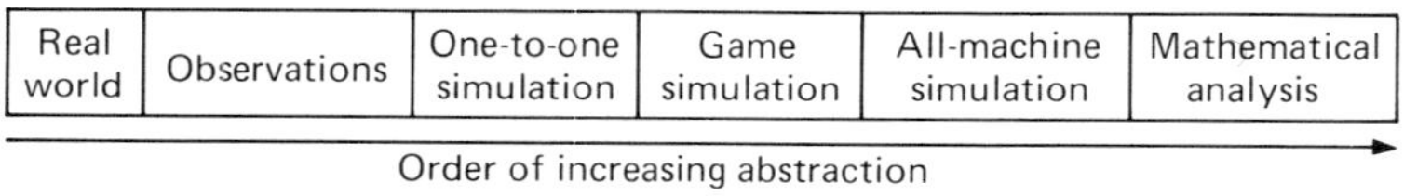

Real world	Observations	One-to-one simulation	Game simulation	All-machine simulation	Mathematical analysis

Order of increasing abstraction →

Figure 1-2. Spectrum of systems analysis.

Most of these levels are apparent in the literature of urban land-use studies. At the lower level, there have been numerous qualitative statements based wholly on empirical observations. For example, the idealized statements of city form known as the concentric zone theory (Burgess, 1925), the sector or wedge hypothesis (Hoyt, 1939), and the multiple nuclei theory (Harris, 1945) are all empirically based and together represent fairly low levels of abstraction.

In Figure 1-2 there are three levels involving some form of *simulation,* and some different applications of these analyses to urban land-use studies are reviewed in the following section. So-called "simulation studies" include a variety of different approaches and levels of abstraction. At one extreme are "hand simulations" such as those performed by the Northeastern Illinois Planning Commission (1968). In that study, the patterns of Chicago's urban growth from 1965 to 1990 were forecast using five different models — the "dispersed regional city design," the "finger design," the "multi-cluster design," the "satellite cities-greenbelt design," and the "current trends development design." Each model was considered in turn and its implications were noted and evaluated by the researchers. The models were essentially qualitative statements of urban form, and no computer systems analysis was involved. By contrast, the simulation model developed by Crecine (1964) is far toward the other end of the systems-analysis continuum. In this study, "simulation" implies a particular approach using the computer to obtain the solution for a set of mathematical equations.

In this paper, hand simulations are ignored in regard to their content, and only those simulations involving the use of computers, in one way or another, are reviewed.

One-to-one simulations (the second level of abstraction in Figure 1-2) do not appear very relevant in urban land-use studies. In such simulations, reality is replicated, but at a different scale. The Link trainer used in flight training, or the wind tunnel testing of models, are essentially one-to-one simulations. Obviously, analogous models of the city would be prohibitive in cost even if they were useful in research and training, which is most doubtful. Urban situations are typically competitive ones, often involving conflict and stress, and reflecting a complex range of decisions made by both the private and public sectors. Hence, game simulations appear more appropriate, and three attempts at developing such simulations are reviewed in the following section.

Game simulations involve inputs from teams of players who act out certain decision-making roles within the constraints of a set of rules. By contrast, all-machine simulations involve samplings from probability functions, and the sampled values are the inputs to the models. Some of these probabilistic approaches to land-use modeling are also reviewed in the next section.

At the highest level of abstraction are the mathematical models for which the solutions are derived analytically. In land-use modeling there have been different forms of mathematical models employed. Some have involved sets of simultaneous linear equations, other linear programming formulations, and still others, nonlinear differential equations and recursive programming. These efforts are also considered in the following section.

The importance of computer facilities varies from level to level. In game simulations, a computer typically serves as the central banker or information bank and monitors the operation of the game. In the City I game (Washington Center for Metropolitan Studies, 1968), for example, an IBM 1130 is involved. The development of software for these game simulations is costly; therefore, there are high computer expenses involved in the running of the game. All-machine simulations depend even more heavily upon computer facilities, and in the case of models such as that developed at the University of North Carolina, there is considerable expense involved in both program adaptation and machine runs.

The mathematical analyses, on the other hand, involve computers in a less intimate manner than do the simulation models. Problems of statistical estimation of parameters and solution of equations are easily programmed for the computer, and the time and costs involved usually are not as great as with the simulation studies. These comparisons are noted in more detail in the following review of specific models.

Models of Urban Land-Use Development

The major structural features of different land-use models are briefly reviewed below within the framework suggested by Figure 1-2

Game Simulations

By definition, a simulation is an attempt to replicate or to create a likeness of reality. But, since the effort is directed toward an understanding of the real-world system in question, there is always some simplification of reality involved. Orcutt (1963, p. 22) has noted that "simulation of a social system involves building and operating a model designed to represent those features of the system which are deemed to be significant in view of the objectives behind the simulation."

With regard to game simulations in particular, Geisler, et al. (1962) note that their purpose is "the study of decision rules in the context of a given organization and environment." From the point of view of urban land-use modeling, this means an emphasis on the decision-making processes which determine the city's land-use pattern. The complexity of designing such game simulations for urban problems is obvious; for one thing, urban land-use patterns are in part determined by public sector decisions (for example, in highway planning, education, municipal services, and zoning) and also by private sector decisions (for example, in the location and development of businesses and residences and in travel patterns). Further, the intersectoral relationships — for example, between the public and private sectors, between employers and workers, and between productive activities — are exceedingly complex and hence difficult to untangle and to allow for in the game simulation. Notwithstanding the conceptual problems, the design problems, and the high development and operating costs of game simulations, some notable progress has been made along these lines by at least three groups. These are discussed below. Kibel (1970) has provided a much more detailed and informative review of the topic of urban gaming.

Cornell Land Use Game (CLUG). The efforts at game simulation by the Cornell planning department have been directed by Dr. Alan G. Feldt (1965). Essentially, the model allows for the development of an urban community, beginning with an open area in which the land is owned only by the game operator. The players begin with small amounts of capital, and they may use this to bid for land and to develop the properties they purchase. The model allows for residential, commercial, and industrial development, some simple input-output relations concerning payments and purchases among these sectors, and for property assessments to pay for the cost of municipal services. A number of variations on the basic game are possible (Feldt, 1966).

LAND-USE DEVELOPMENT

Feldt (1965) notes several significant points with respect to this game simulation:

(1) It is "fundamentally a communications device, intended for an educational milieu — whether that be in a formal classroom or in actual planning practice." The CLUG model is already widely known in both educational and professional circles in this country.
(2) The game generally allows for the development of a city of approximately 250,000 population over 25 or so rounds. This takes about 15 to 20 hours, including instruction time. But, beyond this, the operation of the game becomes too awkward in terms of the amount of information to be processed. As reported to date, this game simulation has not made much use of computers; the CITY I game reported on below is in many respects a computerized version of CLUG.
(3) An attempt to modify the model to fit a real-world situation, specifically Syracuse, New York, revealed among other things that "the scale utilized in the elementary version of CLUG was too gross to allow for detailed handling of patterns of intraurban land-use development." For example, the basic residential unit in the early model consisted of 1000 employed persons and around 4000 total population.

No recent literature on this model seems available; presumably, work on the project is continuing.

METRO Urban Game Simulation. This game simulation is directed by Dr. Richard Duke and has been developed with support from Michigan State University, the University of Michigan, and the Tri-County Regional Planning Commission (Duke, 1964). The game simulation is a fairly complex one and is based on some earlier efforts in this field by the same group. Their *METROPOLIS I* was a hand simulation which was subsequently programmed for a computer as *METROPOLIS II*. All three models are tailored to the particulars of the urban community of Lansing, Mich., and data for this city are used to provide many of the parameter estimates.

Some brief comments are made here on three features of the game simulation, namely the player roles, the types of decisions which have to be made, and the specific simulation models which are involved.

The players each have two roles: one as a member of a government team (either central city or suburb or urbanizing township), and the other as a member of a professional association team (politicians, planners, land developers, and educators).

Decisions have to be made by each team concerning budgets, issues, and policies. These decisions are important inputs to the simulation models of voter response, macroeconomic and demographic growth, and population and economic-firm redistribution.

The game simulation, then, involves sequences of activities and interactions both between the players themselves and between the players and the computer.

Duke (1966) stresses that the aims of the METRO project are to:

(1) simulate growth patterns that would occur naturally, and enable their comparison with planned growth patterns;
(2) illustrate the kinds of information which are available to decision makers;
(3) similarly inform decision makers about the analytical techniques and models that are available for evaluating and implementing decisions; and
(4) to provide information on the implications for urban development of alternative action programs.

Environmentrics. The original CITY I model developed by this group under the direction of Dr. Peter House (Washington Center for Metropolitan Studies, 1968) was a computerized version which incorporated elements of both the CLUG and METROPOLIS models. The game simulation was programmed for an IBM 1130 computer. Typically, it involved nine teams of four to five players each, and there were two main groups in the game — the public and the private sectors. The former controlled by a "bureaucracy" comprising an elected mayor and two councillors, and the department of zoning, highways, education, public works and safety, and finance. Eight of the teams were thereby represented on this bureaucracy, while the ninth remaining team functioned as the "mass media." The other players on the eight teams and the "mass media" team functioned as the private sector.

The public sector had to work out a budget and plan for different public-sector activities — for example, providing fire and police services and building highways and schools. In addition, they acted on requests from the private sector — concerning zoning changes, etc.

The private sector could purchase and develop properties as they chose. A number of industrial, commercial, and residential developments were possible, and each of these involved certain development costs, service and transportation costs, taxes, and income. A set of intersectoral relations were specified in the model.

As in the METRO project, the computer provided projections of population and employment levels, and subregional allocations of these variables.

There were a number of more subtle possibilities in the model, including provisions for borrowing money from the central computer, for renovating or even demolishing properties, and for variations in pricing policies associated with service establishments.

The successor to the City I game, developed by House and his colleagues, is the City II model, which incorporates further refinements. A regional model has also been developed.

LAND-USE DEVELOPMENT   11

These game simulations are not strictly land-use forecasting techniques. By their very nature, they do not involve a set of mathematical solutions and depending to some extent upon the inclinations of the players, they may or may not emphasize questions concerning the land-use pattern of the city. They are all nonzero-sum games, which means that the gains by any one team do not have to be balanced by the losses of another, and certainly in the case of CITY I game, it is possible for the players to emphasize the role-playing activities without any realistic concern for the spatial patterning of the urban complex. But, the pedagogical values of these game simulations for policy-makers, planners, and educators cannot be stressed enough. They give a player a "feel" for the complexity of relationships and decision-making processes which dictate the land-use pattern of the city. Also, it would seem quite possible to use these game simulations under fairly well-controlled rules to consider the implications of certain alternative policies and programs. Duke (1966) has noted this possibility with regard to the METRO project.

Machine Simulations

Simulations which focus on what are assumed to be random or chance elements in the determination of urban land-use patterns are considered here. These models involve variables whose behaviors are best described by probability distributions. Random samplings are made by the computer to simulate these probability distributions, and the solutions to the models are inferred from the behavior of these random numbers. It is because these models involve the use of randomly chosen numbers that they have been called "Monte Carlo" methods.

There are three qualifications which should be made at this point. The first is a technical one and need not concern us further. It is that Monte Carlo methods are much more general and powerful than their application in simulating probabilistic processes (which is the role described here) might suggest. Hammersley and Handscomb (1964) make this point very clear. Second, in urban land-use modeling, a number of other machine simulations have been proposed that are not properly classified as Monte Carlo models. In fact, B. Harris (1961) has noted four conditions, any one or combinations of which might justify the use of simulation techniques:

(1) a mathematical solution is impossible because too many variables are involved;
(2) the relationships between variables may not be simple linear ones;
(3) the model is dynamic and the important lags are long ones; and
(4) the processes involved are stochastic (probabilistic).

There are studies by Crecine (1964), Ellis (1967), Schlager (1964), the Arthur D. Little Company (1966), Forrester (1969), and the Center for Real

Estate and Urban Economics (Berkeley) (1968) that all use machine simulation techniques, especially in solving sets of difference equations to obtain land-use and related forecasts. Some of these models are described in the section below on mathematical analyses.

The third qualification is that Monte Carlo models represent an essentially low-level approach to the study of probabilistic systems, and again there are other land-use studies, notably by Curtis Harris (1968) and the Arthur D. Little Company (1966), that develop more formal stochastic models of land-use processes. These also will be mentioned later.

In the context of systems analysis of urban land-use, Monte Carlo models are associated especially with the University of North Carolina planning group (Donnelly, et al., 1964). Their model simulates the conversion of open space into residential land use. A map of the study area is divided into a large number of square grid cells, and for each cell available for development an "attractiveness measure" is computed. A given number of new residential units have to be located in each prediction period, and these are assigned to the different cells by the use of random numbers and probability functions which reflect the distribution of attractiveness measures.

This North Carolina model is highly aggregative (emphasizing development), and it is restricted to only residential land use. Carlson (1968) has reviewed the operational aspects of the model and reported on the results of a questionnaire survey of 175 planning agencies in the United States concerning its use. Problems loomed large concerning a lack of staff programmers capable of adapting the model and the inability or unwillingness to collect the data required in computing the attractiveness measures. Carlson, however, is optimistic as to the utility of the model, and he provides some useful guidelines for its adaptation.

A Monte Carlo approach to predicting future land-use changes, which is similar in its design to the North Carolina work, has been used by Morrill in studying the expansion of the residential urban fringe (Morrill, 1965) and the negro ghetto (Morrill, 1965).

Mathematical Analyses

Models employing sets of mathematical equations that are solved to yield forecasts of economic activity and land-use requirements for different subregions of the city are considered below. The types of mathematical equations vary from model to model, and the methods of obtaining solutions to these equations may involve mathematical analysis or some form of simulation.

The classical approach to mathematical prediction, at least in the physical sciences, has been to structure a set of differential equations. Such equations express the rate of change in particular variables as functions of the changes in other variables, and they can be solved to yield values for the system variables for any points in time in the future (or in the past). In the social sciences, differential equations have been used in studying phenomena such as population growth and changes in different economic variables, and it is perhaps not surprising that attempts have been made to structure differential equations for the prediction of urban land-use levels.

The best documented attempt along these lines was the work done on the POLIMETRIC model in Boston. This model, which has since been discarded by the Boston group, has been described by Irwin and Brand (1965):

"Basically, it is comprised of a series of nonlinear differential equations of the following form:

$$\frac{d R_i \ell}{dt} = f\left[R_i \ell \left(\sum_{p}^{L} M_{p\ell} \sum_{p=1}^{L} M_{\ell p}^i\right)\right],$$

where

i = number of the located variable (i = 1, 2, ..., i, ..., N)
ℓ = number of the subregion (ℓ = 1, 2, ... ℓ, p, ..., L).

Stated in words, the rate of change over time t of activity i in subregion ℓ is a function of the present level of the activity in subregion ℓ, $(R_{i\ell})$, plus a function of all movements of the activity i from all other subregions p into subregions ℓ,

$$\left(\sum_{p=1}^{L} M_{\ell p}^i\right),$$

minus all movements of that activity i from the subregion ℓ out to all other subregions

$$\left(\sum_{p=1}^{L} M_{p\ell}^i\right).$$

These in- and out-movements are called in-migrations and out-migrations."

This model appears to have been discarded largely because of problems inherent in the data requirements (Irwin and Brand, 1965). The matrix of in- and out-migrations which is suggested by the model presumably would involve extremely difficult estimation problems. The model subsequently was modified by the Delaware Valley Planning Commission (Seidman, 1969) as the basis of their residential and manufacturing location submodels, but in these versions, the differential-equation form was not retained.

Aside from its use of differential equations to predict changes over time, the POLIMETRIC model was somewhat distinctive in its attempts to handle nonlinear relationships. By contrast, most of the other well-known land-use models deal with linear relationships, often in the form of multiple-regression equations. The EMPIRIC model developed for the Boston area illustrates this point. This model distinguishes between certain output or *located variables* (specifically, white-collar and blue-collar population, retail and wholesale employment, manufacturing employment, all other employment, total resident population, total employment) that are to be predicted for each subregion in the city and the predictor or *locator variables* (namely, intensities of land use, automobile and transit accessibilities, quality of water and sewage-disposal systems). The model is based on the notion that "the change in the subregional share of located variable i in subregion ℓ is proportional to (1) the change in the subregional share of all other located variables in subregion ℓ, (2) the change in the subregional share of a number of locator variables in subregion ℓ, and (3) the absolute value of the subregional shares of other locator variables." (Irwin and Brand, 1965)

In equation form, the model is

$$\Delta R_i = \sum_{\substack{j=i \\ j \neq i}}^{M} a_{ij} \Delta R_j + \sum_{k=1}^{M} b_{ik} (Z_k \text{ or } \Delta Z_k) ,$$

where

ΔR = change in located variable $(i, j = 1, 2, \ldots, N)$
Zk = value of kth locator variable at start of forecast period
ΔZ = change in locator variable

and a_{ij} and b_{ik} are coefficients estimated from data for 1950 and 1960.

There is one such equation for each located variable and "the equations are used to estimate future subregional shares of each located variable by substituting into each equation the pertinent values of the locator variables for the subregion and solving the equations simultaneously for the subregional located variables." (Hill, Brand, and Hanson, 1965). These shares are then converted into absolute levels through multiplication by the exogenously determined control levels for each of the located variables.

The EMPIRIC model is operational and is currently used for projection and analysis in Boston; it will likely be applied further in other cities.

Another well-documented model involving sets of equations is the one developed by Lowry (1964). This model uses an iterative procedure to forecast the spatial distribution of population and employment in a city given an exogenously determined level of basic employment, that is, employment in "export" industries which "are relatively unconstrained in local site selection by problems of access to local markets."

The Lowry model consists of nine structural equations which generate retail employment and number of households in the city, allocate these totals among the subregions of the city by use of functions in which accessibility indices appear, and compute the amount of land required for retail establishments in each subregion.

The Lowry model was developed originally for Pittsburgh, and subsequently it appears to have been adapted to the needs of other groups, particularly the Bay Area Simulation Study. (Center for Real Estate and Urban Economics, 1968.) Garin and Rogers (1966) have discussed possible alternative formulations of the model in matrix algebra terms, while Crecine (1964) has developed a time-oriented version of the model. Crecine's work apparently was prompted by dissatisfaction with three of the characteristics of the Lowry model. First, the original model is a static-equilibrium one and assumes that, in any particular forecast period, all retail establishments and households can move. Second, the households in the model are not differentiated by type, and finally, the model relates to a "region" rather than to the particular boundaries of a city. In Crecine's TOMM model, therefore, only a portion of the establishments and households can move in any time period, households are differentiated by income, housing, and social characteristics, and city census tracts are used as the areal units for forecasting. Many of the equations in the model now become difference equations relating the levels at one time period to those of the previous time periods.

There are other models involving sets of equations which might be cited. The Activities Allocation model developed by the Delaware Valley Regional Planning Commission (Seidman, 1964), for example, actually involves a set of seven submodels which are run sequentially for five-year recursion periods for the nine-county Philadelphia region.

In all of the above models, whether they are linear or nonlinear in form and whether they are solved iteratively to arrive at an equilibrium situation or recursively to project the amount of change occurring in the future, there is no explicit consideration of an overall objective function and related constraints and the types of normative solutions which these features would suggest. There have been attempts, however, to structure normative models of urban land use by way of mathematical programming techniques.

Perhaps the best known of these attempts is the Herbert-Stevens (1960) model. This involves a linear program in which households are distributed spatially so as to maximize the aggregate "rent-paying ability." The objective function for the model is

$$\max Z = \sum_k \sum_i \sum_h x_{ih}^k (b_{ih} - c_{ih}^k),$$

where

Z = aggregate rent-paying ability
k = subscript for regions
i = subscript for household groups or types
h = subscript for residential bundles or packages of characteristics
x = solution variable for number of households
b = the residential budget (including transportation)
c = annual residential cost, exclusive of site cost.

The solution was subject to three constraints:

$$\sum_i \sum_h s_{ih} x_{ih}^k \leqslant L^k \qquad (1)$$

$$\sum_k \sum_h - x_{ih}^k = N_i \qquad (2)$$

all $x_{ih}^k \geqslant 0$, (3)

where

s = site area
L = land area available for residential use
N = exogenous number of households to be located.

As in any linear programming solution where the primal problem involves maximization, there is a dual problem of minimization. In this case, it is total aggregate costs which are minimized.

The model, then, provides for the maximization of the sum of the budget residuals available for land rent. But, in fact, this solution proved elusive, and subsequent modifications of the model sought only to maximize the "bid rent," defined as "a budget residual covering the entire residential package of site and structure (but not the cost of transportation)." (Lowry, 1968). Because of the detailed data requirements of this model, few planning agencies have applied it in practice (Hemmens, 1968).

Linear programming also has been used in the Southeastern Wisconsin Regional Planning Commission (SEWRPC) Land-Use Simulation Model. (Southeastern Wisconsin Regional Planning Commission, 1966). In the residential and industrial sectors of this model, linear programs are formulated that provide for the minimization of land-development costs. In addition, the residential land-development process over time is handled by way of recursive linear programming, in which the solution of a program for one time period provides the parameters for the succeeding linear program. (Schlager, 1966). Housing demand is thus allowed to build up over time.

In its early work on the land-use design model (as distinct from the land-use and economic simulation studies), the SEWRPC group contemplated the use of linear and dynamic programming. However, these efforts have given way to a model based on an alternative form of mathematical analysis, linear graph theory. (Southeastern Wisconsin Regional Planning Commission, 1968).

For completeness, one approach to the mathematical modeling of urban land-use systems is mentioned briefly. This involves the formulation of stochastic models, that is, models of probabilistic processes operating over time. As part of the San Francisco CRP study, a Markov chain analysis of the deterioration of housing units was undertaken. (Wolfe, 1967) The states of the model were different levels of housing quality, and there were transition probabilities for the movements from one state to another. Deterioration was an absorbing state, and the behavior of the system over time with respect to this state could be studied.

Harris (1968) has outlined a more general stochastic model for residential development. A parcel of land may be developed or undeveloped, and given m parcels of land, there are thus 2^m states of development for the whole area. The model is semi-Markovian in the sense that there is a waiting time, in itself a random variate, associated with the move from one state to another. More recently, Bourne (1969) has suggested the use of a transition probability matrix in conjunction with regression equations as a means of allocating land-use development. For each subarea of the city, regression analyses yield estimates of the levels of new construction. Also derived for each subarea is a matrix of transition probabilities describing the change over time from one land-use type to another. The regression estimates are combined with these probabilities to predict the future land-use structure of the subarea.

Characteristics of Land-Use Models

The history of the attempts to forecast urban land development is comparatively short, most of the efforts having been made in the current decade. Most of the models reviewed above, then, are essentially first-or second-generation models and the technical features and shortcomings of the models are not yet documented in much detail. But there are five characteristics which can be noted, starting with computer-system requirements.

Computer-System Requirements: A recent survey by Hemmens (1968) has provided some valuable information on this point. As part of a questionnaire survey of large planning agencies, the extent and level of computer use was probed. Hemmens reports that

"Most of the agencies which reported their computer usage utilize more than one computer system. Typically, they use a small computer which is operated by the agency itself or by another public agency, and they rent time on a large computer from a service bureau or other vendor."

The reliance upon service bureaus is more pronounced in the case of those agencies heavily committed to land-use forecasting by use of the mathematical models discussed above. The Bay Area Transportation Commission models are to operate on a CDC 3800 computer with 65K memory; the Delaware Valley RPC models and the Boston EMPIRIC model require IBM 7094 or equivalent capability; the SEWRPC land-use simulation was originally programmed only for an IBM 1620, but the later models are designed for the IBM 360 system.

Given the complexity of the simulations which may be involved and/or the large number of multiple-regression equations which may have to be solved, it is clear that the use of sophisticated land-use forecasting models will require access to computers of at least the IBM 7090 series level and, increasingly, of the 360 series level. Even allowing for access to such computer facilities, the operating costs of these models are high. The metropolis model, for example, requires more than 15 minutes of IBM 7090 time per time period; while the activities allocation model of the Delaware RPC requires as much as 50 minutes of IBM 7094 time for one run. (Lamb, 1967).

Aggregation Problems: In most of the urban land-use studies there are at least three forms of aggregation problems which have to be resolved.

The first is the level of spatial aggregation, which has to do with the number of subregions comprising the city for which forecasts are to be made. Lowry in his empirical analysis of the Pittsburgh data used 650 one-square-mile tracts; the EMPIRIC model on the other hand, was tested originally for 29 subregions representing the Boston region and later, for 123 and 134 subregions. In the context of estimating parameters and analyzing relationships, this decision as to the level of spatial aggregation is not unimportant. It is clear, for example, that parameter estimates for one level of aggregation will not be applicable at another and consequently, many computations will have to be repeated if forecasts are required for these different levels. Again, relationships which hold at one level may not be as significant at another. This was apparent in some of the sensitivity analyses on the EMPIRIC model. (Irwin and Brand, 1965). These kinds of considerations, which in one sense are problems of spatial filtering, are discussed in the spatial-statistics literature (King, 1968), and in the statements on ecological fallacies in theory construction (Goodman, 1959). Fleet and Robertson (1968) have at least drawn attention to the issues in the context of tri-generation studies.

A second problem of aggregation has to do with the number of variables employed in the model. Most of the models are highly aggregative in this respect; the EMPIRIC model, for example, deals with only seven located variables, and the Lowry model deals with even fewer. Obviously, the utility of the models would be enhanced by greater detail in the number of forecasted variables, but problems of data availability loom large in this regard. In speaking of the variables used in land-use and urban development studies, there is also another important aspect to the problem of aggregation. This has to do with the macro-level on which the studies focus, and the fact that questions of individual behavior are ignored. The need for disaggregation along these lines will be discussed in greater detail in the subsequent section on "underlying theory."

Finally, there is aggregation over time with respect to the length of the forecast periods. Most of the models employ five- or ten-year periods, which appear satisfactory in view of the typical goal for most planning agencies of developing a master plan for some future date near the turn of this century. Again, disaggregation with respect to this feature would pose serious problems in regard to data for parameter estimation and forecasting.

Data Availability: The urban development models, for the most part, are particularly demanding regarding data requirements. Carlson (1968) in his survey related to the potential use of the North Carolina model, reported that only 9 of the 135 agencies responding had already collected all the necessary data for the model, while 23 percent of the respondents felt that the data requirements were excessive. The main difficulty in all the models is that the data have to be available for the areal subregions of the city, and there must also exist some historical data for the city, to obtain estimates of the model's parameters (that is, to calibrate the model). The latter point emphasizes again one of spatial-aggregation problems, namely, that the model parameters typically are estimated from historical data for the city as a whole and are then used in obtaining forecasts for very detailed subregions of the city!

Alonso (1968) has drawn attention to some important problems concerning data quality. He cautions against measurement error and the compounding of such errors in modeling situation, and questions whether, in urban land-use studies, the models might not have outrun the capacity of the data. Alonso suggests that, if this is the case, then the quality of the data might have resulted in a deterioration of the predictions. Alonso offers the following "rules of thumb" for model building:

(1) avoid intercorrelated variables;
(2) add where possible;
(3) if addition is not possible, multiply or divide;
(4) avoid, as far as possible, taking differences or raising variables to powers; and
(5) avoid as far as possible models which proceed by chains.

Underlying Theory: Some comments on the theoretical bases of urban land-development models are in order, because as Lowry (1968) notes, "in choosing a model for a particular purpose, the planner will do well to understand what is left out as well as what is left in."

For the most part, the models reviewed in this report have dealt with macro-level variables and relationships. Indeed, with but few exceptions, the models have been structured along the lines of macroeconomic models, with the emphasis being placed typically upon problems of estimation and forecasting, rather than upon questions related to the underlying theory. This is true, for example, of the EMPIRIC, the BASS, and the Lowry models. Not surprising, Lowry (1968) can find little explicit consideration of a theory of the urban land market in his review of seven well-known models.

It is becoming clear, however, that these aggregative statements are not enough, and that increased attention must be given to the theory of individual behavior and the nature of the decision-making processes. B. Harris, et al. (1968) in summarizing the conclusions of the Dartmouth conference notes that, "there is a strong but not unanimous feeling among model-builders that one direction for improving the accuracy with which models reproduce the real world lies in the expansion of studies of the behavior of decision units." Once this possibility is admitted, however, the problems of data availability are increased many times. By the same token, it is well established that the use of aggregative spatial data does not allow for meaningful statements to be made about individual behavior, and that if the new direction in modeling is to be pursued, then individual survey data tabulated by subregions and cross classified must be obtained. It is important to note that considerable progess is being made in the direction of developing behavioral models of urban spatial structure which should have important ramifications for the modeling of urban land use. The papers by Cox and Kaiser in Part II, for example, are illustrative of these efforts.

Lowry's (1968) criticism of existing land-use models concerning their apparent disregard of any theory of land market mechanisms, can be extended also to other theoretical topics of urban spatial structure. Reference has already been made in the preceding paragraph to the paper by Cox, and the work that he and others are pursuing on the spatial dimensions of urban political activity, as represented by this paper, is clearly relevant to the planning of land-use decisions. Similarly, the papers by Casetti and Weicher in Part II represent areas of theoretical work which to date have been poorly acknowledged by the modelers of urban land-use patterns. Casetti's paper, in fact, should be viewed in the content of a fairly extensive literature on urban rent theory, residential utility theory, urban population densities, and spatial equilibrium analysis. Much of this work is referenced in Casetti's own paper, but it seldom is considered in the modeling of land use patterns along the lines discussed earlier.

In general, the argument could be made that the urban land-use models developed to date, have not been strongly *spatial* in character. Admittedly, they have sought to allocate land-uses by subregions and they have in different cases employed certain distance-decay relationships in handling accessibility questions and travel patterns, but for the most part, they have ignored the quite extensive and varied literature on urban spatial structure developed especially by the economists, geographers, regional scientists, and sociologists.

The third point with regard to the theoretical bases of the land-use models has to do with the lack of any broader contexts within which the models are set. That is to say, the models are often neatly structured as regards the particular analytical questions they were designed to solve, but there is generally lacking any consideration of the relationships and feedback loops between the analysis and other facets of the social planning task. Clearly, a land-use allocation model must take for granted certain goals and objective functions and in turn, the solutions which it yields may be only some of the alternatives confronting society. These questions of goal formulations, of defining appropriate utility functions, of evaluating and choosing between alternatives, and of deciding upon means and policies whereby implementation takes place are themselves proper subjects of study and topics for theoretical reasoning. It is these considerations which scholars such as Boyce, Day and McDonald (1969) and Harris, B. (1970) are pursuing.

One final point which should be made concerning the theoretical bases of the urban-land-development models is that they deal with the city essentially as a *closed system*. The models generally take as given certain exogenous forecasts of regional employment and population. In the cases of most of the models discussed up to this point, this feature imposes no really serious constraint since the models are developed for large metropolitan regions and the possible errors stemming from a lack of closure and probably less serious than those associated with the internal workings of the model. But, for small urban areas, the exogenous factors are certain to be much more important in a relative sense, and the internal urban forecasts may be rendered invalid by only a small variation in these exogenous levels. The notions of spatial linkages and spatial hierarchies

Application of Models: In a review of the applications of the above models to specific planning problems, two interesting points emerge. First, it is clear that much of the model development has been accomplished by "in-shop" research but that this work often has not been tied too closely to the immediate problems faced by the planning group in question as regards developing a master plan for its region. This is illustrated by the experiences of SEWRPC. This group has published some of the more intriguing and advanced mathematical statements of urban land-use forecasting, but, in fact, their own regional land-use plan for 1990 was developed by conventional, nonanalytic methods and the land-use simulation model was used merely in testing the consequences of alternative policies. (Southeastern Wisconsin Regional Planning Commission, 1968). The more recent work of this group on the land-use design model is purely an in-shop research project sponsored by HUD.

Second, many planning agencies, in some cases those of large metropolitan areas, are not involved as yet either in model-building or analytical land-use forecasting. The work of the Northeastern Illinois Planning Commission illustrates this point. Their recommended land-use plan for Chicago for 1990 was derived from a hand simulation in which the consequences of five different qualitative models of urban form were evaluated.

The limited extent of the application of the land-use models is borne out in several recent reports. Hemmens (1968) in his survey of some 34 major planning agencies received responses from 26, and of these, only 16 "reported on either current usage or active development of models." Hemmens notes the difficulties these agencies experience in developing the models and making them operational from the point of view of staffing and data facilities. Further, he stresses the lack of communication between agencies and the related absence of any serious cumulative work on the different models. Boyce, Day and McDonald (1970), in a survey of the plan-making process and evaluation methodologies associated with the work of the 13 largest planning programs, notes that as of 1969 only four of them — for Baltimore, Boston, Philadelphia, and the Twin Cities — have actually used computer models of urban growth and development to elaborate a set of alternatives

The work on urban development models, then, has still a long way to go before operational packaged models are available for wide dissemination and use by small planning agencies. The increasing involvement of several commercial consulting firms in this area of land-use planning will possibly facilitate the development of these standard model procedures, although, typically, these privately developed models suffer from a lack of exposure in the published literature. On a national level, HUD could provide a valuable service by promoting the development of a land-use-model package similar to the transportation-network-analysis package provided by the Bureau of Public Roads.

Given the likelihood that these packaged models will be available in the not-too-distant future, and assuming that the numbers of agency personnel better trained in analytical techniques will slowly increase, then it might seem premature for small planning agencies to contemplate seriously the implementation of expensive and "low-reliability" forecasting schemes at this time.

Conclusions and Recommendations

This paper was prepared originally as part of a specific report to the planning agency of a city of under 100,000 population. The recommendations included in that report are reproduced here in summary of some of the points made above. In structuring such recommendations for small metropolitan centers it is important to keep in mind certain background considerations:

(1) It is unlikely that small planning agencies either will have, or can afford, the necessary resources of hardware and manpower for the development, implementation, and monitoring of complex, computerized models of urban land use. At present, these models are far too expensive, both in development and operating costs, for small agencies to experiment with.
(2) The overall state of the art in land-use modeling is not that advanced, and no agency or consulting firm can provide a readily adaptable, packaged land-use model which small cities might be able to use.
(3) The sensitivity of land-use model projections to changes in the exogenous factors has not yet been investigated in detail. Therefore, for urban economies in which the external spatial linkages are strong, the relevance of existing land-use-forecasting techniques is not clearly established.
(4) The previous point notwithstanding, small urban centers with specialized economies may be comparatively easy to model as regards the relevant endogenous variables and the important relationships.

The following general recommendations might be emphasized:

(1) Interested planning agencies undertake a serious evaluation of the overall goals towards which their efforts in land-use analysis are to be directed. If the aim is simply to derive parameters for input to transportation programs, then one set of procedures will be adequate. If the goal is to design land-use plans for the city consistent with certain objectives and constraints, then other approaches will be necessary. Specification of goals is critical.
(2) Agencies might begin simply with the development of regression analyses for the prediction of land uses by census tracts or traffic zones within the city. These models could utilize standard stepwise regression programs, could

emphasize the effects on land-use patterns of a few easily obtained variables, and could be calibrated with historical data. These efforts would at least provide a framework for organizing existing land-use data and, depending upon the results, they may offer a convenient approach to forecasting and sensitivity analysis. There are some simple techniques such as shift analysis which also could be incorporated into the regression analyses.

(3) Agencies seriously consider the pedagogical value to be derived from the participation of their personnel and selected community leaders and citizens in game-simulation sessions conducted by Environmetrics or the METRO project group.

References

Note: Since this paper was prepared a number of other related statements have appeared in journals such as *Land Economics, Environment and Planning,* and *The Journal of the American Institute of Planners.*

Alonso, W., "The Quality of Data and the Choice and Design of Predictive Models," Highway Research Board Special Report, No. 97, Highway Research Board, Washington, D.C., pp. 178-192 (1968).

Arthur D. Little Corp., "Model of San Francisco Housing Market," San Francisco CRP C-65400 (1966).

Bourne, L.S., "A Spatial Allocation-Land Use Conversion Model of Urban Growth," Journal of Regional Science, 9, pp. 261-172 (1969).

Boyce, D.E., Day, N.D., and McDonald, C., Metropolitan Plan Making, Regional Science Research Institute Monograph Series: No. 4, Philadelphia (1970).

Burgess, E.W., "The Growth of the City: An Introduction to a Research Project." in *The City,* R.E. Park et al., University of Chicago Press, Chicago pp. 47-62, (1925).

Carlson, E.D., "Operational Aspects of a Probabilistic Model for Residential Growth," Environmental Policies and Urban Development Thesis Series," University of North Carolina, No. 10 (1968), 89 pp.

Center for Real Estate and Urban Economics, "Jobs, People and Land. Bay Area Simulation Study," Special Report No. 6, Berkeley (1968).

Crecine, J.P., "TOMM," Pittsburgh CRP Tech. Bull., No. 6 (1964), 18 pp.

Donnelly, T.G., et al., "A Probabilistic Model for Residential Growth," *Urban Research Monograph,* University of North Carolina (1964).

Duke, R.D., *Gaming-Simulation in Urban Research,* Institute for Community Development and Services, MSU, East Lansing (1964).

Duke, R.D., "The METRO Urban Game Simulation: An Experiment in In-Service Training," *Proceeding of the Fourth Annual Conference on Urban Planning and Information Systems,* Berkeley, pp. 142-154 (1966).

Ellis, R.H., "Modeling of Household Location: A Statistical Approach," Highway Research Record No. 207, pp. 42-52 (1967).

Feldt, A.G., "The Cornell Land Use Game," *Miscellaneous Paper No. 3*, Center for Housing and Environmental Studies, Cornell (1965).

Feldt, A.G., Current Developments in Heuristic Gaming at Cornell University," *Proceedings of the Fourth Annual Conference on Urban Planning and Information Systems,* Berkeley, pp. 160-167 (1966).

Fleet, C.R., and Robertson, S.R., "Trip Generation in the Transportation Planning Process," Highway Research Record, No. 240, pp. 11-31 (1968).

Forrester, J.W., *Urban Dynamics,* The M.I.T. Press, Cambridge (1969).

Garin, R.A., (comment by A. Rogers), "A Matrix Formulation of the Lowry Model for Intrametropolitan Activity Allocation," J. Amer. Inst. Planners, *32,* pp. 361-366 (1966).

Geisler, M.A. Haythorn, W.W., and Steger, W.A., "Simulation and the Logistics Systems Laboratory," Rand Corp. Mem. RM-3281-PR (1962).

Goodman, L.A., "Some Alternatives to Ecological Correlation," Amer. J. Sociology, *64,* pp. 610-625 (1959).

Hammersley, J.M., and Handscomb, D.C., *Monte Carlo Methods,* Methuen and Co., Ltd., London, pp. 1-9, (1964).

Harris, B., "Quantitative Models of Urban Development: Their Role in Metropolitan Policy-Making," in *Issues in Urban Economics,* H.S. Perloff and L. Wingo (Eds.), The Johns Hopkins Press, Baltimore, pp. 363-412 (1968).

Harris, B., "Some Problems in the Theory of Intra-Urban Location," Operations Research, *9,* pp. 695-721 (1961).

Harris, B., et al., "Construction of Models" (Panel discussion), Highway Research Board Special Report, No. 97, Highway Research Board, Washington, D.C., pp. 193-216 (1968).

Harris, C.C., "A Stochastic Process Model of Residential Development," Journal of Regional Science, *8,* pp. 29-39 (1968).

Harris, C.D., and Ullman, E.L., "The Nature of Cities," The Annals of Sociology, *242,* pp. 7-17 (1945).

Hemmens, G.C., (Ed.), "Urban Development Models," Highway Research Board Special Report, No. 97, Appendix A, pp. 253-262 (1968).

Herbert, J.D., and Stevens, B.H., "A Model for the Distribution of Residential Activity in Urban Areas," Journal of Regional Science, *2,* pp. 21-36, (1960).

Hill, D.M., Brand, D., and Hansen, W.B., "Prototype Development of a Statistical Land Use Prediction Model for the Greater Boston Region," Highway Research Record, *114,* pp. 51-70 (1965).

Hoyt, H., *The Structure and Growth of Residential Neighborhoods in American Cities,* FHA, Washington, D.C. (1939).

Irwin, N.A., and Brand, D., "Planning and Forecasting Metropolitan Development," Traffic Quarterly, pp. 520-540 (October, 1965).

Kibel, B.M., *The Evolution of A Dynamic Planning Model,"* unpublished Ph.D. dissertation, University of California, Berkeley (1970).

Kilbridge, M.D., O'Block, R.P., and Teplitz, P.V., "A Conceptual Framework for Urban Planning Models," Management Science, *15,* B pp. 246-266 (1969).

King, L. J., *Statistical Analysis in Geography,* Prentice Hall, Englewood Cliffs, pp. 154-162 (1968).

Lamb, D.C., "Research of Existing Land-Use Models," Report Number 00010045, Southwestern Pennsylvania Regional Planning Commission, Pittsburgh, 1967.

Lee, D.B., "Models and Techniques for Urban Planning," CAL Rep. No. VY-2474-G. 1, Cornell Aeronautical Lab., Inc. (1969).

Lowry, I.S., "Seven Models of Urban Development: A Structural Comparison," in "Urban Development Models," G.C. Hemmens (Ed.), *Highway Research Board Special Report,* No. 97, pp. 121-163 (1968).

Lowry, I.S., "A Model of Metropolis," Rand Corp. Memorandum RM-4035-RC (1964).

Morrill, R.L., "Expansion of the Urban Fringe: A Simulation Experiment," *papers* Regional Science Assoc., Vol. 15, pp. 185-202 (1965).

Morrill, R.L., "The Negro Ghetto: Problems and Alternatives," *Geographical Review,* Vol. 55, pp. 339-361 (1965).

N. E. Illinois Planning Commission, *The Plan Study: Methodology,* NIPC, Chicago (1968).

Orcutt, G.H., "Views on Simulation and Models of Social Systems," in *Symposium on Simulation Models,* A.C. Hoggatt and F.E. Balderston, South-Western Publishing Co., Cincinnati (1963).

Schlager, K.J., "Simulation Models in Urban and Regional Planning," *SEQRPC* Technical Record, *2,* p. 36 (1964).

Schlager, K.J., "A Recursive Programming Theory of the Residential Land Development Process," Highway Research Record, *126,* pp. 24-32 (1966).

Seidman, D.R., "The Construction of an Urban Growth Model," DVRPC Plan Report No. 1, Technical Supplement, Vol. A, Delaware Valley Regional Planning Commission, Philadelphia (1969).

Seidman, D.R., "Report on the Activities Allocation Model," Penn-Jersey Study Paper, No. 22 (1964).

Southeastern Wisconsin Regional Planning Commission, "A Land Use Plan Design Model," Technical Report No. 8, p. 102 (1968).

Southeastern Wisconsin Regional Planning Commission, "A Mathematical Approach to Urban Design," Technical Report No. 3, p. 54 (1966).

Washington Center for Metropolitan Studies, *City I Player's Manual,* Unpublished draft copy (October 3, 1968).

Wilson, A.G., "Models in Urban Planning: A Synoptic Review of Recent Literature," Urban Studies, *5,* pp. 249-276 (1968).

Wolfe, H.B., "Models for Condition Aging of Residential Structures," J. Amer. Inst. Planners, *33,* pp. 192-196 (1967).

2 The Role of Urban Development Models in Metropolitan Plan-Making[a]

David E. Boyce

The term "urban development models" is generally reserved to designate a class of operational models of urban structure for predicting the location, type and relative intensity of urban activities, conditional on assumptions regarding the type and extent of public facilities systems in the metropolitan region. Serious attempts to construct such models have been in progress for over ten years in several metropolitan regions; however, the number of models that have achieved an operational status and have been used productively in metropolitan planning is relatively few.

The intent of this paper is not to examine the structure of these models, as such, but rather to focus on their role in preparing metropolitan land use and transportation plans. First, the reasons for developing and applying such models are examined. Second, the status of actual applications of these models is reviewed. Some of the results of the applications of these models are then discussed, particularly with respect to their sensitivity to public policies. The chapter concludes with a brief look at on-going research on these models and future expectations for their applications.

To have a better perspective for reviewing the status of these models, a brief summary of the history of their development is warranted. The first major attempt to construct an operational model for forecasting urban growth in response to metropolitan transportation policies was the well-known Penn Jersey Transportation Study. Its "regional growth model," later simplified to an "activities allocation model," was a most ambitious undertaking, at least for that time. Spurred on by the attempts underway in Philadelphia, the Baltimore and Milwaukee regional planning agencies undertook the construction of models for simulating urban growth and development.

In the Boston region, research was begun on two urban activities models that led to the EMPIRIC model, which is now also being applied in Washington, D.C. An adaptation of M. Schneider's intervening opportunities concept was made for allocating urban activities in the Upstate New York metropolitan areas. In the Twin Cities, planners with a somewhat more pragmatic orientation in-

---

[a]The support of the Federal Highway Administration, U.S. Department of transportation, is gratefully acknowledged.

cluded a program of simple model development in a broad program of plan preparation and evaluation. Model development studies initiated by the Bay Area Transportation Study Commission in the mid-1960s represent the last major effort on the Penn Jersey scale to bring to operational status a range of models of urban structure and growth. Since that time, Detroit and Pittsburgh have embarked on smaller-scale programs of model development.

In addition to the operationally-oriented models mentioned above, four other research projects should be cited at this point. The path-breaking work by Lowry (1964) is of particular importance because it gave initial clues to the difficulties and complexities of adequately representing urban structure to be useful for forecasting purposes. For smaller metropolitan areas, the research conducted at the University of North Carolina (Donnelly, Chapin and Weiss, 1964), gave similar indications for modelling residential growth. More recently, Schneider (1968) combined the early transportation oriented approach with a new and more powerful formulation of the travel decay function for representing the spatial relationship among urban activities. Finally, the theoretical work of Alonso (1964), though more simplified in its assumptions, has provided a useful basis for several model development efforts.[b]

Reasons for the Construction of Urban Development Models

A detailed examination of the plan-making process followed by the several metropolitan planning agencies that chose to construct and apply these models suggests several specific reasons for their use. Four metropolitan planning agencies — Philadelphia, Boston, Bay Area, and Twin Cities — initially set out with the specific intent of predicting land development patterns arising from or associated with alternative transportation and other public facility plans. The purest cases of this reason for constructing such models are found in Philadelphia and Boston. The Bay Area and Twin Cities programs began with this specific reason for preparing alternative land use plans, but later modified or expanded their reasons in response to other substantive issues.

Four other metropolitan planning agencies — Baltimore, Milwaukee, Detroit, and Pittsburgh — applied such models to predict land development and urban activities for specific elements of the land use plan, given the location of other elements. For example, in Baltimore it was desired to predict total retail sales at regional shopping center locations, given the distribution of households and the

---

[b]Descriptions of many of the above models, together with reflections and comments on their attributes, are found in the two major collections of publications to date in this field: (1) "Urban Development Models: New Tools for Planning," *Journal of the American Institute of Planners, Special Issue,* Vol. 31, No. 2 (May, 1965); and "Urban Development Models," Special Report 97, Highway Research Board, Washington, D.C. (1968).

travel times from households to the shopping locations. In Detroit and Pittsburgh, models were being developed to forecast residential and retail-service employment, given both public facility plans and locations of other activities such as basic employment.

A quite different approach was taken by the Milwaukee metropolitan planning agency. In this case the intent of the model was to identify the optimal arrangement of activities, rather than to forecast or simulate the pattern of growth. Here, mathematical programming and other optimizing approaches were employed in two versions of an urban design model.

Finally, several procedures have been developed for making unconditional predictions of land development. Representative of one of the best simple approaches is the work by the Chicago Area Transportation Study in the late 1950s.

The Status of Applications of
Urban Development Models

Despite a relatively large amount of research and model development over the past 10 years, as of 1969, relatively few metropolitan alternative plans have been prepared using urban development models. Three metropolitan areas — Boston, Baltimore, and Twin Cities — have completed the preparation and evaluation of alternative plans using these procedures. The Bay Area, Pittsburgh, Washington, D.C., and Detroit, were in the process of preparing such alternatives using these methods. A single prediction of land development was prepared for Philadelphia using a sequence of urban development models originally intended for preparing alternative land use plans.

Another aspect of the status of these models pertains to the mathematical procedures employed in their specification and application. In four cases — Boston, Philadelphia, Twin Cities and Detroit — various types of regression analysis have been applied. In five metropolitan areas, distributional algorithms based on trip length or travel decay functions have been developed. In some cases these are straightforward applications of gravity model or opportunity model concepts. In others, more complex relationships have been added. Models of this type have been developed for Baltimore, Pittsburgh, Bay Area, Philadelphia, and the Upstate New York metropolitan areas. Mathematical programming and optimal search procedures have been applied primarily in the Milwaukee and Philadelphia metropolitan planning agencies. In some cases in which a sequence of models has been developed, as in Philadelphia, each of the above methods has been applied in the set of models developed.

For models intended for conditional forecasting, one ultimate test is the success attained in preparing alternative land-use plans. In this regard, the evidence assembled to date pertains to only four metropolitan areas — Baltimore,

Boston and the Twin Cities, which have succeeded in preparing alternative land-use plans, and Philadelphia, which attempted the preparation of such alternatives. As already described, in Philadelphia and Boston, the intent was to prepare a series of land-use plans in response to alternative transportation and other public facility plans. The results of the Philadelphia experience are well documented by Seidman (1969, p. 211): "We were surprised to discover that, except for non-manufacturing employment, there were no significant differences between the land use patterns forecast for the different transportation plans and policies inputed. That is, even at the district level most differences were no greater than 5 percent. Non-manufacturing employment, on the other hand, showed differences in the CBD of up to 25 percent; in a few cases it showed differences greater than 100 percent at the district level."

Seidman goes on to discuss whether the small amount of variation achieved among the alternatives represents a true prediction of land development for the narrow range of the politically feasible transportation alternatives considered, or whether the models developed were unrealistically insensitive. He concludes that both explanations are probably at work, as well as the probable true lack of differences in urban structure for the rather large districts (20 square miles on the average) that were used in making the predictions.

The second set of alternatives prepared using urban development models in which transportation and other public facility policies were varied is Boston. In this case, a more direct comparison of the alternatives is possible, and a simple analysis based on the available information is given in Table 2-1. Here, the change in population by ring from 1963 to the mean of the four 1990 alternatives is compared with the differences among the two extreme 1990 alternatives. In making such a comparison, if the change in population from 1963 to 1990 is much, much greater than the differences among the 1990 alternatives, then one might conclude that the alternatives were not very different. If, on the other hand, the difference among the alternatives is as great as the change, then one might conclude that the alternatives were quite different. An examination of Table 2-1 shows that for the most rings in the Boston region the differences among the alternatives are quite small.

The analysis in Table 2-1 is only one of several kinds that could be made. Other comparisons might be made for sectors and for the forecast districts themselves. It is quite possible that differences could occur at a small geographic scale, but not for the ring. However, in this case in which transportation and water-sewer policies are the only input variables being manipulated, one might expect that for the alternatives to have validity, the differences should appear at a highly aggregated scale. Otherwise, one could not expect that the differences among the alternatives would lead to different levels of performance for the transportation system.

Two metropolitan planning agencies to date have prepared land-use and transportation alternatives in which land-use policies and controls were the

Table 2-1
Comparison of Change in Population in Boston From 1963 to 1990 With the Extreme Differences Among the 1990 Alternatives

Ring	Percent Change	Percent Difference	Change / Difference
1	$-\ 16.5$	2.4	6.9
2	$+\ \ 4.3$	5.2	0.8
3	$+\ 54.2$	4.2	12.9
4	$+\ 93.3$	5.6	16.5
5	$+\ 66.8$	2.2	31.1

$$\text{Percent Change} = \frac{\bar{P}_{90} - P_{63}}{P_{63}} = \text{Change in population from 1963 to the mean of the four 1990 alternatives as a percentage of 1963 population}$$

$$\text{Percent Difference} = \frac{P_{90}^H - P_{90}^L}{P_{63}} = \text{Difference in population between the extreme 1990 alternatives as a percentage of 1963 population}$$

$$\frac{\text{Change}}{\text{Difference}} = \frac{\bar{P}_{90} - P_{63}}{P_{90}^H - P_{63}^L} = \text{Ratio of the change in population from 1963 to 1990 to the difference in population between the extreme 1990 alternatives}$$

$\bar{P}_{90}$ = mean population for the four 1990 alternatives

P_{90}^H = highest population among the 1990 alternatives

P_{90}^L = lowest population among the 1990 alternatives

P_{63} = 1963 population

Source: Boyce, Day, and McDonald, (1970) p. 71.

major variables manipulated. In the case of Baltimore, three alternatives were developed in which major emphasis was placed on the number, location and size of regional shopping centers. In one of the alternatives, these shopping centers were considered to be the cores for several new towns, and the location and density of residential development were strongly controlled in order to achieve compact new-town development.

At the other extreme, a sprawl type of alternative was developed in which relatively few controls were imposed. An analysis of these alternatives comparable to the Boston analysis is given in Table 2-2. In this case the ratio of change to difference among the alternatives is much smaller than for the Boston case. Here, one can conclude that large differences were obtained among the alternatives prepared by imposing rather arbitrary restrictions on the location and intensity of development.

In the Twin Cities program, four alternative land-use and transportation plans were prepared. Variations were made in highway speeds, but for the same

Table 2-2
Comparison of Change in Population in Baltimore From 1965 to 1985
With the Extreme Differences Among the 1985 Alternatives

Ring	Percent Change	Percent Difference	Change/Difference
1	− 5.0	2.9	1.7
2	+ 48.6	12.4	3.9
3	+ 198.3	76.3	2.6
4	+ 141.6	47.4	3.0
5	+ 75.8	100.8	0.75

Percent Change $= \dfrac{\overline{P}_{85} - P_{65}}{P_{65}} =$ Change in population from 1965 to the mean of the three 1985 alternatives as a percentage of 1965 population

Percent Difference $= \dfrac{P^H_{85} - P^L_{85}}{P_{65}} =$ Difference in population between the extreme 1985 alternatives as a percentage of 1965 population

$\dfrac{\text{Change}}{\text{Difference}} = \dfrac{\overline{P}_{85} - P_{65}}{P^H_{85} - P^L_{85}} =$ Ratio of the change in population from 1965 to 1985 to the difference in population between the extreme 1985 alternatives

(See Table 1 for additional definitions of symbols.)
Source: Boyce, Day, and McDonald (1970), p. 73.

network configuration. Alternate transit proposals were input to each plan, and several other land-use policies and controls were manipulated including the number, size and location of major retail centers, the location of multifamily housing, and the location and extent of the open-space system. Within the framework of policies provided for each alternative, a series of regression equations forecast the distribution of single family residences and several classes of employment.

No information comparable to Tables 2-1 and 2-2 is available for the Twin Cities alternatives. However, tests of the performance of the transportation network did not result in any differences in the cost of constructing the alternative transportation plans that were considered to be significantly different by the highway planners. Other evaluations of the alternatives that were performed showed some differences, but not as large as were expected.

Unfortunately, the Philadelphia, Boston and Baltimore programs did not conduct extensive tests and evaluations of the alternatives prepared. Therefore, despite the large quantity of research and planning funds that have been devoted to the development of these models to date, no substantial evidence yet exists that alternative plans prepared with such models lead to more efficient or effective performance of public facilities such as transportation, water and sewer systems and open-space systems. For the case of the Baltimore and Twin Cities programs, there seems to be some evidence that the number, location, and size of regional retail-service centers can be manipulated to achieve a system of subregional centers that more effectively serves the households in the region. To date, however, no specific proposal has been brought forth as to how these centers can be controlled in their location and size except to say that their development might be undertaken by a public development corporation.

In two metropolitan areas — Milwaukee and Chicago — rather extensive tests of highway and transit networks were undertaken with land-use alternatives prepared by more conventional methods. Using the same analysis presented above for Boston and Baltimore, these alternatives were found to be quite different. However, the evaluations performed for the transportation systems resulted in network performance measures that were very similar for each of the land-use alternatives tested. Therefore, even if the models were able to forecast land-use alternatives that were quite distinct, there is no strong evidence that the evaluation of the associated transportation networks would detect that one alternative is more efficient or effective than the others.

Reasons for the Few Successful Applications of Urban Development Models

The small number of successes to date in preparing alternative land-use plans using forecasting models is the result of a large number of circumstances and events. Many of these are documented in more detail by Boyce, Day, and McDonald (1970). A primary reason, which is closely related to the concern of this paper, is that the model building activity itself consumed so much of the time and financial resources of each agency that little attention could be given to the question of how to use the model once it was operational.

For example, in the work programs of several planning agencies examined, little if any attention is given to the problem of how to evaluate the alternatives prepared by the urban development models. It was implicitly assumed, with the possible exception of transportation network testing, that the alternatives would be so different and so clearly desirable or undesirable that no thorough evaluation would be required. Instead, some of the alternatives prepared were so similar that they could not even be readily distinguished from each other.

Another example of the preoccupation with the models themselves is the lack of attention to the preparation of inputs to these models. In several cases, planning agencies prepared preliminary sketch plan alternatives as a basis for specifying the detailed transportation and other policy inputs to the urban development models. While these sketch plans were executed with considerable intellectual effort, they were done at an highly aggregated level and in such a way that the inputs prepared from them could not be rigorously compared even to determine if there was much difference among them.

In the case of transportation systems, for example, typically alternative networks were prepared, or different levels of service or speeds were assumed on the same basic network. From these assumptions, accessibility measures from each zone to activities in all other zones were calculated. Knowing that the accessibility variables in the models were not strongly related to the forecast variables, it should have been of primary importance to test whether the accessibility measures input to the model were really different. However, no agency appears to have even casually examined this rather basic assumption about their model inputs. Similar examples could be cited for other inputs to the models.

In summary then, several past efforts to apply urban development models absorbed so much of the agencies' energy in constructing the models that little resources remained for either preparing inputs to the model or evaluating the model outputs. Presently, most planning agencies have corrected for this initial overemphasis, and some may have overcorrected.

Research currently in progress (Boyce, McDonald and Fahri, 1971) is examining this question of preparation of model inputs and evaluation of model outputs as a general planning procedure. The research objective is not to build a new model or to revise existing models, but rather to facilitate the use of existing or improved models by constructing a working environment for the model's operation. Such a working environment could facilitate the preparation of model inputs through systematic procedures for manipulating the input variables, and for processing model output so as to facilitate its evaluation.

For example, the transportation inputs to urban development models have usually been prepared on the basis of a network description requiring hundreds of man-hours for detailed coding. Such networks for highway and transit are required for each alternative. Using these procedures, it is not surprising that only a few alternatives could be prepared, and that no serious attention could be given to the testing of differences among the inputs to each alternative. As a revised procedure, consider that the necessary travel times and costs between each pair of zones could be quickly generated from very simple assumptions about the nature of the regional transportation network. For all pairs of zones on radials from the metropolitan core, speeds of 30 miles-per-hour might be assumed; for circumferential zones, 40 miles-per-hour might be the case.

Schneider (1969) explores some aspects of such a procedure. Based on such assumptions, the model inputs could be quickly computed and the effects of alternative assumptions could then be determined. In a similar fashion, the effect of manipulating open space by excluding a certain proportion of land from development in each forecasting district could be examined. When simple assumptions leading to desirable outputs are identified, more specific plans and policies consistent with these assumptions can be devised.

Another aspect of urban development models that was virtually ignored in past model construction efforts is the geographic scale, time dimension, and level of detail of activities represented in the models. Often, decisions on these model properties had to be made on grounds of data availability or for other reasons that in retrospect may have contributed greatly to the model's demise. For example, in several cases the time span for which alternative development patterns were forecast was limited to 10 or 15 years, following a 10 or 15-year period of inertia of present development trends. With only this relatively short time available for different alternatives to emerge, it is not so surprising that the variation among the output variables was small. A similar lack of attention to the geographic scale and the detail of the activity types to be forecast also led to unsatisfactory results.

Conclusions

Clearly, urban development models are not the glamour area of metropolitan planning as was the case in the early and middle 1960s. This shift of emphasis at the agency level is partly a negative reaction to the considerable lack of success in bringing these models to bear on the actual plan making activity, and partly because other problems and methods have attracted the attention of planners in the interim. As a result a more balanced model development and application effort is being pursued today than was the case eight or ten years ago. These current efforts are also much more realistic in terms of what can be accomplished through the use of these methods. This situation should lead to a more careful examination of the problems associated with these methods and can be expected over time to result in considerable improvements.

Despite the lack of immediate success in the use of these models, much can still be learned from the intense model construction activity that has been undertaken. However, this can only really occur if the individuals involved in the research over the last ten years carefully document their findings before shifting their attention to other problems. In some cases, notably Philadelphia and Boston, this has been done. Another excellent example of well-documented research on urban development models is Barras et al. (1971).

If past experience and understanding are to be conserved and the mistakes of the past avoided in the future, it is essential that this work be accomplished. Hopefully, research during the next few years will result in a literature further documenting and clarifying the reasons for the successes and failures of urban development models.

References

Alonso, W., *Location and Land Use,* Harvard University Press, Cambridge (1964)

Barras, R., T.A. Broadbent, M. Cordey-Hayes, D.B. Massey, K. Robinson, J. Wills, J. Wills, "An Operational Urban Development Model of Cheshire," *Environment and Planning,* Vol. 3, 115-233 (1971).

Boyce, D.E., Day, N.D., and McDonald, C., *Metropolitan Plan Making,* Regional Science Research Institute, Monograph Series: No. 4, Philadelphia, (1970).

Boyce, D.E., C. McDonald and A. Farhi, *An Interim Report on Procedures for Continuing Metropolitan Planning,* Regional Science Department, University of Pennsylvania, Philadelphia, (1971).

Donnelly, T.G., Chapin, F.S. Jr., and Weiss, S.F., *A Probabilistic Model for Residential Growth,* Center for Urban and Regional Studies, University of North Carolina, Chapel Hill (1964).

Lowry, I.S., *A Model of Metropolis,* RAND Corporation, Santa Monica (1964).

Schneider, M., "Access and Land Development," *Urban Development Models,* Special Report 97, Highway Research Board, Washington, D.C. (1968).

Schneider, M., *Transportation and Land Development,* Creighton, Hamburg Inc., prepared for the U.S. Department of Transportation, Washington, D.C. (1969).

Seidman, D., *The Construction of an Urban Growth Model,* Delaware Valley Regional Planning Commission, Philadelphia (1969).

3 A Model for the Distribution of Residential Activity in Urban Areas[a]

John D. Herbert and Benjamin H. Stevens

Introduction

The model presented here is designed to distribute households to residential land in an optimal configuration. The model was constructed for the Penn-Jersey Transportation Study as part of a larger model designed to locate all types of land-using activity.

Since the model had to be suitable for practical application, a certain amount of conceptual elegance has been sacrificed in favor of operational simplicity. The larger model operates in the following way: the total relevant time period is subdivided into a number of short iterative periods. For each iterative period different types of land-using activity are handled separately. A particular type of activity is distributed in a configuration that is optimal only with respect to all previously located activities.[1] Interactions that are expected to occur among simultaneously locating activities are ignored. We are assuming that they can be ignored if iterative periods are kept short enough to ensure that the number of users located in a single run of the model is small. Operating in this way we are able to achieve computational simplicity and, at the same time, recognize most of the basic interactions among land users.[2]

For the residential model, in a particular iterative period, the number of households to be located and the amount of land that is expected to be available for residential use is forecast exogenously.[3] A linear program is used to produce, for the end of that period, an optimal configuration of the new households on the available land. This configuration is optimal with respect to the configuration of all previously located activities, and constitutes a prediction of the way in which the forecast households will locate.[4]

---

[a]This paper was adapted from a report prepared for the Penn-Jersey Transportation Study and is reprinted with permission from *The Journal of Regional Science,* Vol. II, No. 2 (1960). The authors wish to acknowledge the contributions of Britton Harris, who directed the section of the study under which the model was prepared and who made invaluable criticisms and suggestions throughout its development, Nan Fetter and the other members of Penn-Jersey staff who participated in discussions of the problem. The paper also draws on the excellent theoretical development of similar materials in Alonso (1960). The authors accept full responsibility for the model's shortcomings.

Definitions

Household: A household is a person or group of persons with a common budget purchasing a single residential bundle.

Household Group: A household group is a collection of households which have similar residential budgets and similar tastes with respect to residential bundles.[5]

House: A house is the physical structure to be occupied by a single household.

House Cost: House cost is the dollar cost of constructing, operating, and maintaining a house over a specified time period, computed on an annual basis.[6]

Amenity Level: The amenity level associated with a site is the level of psychic satisfaction which a household has an opportunity to enjoy because of certain characteristics of that site.[7]

Trip Set: A trip set consists of the numbers of each type of trip generated by a household.[9]

Trip Pattern: The trips in a trip set when their origin and destinations have been identified.[10]

Travel Cost: Travel cost is the annual dollar cost to the household of carrying out a trip pattern.[11]

Site: A site is the parcel of land assignable to a particular household.[12]

Total Site Rent: Total site rent is the dollar value of the amount received annually by a site owner for the use of the *land* in the site. It is exclusive of the value of the house, amenity level, and travel pattern associated with the site.

Residential Bundle: A residential bundle is a unique combination of a house, an amenity level, a trip set, and a site of a particular size.

Market Basket: A market basket is a unique combination of a residential bundle and a bundle of all other commodities (which we shall call the "other commodities" bundle) consumed annually by a household.

Total Household Budget: A household's total budget is the dollar amount that a household allocates annually to the purchase of a market basket.

Residential Budget: A residential budget is that part of a household's total budget that is allocated annually to the purchase of a residential bundle.

Region: A region is the geographical space within which our model is required to allocate a given number of households to a given supply of land.

Area: An area is a regional subdivision whose characteristics are homogenous with respect to the costs of construction, amenity costs, and the costs of transportation to other areas.

Conceptual Framework

We assume that the factors which a household considers in choosing an area in which to locate are its total budget, the items which constitute a market basket, and the costs of obtaining those items. For each household group we posit a set of market baskets among which each household in that group is "indifferent."[13] We posit the set which includes, but is not necessarily limited to, the market baskets currently consumed by households of that type.[14] We permit the household to optimize, not by selecting a market basket from *all* the conceivable sets from which it could obtain satisfaction, but by selecting from the posited set the market basket which maximizes that household's "savings."

These "savings" arise in the following way. A household has a fixed total budget. For a particular market basket the prices of the items in the "other commodities" bundle are given. The residential budget is therefore a residual determined by the size of the total budget and the cost of the "other commodities" bundle. Clearly, it may vary from market basket to market basket. Notice that the character of each of the four items that constitute a residential bundle may vary from market basket to market basket also. Each market basket in the indifference set will have in it a unique residential bundle which has a unique residential budget associated with it. Disregarding site for a moment, the costs of each of the other three items in a residential bundle may vary from area to area. For a particular area, the difference between the residential budget assigned to a particular residential bundle and the cost of the bundle exclusive of the site in it is the maximum amount the household can pay in that area for that site. And it will be the maximum amount that the landowner could extract from the household as site rent. If land were free, it would be a measure of the savings enjoyed by the household because of the locational advantages of the area. We define this difference as the household's rent-paying ability for that site in that area.

Although we have said that a household is "indifferent" among the market baskets in its indifference set, it seems reasonable to suppose that such savings would have a positive marginal utility for the household. Therefore, in the model, a rational household will attempt to obtain from its indifference set the market basket in which those "savings" are a maximum. In reality, the functioning of the land market may make it possible for the landowner to draw off the "savings" as rent. Nevertheless, the *attempt* of each household to maximize its savings will result in households being allocated to land in configuration that is optimal from the point of view of all the households that are to be located. This allocation will be optimal in a Pareto sense: no household can move to increase its savings without reducing the savings of some other household and simultaneously reducing aggregate savings. Since we have made savings synonymous with rent-paying ability, an optimal allocation is achieved by the maximization of aggregate rent-paying ability.[15]

The Primal Problem

Notation:

U areas which form an exhaustive subdivision of the region. Areas are indicated by the superscripts $K = 1, 2, \ldots, U$.

n household groups indicated by subscripts $i = 1, 2, \ldots, n$.
m residential bundles indicated by subscripts $h = 1, 2, \ldots, m$.
b_{ih} is the residential budget allocated by a household of group i to the purchase of residential bundle h.
c_{ih}^K is the annual cost to a household of group i of the residential bundle h in area K, exclusive of site cost.
s_{ih} is the number of acres in the site used by a household of group i if it uses residential bundle h.
L^K is the number of acres of land available for residential use in area K in a particular iteration of the model.
N_i is the number of households of group i that are to be located in the region in a particular iteration.
X_{ih}^K is the number of households of group i using residential bundle h located, by the model, in area K.

The allocation model:
    The primal linear programming model for allocating households to land has the rather simple form:[16]
Maximize

$$Z = \sum_{K=1}^{U} \sum_{i=1}^{n} \sum_{h=1}^{m} X_{ih}^K (b_{ih} - c_{ih}^K) \qquad (1.0)$$

subject to:

$$\sum_{i=1}^{n} \sum_{h=1}^{m} s_{ih} X_{ih}^K \leq L^K \qquad (K = 1, 2, \ldots, U) \qquad (1.1)$$

$$\sum_{K=1}^{U} \sum_{h=1}^{m} X_{ih}^K = -N_i \qquad (i = 1, 2, \ldots, n) \qquad (1.2)$$

and all $X_{ih}^K \geq 0$ $(K = 1, 2, \ldots, U)$
                         $(i = 1, 2, \ldots, n)$
                         $(h = 1, 2, \ldots, m)$

    Constraints (1.1) prevent the consumption of land in each area from exceeding the land available. Constraints (1.2) require the model to locate the projected numbers of households of each group. These constraints are equalities because inequalities (of either sense) would not fit the overall requirements of the model. Suppose these constraints were written in such a way that the model were prevented from locating *more than* the projected numbers of households. This would be logical since we are interested in the situation where a particular number of households are located, not where the model can continue locating households in unlimited numbers until all the available land is used up. On the other hand, it is just as logical to write the constraints in such a way that the model is required to locate *at least* the projected numbers of households. This is particularly important where there are household groups which have negative or zero rent-paying ability in all areas. Without constraint, the model would choose not to locate these households at all, since at best they would not add to, and at worst they would not subtract from, aggregate rent-paying ability. For these reasons, it is difficult to establish a general rule for the sense of the inequalities. Therefore it is preferable, and perfectly reasonable, to make the constraints equalities.[17] The objective function (1.0) to the maximized is, of course, aggregate rent-paying ability.

Households may be allocated to land in the following ways: (1) One type of household may use all the land available in an area. This will occur where that type of household can yield the highest unit rent for the land in the area and there is a sufficient number of such households to fill the area. (2) The land available in an area may not be used up entirely. Partial utilization will occur where the area has strong locational advantages for only one of the household groups and there are not enough households of this type to fill the area, or where the area has strong locational advantages for two or more household groups and these groups, *in toto,* cannot fill the area. (3) The available land in an area may be left vacant if all households have higher unit rent-paying abilities in other areas and can find sites in other areas. (4) The land available in an area may be used by more than one type of household. This will occur where there are not enough households in the group with the highest unit rent-paying ability in the area to fill that area and they are joined by other households with unit rent-paying abilities the same as, or lower than, the highest group but higher in this area than in other areas. Joint utilization can occur also in the unusual circumstance where two or more household groups have identical unit rent-paying abilities in the area and in all other areas where they could outbid other groups for sites.[18]

The Dual of the Allocation Model

The notation of the dual problem is identical to that of the primal except that the solution variables, X_{ih}^{K} are replaced by:

r^K the annual rent per unit of land in area K. ($K = 1, 2, \ldots, U$)

v_i the annual subsidy per household for all households of group i. ($i = 1, 2, \ldots, n$) The use and meaning of the subsidy variables will be made clear below.

The dual problem is to minimize:

$$Z^1 = \sum_{K=1}^{U} r^K L^K + \sum_{i=1}^{n} v_i(-N_1) \tag{2.0}$$

subject to:

$$s_{ih} r^K - v_i \geq b_{ih} - c_{ih}^K \quad (K = 1, 2, \ldots, U), (i = 1, 2, \ldots, n) \tag{2.1}$$
$$(h = 1, 2, \ldots, m)$$

all $r^K \geq 0 \quad (K = 1, 2, \ldots, U).$
$v_i \geq 0 \quad (i = 1, 2, \ldots, n).$[19]

In most linear programming models, the dual presents a problem in interpretation. The existence of the dual is a mathematical fact. But often it also contains information and provides insights which are as important as those provided by the primal itself. This is particularly true in the case of the present model. If we look at the objective function (2.0) and neglect for a moment the second summation, we can interpret the first summation as the total land rent.[20]

It may seem peculiar to minimize total land rent in the dual when we are maximizing aggregate rent-paying ability in the primal problem. It can be shown that the optimal solution of the primal problem must be exactly equal to the optimal solution of the dual. But there is also an important economic interpretation of the dual objective. Suppose all land in all areas were owned by a monopolist. Then the minimization of site rent will minimize the returns to this monopolist. Alternatively, land could be widely held by individual holders. We would then be minimizing returns to the rentier class as a whole. To put it another way, we are obtaining sites for households as cheaply as possible within the constraints of the model.

This is not necessarily a desirable goal if it causes inequities to land owners. But notice that the constraints (2.1) prevent the unit rent on each site from falling below the unit rent-paying ability of *any* household that might locate on that site.[21] This means that the individual landowner can receive at least as much per unit as the highest bidder for his land is willing to pay. This will create certain problems when the household group which can bid highest does not actually purchase the land because it has an even higher unit rent-paying ability elsewhere. It is this latter case, and certain other cases, in which the "subsidy" variables become important.

Bear in mind that a household which can bid the highest unit rent in a particular area is not necessarily of the "wealthiest" household group. Unit rent-paying ability depends upon both total rent-paying ability and size of site purchased. "Poorer" households using small sites may be the highest bidders, per unit of land, in a particular area. Thus "subsidies," in the model, may be assigned in some cases to "wealthy" households.

Interpretation of "Subsidies" and Rents

The foregoing serves to introduce the idea that the "subsidy" variables, v_i, are basically a mathematical device.[22] Now let us consider their economic meaning. Suppose, for example, that all household groups save two have been located. Suppose further that all areas have been filled save one. Assume that one household group can bid more per unit for the land than the other. This high-bidding group will then establish the rent level in the area. Because areas are not divisible within the model and because of the nature of linear programming, the same unit rent must then be charged for *all* units of land in the area.[23] The households with the lower rent-paying ability must be located somewhere and this is the only area left. Since their rent-paying ability is insufficient to meet the high rent level established in the area, households of this second group must be "subsidized." And, as indicated above, the same situation would prevail even if the group with the higher rent-paying ability in this area actually locates in another area or areas.

This simplest interpretation of the subsidy variables is not hard to grasp. However, the existence of these variables creates problems in interpretation which are more difficult to handle. Notice that the v_i are specific to household *groups*. Therefore, once any household in a group receives a subsidy, all of that group must receive the same subsidy. It might be possible to argue that this would be a realistic consequence of an egalitarian public policy, but the argument would be a weak one. For suppose that all "high income" households but one could be accommodated in a particular area. This leftover household would have to locate in another area. If the locational advantages of the first area were extremely large but other areas were highly unsatisfactory to "high-income" households, we might find that this leftover household had a *lower* rent-paying ability in all other areas than competing households of other groups. Since this household must be located somewhere, it will then have to be subsidized. But in the process, all high-income households would be subsidized, raising their rent-paying abilities in the first area to unnecessarily high levels.

We could avoid this problem by disaggregating households and having a constraint (1.2) for each individual household. But this would make our problem extremely unwieldy. A better approach would be to disaggregate areas after a run of the model. This would involve splitting any area in which two or more different household types locate into two or more subareas each occupied by a single household type.[24] Rent levels could be adjusted, ostensibly by taxing away from landowners the "extra" rents made possible by the subsidies. Rents would then be equal to rent-paying abilities for all household types and subsidies, of the type we have been discussing, would be eliminated.[25]

Areal disaggregation would enable us to approximate a continuous model in which each small parcel of land is bid on separately and can carry a different rent from neighboring small parcels. The linear programming approximation to the continuous model is especially important in any practical application since the latter is very difficult to solve.[26] Furthermore, the linear programming model may actually be the more realistic of the two. A truly continuous model assumes a level of information and sophistication on the part of both landowners and households which is not likely to exist in practice. From the landowners' point of view it is hard to imagine a real situation where there are marked variations in residential rent among contiguous sites; from the households' point of view, it seems unlikely that contiguous sites will be regarded as having distinctly different locational cost and advantages.

We still have not dealt with one important problem. Suppose that a certain household group has the highest rent-paying ability in an area but cannot fill it. Assume that all other households have higher rent-paying abilities in other areas and can be completely accommodated in these areas. This would mean that the land constraint (1.1) for the area would remain an inequality at an optimal solution. In accordance with the general structure of linear programming models, this means that the rent variable corresponding to this area should be equal to zero. In economic theory, land, as a resource for this household type, is then not really scarce and should carry a zero rent. Yet the dual constraints (2.1) for the area require that the land rent be no less than the unit rent-paying ability of any household which might locate there. We appear to have a contradiction unless the households which make the highest bid have zero or negative unit rent-paying ability in the area. If their rent-paying ability is strictly positive we appear to find all units of land in the area earning a positive r^K even though some of the units are not consumed at all. This would seem to make the value of the dual objective function larger than the value of the primal objective function.

We may resolve this conceptual dilemma if we recall that the "subsidy" variables, v_i, need not be positive. Therefore, we can fulfill both the condition of zero rent on unfilled areas and the condition of unit rent greater than or equal to unit rent-paying ability in all areas. The negative "subsidy" can be regarded as a "tax" on the households (equal to the rent-paying ability of the households in the area which they occupy but do not fill) to be used as a "subsidy" to the landowner in the area to "pay" him for the land actually consumed.

By now it may have occurred to the reader that we have obtained the information necessary to construct a classical rent surface for the region. Given a map of the region we could place a block on each area with a height proportional to the unit rent in the area. The surface thus constructed would have discontinuities. But perhaps a discontinuous surface is actually more realistic than the smooth surface of classical theory. A multinodal metropolitan region, with an irregular topography and transportation system and a mixed pattern of land uses, should not be expected to exhibit smooth rent gradients.

The sharpness of the rent discontinuities can be reduced if we can assume that households need not bid the full amount of their rent-paying abilities. If they are able to win land by just outbidding competing households, they can save the difference between rent-paying ability and actual amount bid.[27] The landowner may be able to extract the full rent if, as we suspect, he is the more powerful bargainer. But if there are actually a large number of small competing landowners, their bargaining power may not be much greater than that of the households. Then true net rents may be as high as the rent-paying abilities of the households which occupy the land, as low as slightly above the highest bid of competing households, or somewhere in between, and will depend upon the pattern of land ownership and the vagaries of the land market.[28]

Some Limitations of the Model

Many of the limitations of the model are implicit in its construction. They include the following: (1) Data problems: it will often be difficult to obtain consistent data on household budgets and tastes, amenity levels and costs, etc. For the present, in the light of preliminary surveys, we are assuming that it will be possible to obtain data which, though crude, will be adequate to make the model operational. (2) Forecasting problems: successful use of the model depends upon obtaining accurate forecasts of the numbers and characteristics of location-seeking households and of the amounts of available land. (3) Restriction of the choices of a household to a single indifference set: this restriction may prevent the model from achieving a true optimum, since households cannot shift to indifference sets yielding higher levels of satisfaction. Locational savings may or may not constitute an adequate proxy for the satisfactions that might be gained through continuous substitution. (4) Optimization over a number of iterative periods: the model optimizes for individual iterative periods. It may not be rational to assume that an aggregation of such optima will constitute an optimum for the aggregate time period. (5) The sumulation problem: the failure of the model to take into account interactions (other than competition for land) among households locating simultaneously is a serious enough limitation to warrant further discussion.

The problem can be illustrated by considering the cumulation of households around concentrations of job opportunities. Recall that we use a probability interchange model to determine travel cost. This requires the development of a set of expected trip costs for each area on the basis of the number and location of opportunities for trip ends. These expected costs are heavily influenced by the existence of large employment centers which provide trip end opportunities for large numbers of workers.

The difficulty is that too many households may locate in the areas near large employment centers and not enough in the areas surrounding smaller employment centers. At an optimal solution we may find that there are not enough jobs in a large center to accommodate all household wage-earners so that some of them will have to travel relatively long distances to find jobs. This is more a problem with the model than with the real world although there is some evidence to indicate that, given two centers of employment, households tend to orient themselves toward the larger one even if they are not sure to find employment there. It may be that near the larger center they expect to have a wider range of choice of employment and be in a better position to find another job should they be laid off.

Nevertheless, the model may give us erroneous results because of the cumulation phenomenon. There are several ways of handling the problem but none of them is completely satisfactory. One approach would be to assign households to jobs in advance of the model run. For example, suppose we were dealing with a metropolitan area with one major and one minor center of employment for workers of a particular household group. Assuming one worker per household, we could then break this group into two parts in proportion to the number of jobs available at the two centers. One part would have its transport costs computed as if only the major center existed. The smaller part would have transport costs relative to the minor center. Such an approach would give strong locational advantages to approximately the right proportions of households near each of the two centers although a successful solution would still not be guaranteed.

An alternative approach would be to make travel costs a function of the number of households locating in particular employment areas. Unfortunately, this would require a nonlinear program which is much more difficult to solve. It might provide a theoretical solution to the problem, but not a practical one.

Finally, an approach might be developed out of repeated use of the model. If we find that cumulation occurs, we might be able to determine experimentally how probabilities should be altered or weighted so as to produce a more "realistic" solution.

Alternative Approaches

It is appropriate at this point to discuss the question of alternative models. We have used a linear program because it appears to afford the best compromise between theoretical elegance and practical applicability. A nonlinear programming model would be able to handle the cumulation problem as well as problems such as the effect of traffic congestion on travel costs, the effect of growing residential densities on household decisions, and the effects of changing land use on amenity levels and costs. But it will be some time before the new computational techniques for nonlinear programming become economically feasible for large-scale problems.

We specifically reject multiple regression models because they tend to project the past into the future in a way which fails to recognize the basic structural interrelationships of activities and land uses.[29] For somewhat the same reason we feel that simulation models do not provide the most promising direction for further research. However, current developments in simulation models for residential decisions indicate that they will give much better results than multiple regression techniques. And it is difficult to ignore the possibility that residential patterns may be more random than rational.[30]

Finally, it is important to recognize Alonso's unique contribution in the development of a rigorous theoretical model of residential location. His method is difficult to apply directly, but we feel that our linear programming model provides an analogous approach that is both acceptable and workable.[31]

Policy Implications.

The model is applicable to public policy decisions concerning zoning, transportation, redevelopment, public housing, segregation, and other areas of public interest. For example, the model could be run without zoning restrictions. Then restrictions could be applied to determine their effects, if any, on rents and residential patterns. Similarly, the effects of altering transportation costs could be tested by multiple runs of the model.[32]

Where the model gives high rents in areas with little available land and close to existing blighted areas, it may indicate that these areas are ripe for redevelopment. Moreover, the existence of high rent levels would indicate a low cost of writing down the land.[33] Some areas may exhibit extremely low rent levels in comparison with surrounding areas. These may be ripe for redevelopment to raise amenity levels (and reduce amenity costs). Because the model can identify the "savings" that households might enjoy, not only on vacant land but also in partially improved and built-up areas, it should be of interest in problems of conservation and rehabilitation as well as redevelopment. In all of these applications it could be used as one type of cost and benefit analysis.

We may wish to use the model to consider real subsidies to households which have negative rent-paying ability in all or most areas. Tests could be made to determine whether it is more effective to raise these households' location budgets through direct subsidies (thereby shifting them into another household group) or to reduce their location cost through indirect subsidies (e.g., through public housing). The dual variables, together with knowledge of the total and locational budgets of such households, can provide a measure of how large such subsidies should be.

Notice that the model can recognize racial segregation and similar policies if they have measurable dollar consequences for rent-paying abilities. It can do this in much the same way as it recognizes the amenity value of particular areas. For example, we can ascribe to a predominantly white area high "amenity" costs for particular types of Negro household seeking particular locational bundles.

Whenever we use the model as a guide to policy-making, we must be careful that we do not ascribe spurious meanings to its output. There may be social welfare considerations which are noneconomic and which are not reflected in the maximization of aggregate rent-paying ability. And these noneconomic considerations should be taken into account by the policy-maker. He may decide that a true social optimum can be achieved only by deviating from the pattern produced by the model. If he does, the model can tell him how much the deviation will reduce aggregate rent-paying ability. In other words, an "optimal" residential pattern can be found against which to test the effects of alternative programs of public expenditure and control. Although it was designed for use by a transportation study, the model has implications and applications which make it useful in a much broader range of decision problems.

References

Alonso, W., A Model of the Urban Land Market: Location and Densities of Dwellings and Businesses, unpublished doctoral dissertation, University of Pennsylvania, microfilmed (1960). A brief description of this model is to be found in Alonso, W., "A General Theory of the Urban Land Market," *Papers and Proceedings of the Regional Science Association,* Vol. VI (1960).

Carroll, J.D., and Bevis, H.W., "Predicting Local Travel in Urban Regions," *Papers and Proceedings of the Regional Science Association,* Vol. III, pp. 183–197 (1957).

Chicago Area Transportation Study, *Allocating Population to Small Areas,* Chicago (1957).

Dorfman, R., Samuelson, P.A., and Solow, R., *Linear Programming and Economic Analysis,* McGraw-Hill, New York (1958).

Gale, D., *The Theory of Linear Economic Models,* McGraw-Hill, New York (1960).

Garrison, W. L., "Toward a Simulation Model of Urban Growth and Development," paper prepared for the Symposium on Urban Studies, Lund (1960).

Marble, D.F., "Transport Inputs at Urban Residential Sites," *Papers and Proceedings of the Regional Science Association,* Vol. V, pp. 253–267 (1959).

Stevens, B.H., "A Review of the Literature on Linear Methods and Models for Spatial Analysis," *Journal of the American Institute of Planners,* Vol. XXXVI, No. 3, pp. 253–259 (August, 1960).

Stevens, B.H., and Coughlin, R.E., "A Note on Interareal Linear Programming for a Metropolitan Region," *Journal of Regional Science,* Vol. I, No. 2, pp. 75-83 (Spring, 1959).

Notes

1. For a particular type of activity in a particular iterative period, previously located activities comprise all activities located in previous periods plus activities of other types previously located (by other elements in the larger model) in the same period.
2. For example, if we take an extreme case with an iterative period of one week, the number of land users that will be located in that period is likely to be small; it seems reasonable, both conceptually and realistically, to assume that they will make their locational decisions largely independent of one another. However, interactions between users located in a particular week and those located in previous weeks will be recognized, with the result that a vast majority of the important interactions are taken into account. For Penn-Jersey we envisage an iterative period of at least a year, which will certainly introduce inaccuracies; but we can achieve any level of accuracy that we desire, at the cost of increasing computational complexity, by decreasing the length of the periods.
3. The residential model can handle land that is vacant, partially improved, or completely built-up. For expositional simplicity, the discussion will be limited to vacant land unless otherwise noted. Forecasts are exogenous in the sense that they are made outside the overall model (by techniques that are beyond the scope of the present discussion) but can be modified for a particular iterative period to recognize the configurations produced by the model in previous periods.
4. Linear programming is not ordinarily regarded as a predictive tool. However, if we have a prediction of the number of households that is to be located and the model locates them in a realistic configuration then we can use the model to predict configurations. Since the configurations it produces are optimal in a specific economic sense the model may be both predictive and prescriptive.
5. We are assuming that households that have similar tastes give rise to similar phenomena on the sites they occupy. E.g., households with similar tastes with respect to travel patterns generate the same numbers of each kind of trip, regardless of the number of persons in the household.
6. We hope to obtain house costs from contractors' estimates. Clearly, the construction, operating, and maintenance costs for a particular type of house may vary from area to area, and will be dependent in part upon the topography, soil, and microclimate in each area.
7. The site characteristics contributing to the amenity of a site have yet to be selected. It is expected that they will include characteristics such as the

existing households in the area in which the site is located, the levels of public services in the area, the age of the area, other land uses in the area, planting on the site, and views from the site.

8. Tentatively, it is proposed that estimates of amenity costs be obtained in the following way: Realtors and developers will be asked to identify for each area in the region the "premiums" they could add to or subtract from the selling price of a particular type of house, offered to a particular type of household because of the amenity of that area. Where these premiums reflect the accessibility of an area as well as its amenity level, we anticipate that the effects of accessibility can be eliminated. For a particular type of household and house the area in which that premium is a maximum will be regarded as having zero amenity cost for that type of household purchasing the residential bundle in which that type of house occurs. The corresponding amenity cost in any other area will be the difference between the premium associated with it and the maximum premium. Since premiums may be negative, amenity costs in some areas may be so high that they prevent the model from locating particular types of households in those areas. It is worth noting here that the model can recognize, in a similar way, segregation and other policies which affect the prices households are willing to offer for houses.

9. By kind of trip we mean, for example, a trip to a particular type of employment, recreation, shopping, etc. The origins and destinations of the trips in a set are not specified since we assume that the alternative trip sets considered by a household will be independent of that household's location. There is some evidence in support of this assumption. (Marble, 1959). It will be seen below that the assumption may not be unreasonably restrictive since we provide households with a number of alternative trip sets from which to choose.

10. The destinations of the trips in a trip set will vary with the location of the household generating the set. These destinations will be forecast exogenously by a probability interaction model. (Carroll and Bevis, 1957).

11. Travel costs, including out-of-pocket and imputed time costs, can be estimated from data on the transportation system.

12. Land not covered by a house but under the same tenancy or ownership as the house is included in the site associated with that house. Where a parcel of land has more than one house superimposed upon it, as in the case of an apartment building, the site assignable to each household is found by dividing the total area of the parcel by the number of households occupying it.

13. The household is "indifferent" among the baskets only in a limited sense which will be made clear in the subsequent discussion.

14. This is based on the assumption that households have, in the past, come close to achieving optimal levels of satisfaction. However, where empirical evidence suggests that market imperfections have precluded optimization we can add to the indifference set market baskets that could be chosen by the household in a market free of imperfections. Obviously there are conceptual

weaknesses involved in the use of empirical evidence for the identification of indifference sets. We assume that it is possible to construct operationally acceptable sets that are based on such evidence without being tied rigidly to it. The model will not permit the indifference set that is relevant for a particular household to change during an iteration. But this does not preclude the possibility of allowing taste changes to occur from one iteration to another.

15. In a Henry Georgian single-tax economy, the maximization of aggregate rent–paying ability would provide a maximization of public revenue. In a socialist system, if land were free, maximization of aggregate rent–paying ability would provide a maximization of consumer's surplus.

16. Readers with limited knowledge of linear programming are referred to Dorfman, *et al.* (1958) and the bibliography in Stevens (1960). Although there are Umn variables to be determined, it is possible to eliminate many of them in advance of the computation of the program. We can do this for each household in each area by disregarding all residential bundles that yield less than the maximum unit rent–paying ability for that household in that area. These would have to be eliminated in any case in the process of maximization; a prior removal of them can reduce computational time and effort considerably.

17. Actually, it is more likely to be necessary to force the model to locate households with zero or negative rent–paying ability than to restrict the number of households which may be located. This is reflected in the minus signs which appear on both sides of constraints (1.2). If these constraints were written as inequalities they would read:

$$\sum_{h=1}^{m} \sum_{k=1}^{U} -X_{ih}^{K} \leqslant -N_i.$$

But without the minus signs the inequalities would be of the opposite sense. In a maximization problem the inequalities *must* be of the "$\leqslant$" form. Therefore the minus signs are necessary. They could be removed when constraints (1.2) are changed to equalities. But the interpretation of the dual variables is somewhat easier if the minus signs are left in the primal.

18. This is the degenerate case in which there is no unique optimal allocation of the households in the groups which fulfill this condition. A further degenerate case can occur where a particular household group has the same unit rent–paying ability in a number of areas, none of which it can fill completely.

19. An inequality (1.1) in the primal corresponds to a nonnegative variable r^K in the dual. But an equation (1.2) in the primal corresponds to a variable, v_i, whose sign is unrestricted in the dual. Thus the v_i, can be positive or negative. See Gale (1960).

20. The second summation is the total of "subsidies" paid to households. We will see later how these subsidies add to the rent–paying ability of households and thereby to the rental income of landowners. But notice that the

total value of the subsidies is *subtracted* from the total land rent (and could, in fact, be taxed away from landowners without altering the optimal configuration). Therefore, the value Z^1 to be minimized is actually *net* land rent.

21. Neglecting the v_i, we could divide both sides of (2.1) by s_{ih}. Then unit rent (on the left) must be no less than unit rent–paying ability (on the right). Since this must hold for every household–bundle combination in an area, it then must hold for the combination which would yield the highest unit rent.
22. For each constraint in the primal problem, there must be a variable in the dual and for each variable in the primal there must be a constraint in the dual. The U land constraints (1.1) are associated with the U variables r^K. The n constraints (1.2) have a similar correspondence with the n variables v_i. The requirement that all households should be located therefore makes the "subsidy" variables a necessary part of the model.
23. Areas must be fixed in size and number for any run of the model. They may be subdivided or otherwise adjusted after the run.
24. Generally, two or more household types will locate in the same area no more times than there are numbers of household groups since the solution to a linear programming model need contain no more nonzero variables than constraints. Our primal problem contains U land constraints and n household group constraints. Therefore no more than $U + n$ variables need be other than zero at an optimal solution. It should be clear that if at least one household locates in every area, no more than n areas can have a second household type.
25. Subsidies to households with negative rent–paying ability in all areas available to them might still appear, much as subsidies to low–income households may be necessary in the real world.
26. Cf. Alonso (1960).
27. The household could use these savings to purchase additions to any component of its market basket other than site or travel without altering the optimal spatial configuration.
28. The discontinuities can be reduced in another way. If we make the areas smaller and smaller (and hence, more and more numerous), the rent surface will be smoother. As indicated above, however, there is both a conceptual and a practical limit to this process.
29. E.g. See Chicago Area Transportation Study (1957).
30. Cf. Garrison (1960).
31. Alonso (1960).
32. Cf. Stevens and Coughlin (1959).
33. And the rent variables may be of use in establishing fair compensation in other types of land condemnation proceedings.

4 A Land-Use Plan Design Model[a]

Kenneth J. Schlager

Postwar advances in applied mathematics and electronic computation have stimulated great interest in the application of mathematical models and data processing systems to urban and regional planning. Significant progress has been made in the application of these techniques to urban transportation planning, and more recently a number of research projects aimed at the development of land-use models have been initiated. There seems little question that the long-range potential impact of these methods will be revolutionary, but some critics have questioned the relevance of current planning models to the real problems of planners. The obvious question is: What problems are current models able to solve?

Even a brief review of current land-use planning models will reveal a strong emphasis on explaining and predicting human behavior. Quite correctly, many of these models include the word forecasting somewhere in their title description.[1] Such an approach conceives of the urban complex as a phenomenon to be explained scientifically and as a changing configuration that can be predicted in the same way that the solar system can be predicted from the theories of physics. Indeed, such an approach is well designated as applied social physics. The philosophy underlying this approach is the natural result of the direct transfer of the methodology of the physical sciences.

Plan Design: The Central Problem

A contrasting viewpoint conceives of the urban complex as a subject for design. In this approach, the plan is a conscious synthesis of urban form to meet human needs. Rather than serving as a negative restraint on undesirable aspects of human behavior, the plan serves as a positive force for the directed development of the community.

This design viewpoint is not new. It has provided the basis for architectural and engineering achievement for centuries. What is new, or at least overlooked

---

[a]Reprinted with permission from the *Journal of the American Institute of Planners,* Special Issue, Vol. XXXI, No. 2, Urban Development Models: New Tools for Planning, Britton Harris, guest ed. (May, 1965).

in recent years, is the possibility of using recent advances in applied mathematics and electronic computation for plan design. Design, and not explanation and prediction, becomes the primary problem for solution.

The subject of this paper is land-use plan design and a land-use plan design model now under development. Design, however, is but one of a sequence of functions in the planning process. For this reason, the introduction of the design model will be preceded by a discussion of the role of mathematical models in a specific land-use, transportation planning sequence.

A system diagram illustrating the functional relationships in the planning process is shown in Figure 4-1. Although this diagram specifically represents the planning sequence related to the formulation of a regional land-use, transportation plan, it is typical of other planning sequences.

The first function in the planning sequence is that of forecasting population and employment, as a basis for determining future land-use requirements. In the current Land Use Transportation Study of the Southeastern Wisconsin Regional Planning Commission, new methods of socioeconomic forecasting are being investigated in an attempt to provide more accurate and comprehensive employment and population forecasts. These new techniques, which center around the Regional Economic Simulation Model, are the subject of another paper[2] and will not be discussed in detail here. Whatever the method used, population and employment forecasts must be provided as the output of the first step of the planning sequence.

In the second function, aggregate land-use demand requirements are determined by applying a conversion coefficient, usually designated as a design standard, to each employment and population category. Such a multiplication and summation will result in a detailed classified set of aggregate demands for residential, industrial, commercial, and other land uses. These aggregate demands provide one of the primary inputs to the third function: plan design.

Plan design lies at the heart of the planning process. The land-use plan design function consists essentially of the allocation of a scarce resource, land, between competing and often conflicting land-use activities. This allocation must be accomplished so as to satisfy the aggregate needs for each land use and comply with all the design standards (derived from the plan objectives) at a reasonable cost.

The plan selected in the design stage of the planning process must be implemented in the real world. Private decisions of land developers, builders, and households may run contrary to the land pattern prescribed in the plan. This problem of plan implementation is the function of the third stage of the planning process illustrated in Figure 4-1, land-use plan implementation test.

Land-use plan implementation is simulated in the Land Use Simulation Model by detailed representation of the decision processes of households and business firms influential in land development. Public land-use control policies and public works programs are exogenous inputs to the model. In practice, a

LAND-USE PLAN DESIGN

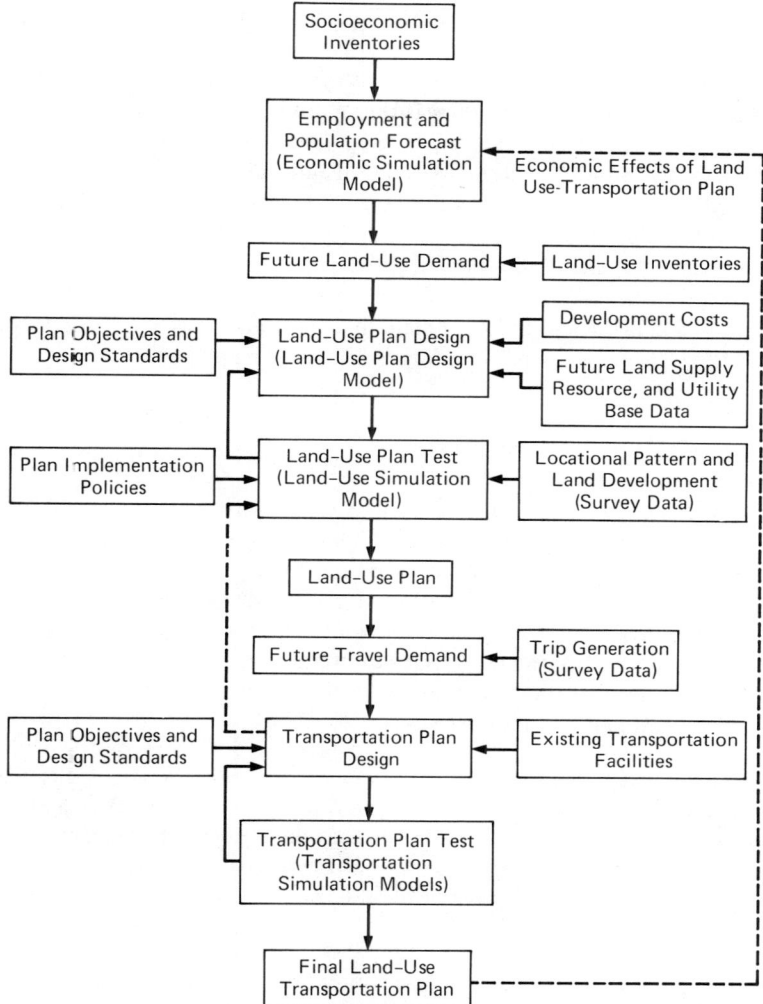

Figure 4-1. Land-Use, Transportation Study Planning System Diagram.

number of experimental simulation runs must be performed with different land-use control policies and public works programs until a set of policies and programs are determined that result in the implementation of the target land-use plan. The feedback on the diagram between land-use development and land-use plan design accounts for the changes that will probably be needed in the plan design to make it realizable. The output of the third stage of the process is a land-use plan capable of practical implementation.

The remaining stages of the planning sequence depicted in Figure 4-1 relate to the development of a transportation plan. The primary inputs to a transportation system are the trips generated as a function of land use. For this reason, the land-use plan is shown in the diagram as an input to the transportation plan design. No models are indicated in the transportation plan design function: none exist, to my knowledge. Trip distribution and traffic assignment models may be used to test the plan intuitively designed by the transportation planner. As a result of model simulation, the transportation plan network is revised until a satisfactory system is developed.

Although each function in the planning process is important to the final realization of a creative and practical plan, the vital role is played by plan design since it is the focal point of all preceding and succeeding planning activity.

The Land-Use Plan Design Process

To appreciate the need and requirements for a land-use plan design model, it is necessary to examine closely the design process in general and the land-use plan design process in particular. Analytical discussion of the design process is rare. Most of the literature on design is based on intuitive and artistic concepts or styles that have predominated in certain periods of history.

An exception to this general scarcity of literature is a recent work by Alexander which defines the design problem in terms of a "fit" between the problem statement and its solution:

It is based on the idea that every design problem begins with an effort to achieve fitness between two entities: the form in question and its context. The form is the solution to the problem; the context defines the problem. In other words, when we speak of design, the real object of discussion is not the form alone, but the ensemble comprising the form and its context.[3]

Achieving this fit between the form and its context is not a simple task, for the many requirements that make up the context of the design problem often interact in a complex manner. Attempts to satisfy one design requirement often lead to a violation of another. Faced with such complexity, the designer may be tempted to ignore the real design problem and substitute a traditional design. Although such an approach may be acceptable in a political sense, the original problem remains unsolved.

Difficulties in the design process derive primarily from the inability of the human designer to manipulate simultaneously a large number of interacting design relationships. Mathematics, particularly in its newer forms such as modern algebra, provides a powerful tool for the manipulation of these relationships for the more effective solution of design problems.

LAND-USE PLAN DESIGN

To be useful in design synthesis, mathematical formulations must comply with two conditions related to Alexander's definition of a "selection problem": one, "It must be possible to generate a wide enough range of possible alternative solutions symbolically"; two, "It must be possible to express all criteria for solution in terms of the same symbolism."[4] While Alexander does not pursue the direct solution of selection problems by means of mathematical techniques, his definition provides useful criteria for the systematic formulation of such problems.

Land-use plan design, despite its admitted complexity, possesses certain inherent characteristics that meet Alexander's requirements of a selection problem. The first requirement, involving the generation of a wide range of alternative solutions symbolically, is naturally achieved in land-use plan design by reason of the common measure of all land-use plans: the land itself. All land-use plans for areas ranging from the smallest subdivision to multi-state regions may be expressed symbolically by three sets of variables:

(1) The type of land use (quality variables)
(2) The density of land use (quantity variables)
(3) The geographic location (location variables).

Typically, the land area concerned will be subdivided into a grid of "zones" of equal area. The location variable is determined by the geographic coordinates of the zone in question. For each zone, the types and densities of land uses may be expressed as a measure of the activities in that zonal area. The amount of detail provided will depend on the coarseness of the grid. For small areas, a zone may be as small as individual residential lot parcels. In large regions, they may be counties or even states. The key point to be observed is that all land-use plans may be expressed by these three classes of variables.

The grid nature of the coordinate system does not limit the results to rectangular plans. On the contrary, the most complex and irregular plan may be expressed with the designated variables if an appropriate grid size is selected.

The second condition, relating to the symbolic relationship between alternative forms and design requirements, is also complied with in the land-use plan design problem. All design requirements or "standards" restrict in some way the set of acceptable land-use plans. For a design model, these requirements may be divided into two primary classes:

(1) Requirements that restrict the minimum or maximum numerical value of a land use or a relationship between land uses *within a grid zone* (intrazonal standard). Examples of these requirements are the exclusion of flood plain areas from development in a given grid zone (maximum value standard) or prevention of the simultaneous development of both industrial and residential land in the same grid zone (relationship standard).

(2) Requirements that restrict a relationship between land uses *between grid zones* (interzonal standard); for example, the need to provide an elementary school within a specified distance (or time) of all residential units.

In either class, the design requirement can be expressed symbolically as an algebraic equality, or more often an inequality, using the three classes of variables noted above. Again, compliance with this condition, like the first, is possible because land-use planning is concerned with a single measurable resource, land. That these claims of symbolic design alternative generation and requirements-alternatives comparison are authentic will become more apparent as the design model methodology is explained further.

It is useful at this point to provide a specific, succinct statement of the land-use plan design problem indicating the nature of both the design requirements and the design alternatives. To an experienced urban planner the problem will certainly not be new, since it is the same basic problem that he has been concerned with intuitively during his past design experiences. The problem, as stated below, may seem excessively quantitative, and the emphasis on minimal costs may appear unnecessary, but fundamentally it is the same problem of urban form design that has challenged man since cities were found useful. In brief, the problem of the designer of urban form is:

(1) Given design requirements expressed as:
    (a) A set of design standards in terms of restrictions on land-use relationships that may exist in the plan
    (b) A set of needs or demands for each type of land use based on forecasts of future urban activity
(2) Synthesize a land-use plan design that satisfies both the land-use demands and design standards considering the current state of both natural and manmade land characteristics, at a minimal combination of public and private costs.

The conceptual basis for minimal costs, it must be emphasized is not to provide a cheap plan but to avoid unnecessary expenditures of precious resources as long as the design standards and land demands are complied with in the plan design.

Intrazonal design standards may take the form of limitations on density or restrictions of the types of land use that may coexist within a zone. An example of an interzonal design standard would be the provision of a regional shopping center within a certain travel time of every residential area. Land-use demand requirements would restrict the set of acceptable plans to those that provided the aggregate total of each land-use need over the entire design area. The current state of the land, whether developed or in a natural state, is a primary consideration in plan synthesis because of the relationship of the land to both the design standards and the costs associated with new or renewed development.

The Design Model

Two related mathematical techniques will now be discussed as possible frameworks for a land-use plan design model. The first technique, linear programming, has a record of successful accomplishment in other fields and has efficient, highly developed computational procedures. Dynamic programming, the second and newer technique, while not as productive in previous applications or standardized computational procedures, is less restricted in its assumptions and, potentially at least, is a more flexible framework for a land-use plan design model.

Both linear and dynamic programming are sometimes classified as subsidiary fields under the general title of mathematical programming. Such a general classification is desirable, inasmuch as both fields have as their objective the solution of problems involving the optimization (maximization or minimization) of some objective, such as cost, within the restrictions of certain constraints such as design standards. The techniques involved differ considerably, however, with linear programming imposing rather severe restrictions on the nature of both the objective and constraints while dynamic programming is almost unrestricted in its formulations of both the objective and constraint functions. Linear programming models, on the other hand, can usually be solved by the use of standardized computational procedures, while dynamic programming usually provides at least a serious challenge and often insurmountable obstacles to an efficient computational solution. With either technique, the sheer size of many land-use plan design problems bring with them what has been called the "curse of dimensionality," which militates against any simple "brute force" approach to solution.

The linear programming formulation of the land-use plan design model problem is straightforward. The objective function relates to the cost of developing land for a given land use:

$$c_t = c_1 x_1 + c_2 x_2 + \ldots + c_n x_n$$

where the variables (x) may represent residential, industrial, or other land uses in given areas and the constants (c) the costs of developing this land. Land-use categories may be subdivided into subsidiary classes such as single family residential, multifamily residential, and the costs may be related to the topography and soil characteristics of the area. With each subdivision, of course, the number of variables grows larger, and the computation time for a model solution is increased. In practice, a compromise must be made between the desire for detail and reasonable solution times. With the rapid developments in computer technology, however, this problem will be of decreased significance in the coming years.

The equality and inequality constraints in the linear programming formulation of land-use plan design include the following:

(1) The total demand requirement for each land-use category (equality constraint):

$$d_1 x_1 + d_2 x_2 + \ldots + d_n x_n = E_k$$

where

E = regional land-use demand requirement for each land use
d = service ratio coefficients which provide for supporting service land requirements, such as streets, which are necessary for primary land-use development

(2) Maximal (minimal) limits on land uses within a zone:

$$x_1 + x_2 + \ldots + x_n \leqslant F_m$$

where

F_m = upper limit on land use n in zone m

(3) Interzonal or intrazonal land use relationship constraints:

$$x_n \leqslant G x_m$$

where

G = ratio of land-use n allowed relative to land-use m with land-uses m and n in the same or different zones.

The land-use demand equality constraint (1) follows a standardized format with one equation for each primary land-use category. Since some land uses such as single family residential are usually subdivided further according to lot sizes, the number of demand equations in a typical design model may exceed 20 relationships. It is important to emphasize that only primary land uses such as residential, industrial, agricultural, and recreational land are directly determined. Service ratios incorporated in the d parameters account for secondary land uses such as local streets and parks.

LAND-USE PLAN DESIGN

The second and third categories of constraints reflect the design standards and may take a wide variety of forms. The maximal constraint will usually reflect a density standard, but it also may provide for the exclusion of an unsuited soil type for a given type of land use. Land-use relationship constraints will result from design standard restrictions on coexistent land uses within a zone or in adjacent zones. Accessibility standards for employment and shopping areas will also be reflected in this type of constraint.

The above constraint relationships reflect the types encountered so far in experimental plan design model runs in test areas. Other constraint forms may be needed when a complete regional plan design is attempted, but they may be easily included as long as they are linear, continuous constraints. Nonlinear discontinuous constraints are not possible with linear programming and account for the primary disadvantages of the method.

For a region subdivided into about 30 zones, the size of a typical linear program for a land-use plan design is about 60 equality and inequality constraints and 400 variables. Computer time on an IBM 1620 computer is about three hours. On larger systems, such as the IBM 7090, it would take less than 30 minutes.

Model Application

Some initial experience with applications of the model will now be detailed in order to provide the reader with an idea of the input data requirements and computational characteristics of the model.

Four primary sets of input data are required for model operation:

(1) The costs of unimproved land and land development for each primary land-use activity for each type of soil
(2) The aggregate demand for each primary land-use activity
(3) Design standards which reflect the plan objectives and restrict the set of acceptable plans by limiting interzonal land-use relationships
(4) The current land inventory, which will include both land-use activities by area and soil characteristics.

Land-development cost data may be obtained either by engineering estimates or by statistical analysis of recent land development in the area. The former approach has been used in the initial tests of the model in the Waukesha city pilot area. Collection of land-development cost data is always expensive and in many cases difficult or even impossible to obtain. Land developers are usually extremely reluctant to reveal their costs, and the cost data obtained is of uneven quality since many developers do not maintain complete records. For all these reasons, engineering cost estimates are usually preferable if competent professional experience is available.

In the Waukesha area, separate land-development cost estimates were made for five sizes of residential lots with their associated service land uses, such as streets, neighborhood shopping, schools, and parks. Additional cost estimates were made for industrial, regional shopping, and regional park land uses. These were not gross estimates but detailed analyses of the costs of each improvement related to both the land use and the type of soil involved. All estimates were subdivided into their component parts, each with its individual cost.

Separate cost estimates were prepared for each of three classes of soil. Soil data were obtained from a comprehensive soil survey made in southeastern Wisconsin as part of the Land Use Transportation Study. Unimproved land costs presented a special problem since they could not be obtained from engineering estimates. Assessed and equalized land-value data were obtained from each of the communities and were adjusted on the basis of prices realized in recent land transactions in the area.

Initial tests of the model used historical aggregate land-use demands for 1950-1962 to provide comparisons between actual and "optimal" land development in the area. Typically, however, a design application of the model will require forecasts of future land-use demands, which may be obtained by applying design standards to forecasts of population and employment in the region of interest.

The various forms of design standards usually provided were described in the previous section. In current tests of the model, design standards were limited to the exclusion of development from areas such as flood plains, along with the provision of service ratios for the amounts of secondary land (streets, parks) required to support the primary land uses. Design standards for the regional land-use plan are still in preparation and will be used in model tests as soon as they become available.

An inventory of both current land-use activities and soil characteristics is critical for model application. In current tests, developed areas were eliminated from consideration for future land development. It is possible, however, to consider redevelopment in the form of urban renewal as a set of alternatives in the design. For this approach, redevelopment costs would be required. Through the use of the soil inventory, it was possible to assign a development cost to each subarea in the test area.

Proper presentation of the Land Use Plan Design Model output is an important consideration in achieving acceptance of its design by planners and governmental officials. Initial model outputs were in tabular form and were meaningful only to someone familiar with the operation of the model. Improved presentation was later achieved by tabular designation of the intensity of each land-use activity in each zone. Printed output was supplemented by colored land-use maps manually prepared from the tabular print-out.

Available Mathematical Models

Although linear programming provides a reasonably satisfactory framework for a land-use plan design model, it possesses certain inherent disadvantages that restrict its usefulness in design. The primary limitation is the need for continuous rather than discrete values for the land-use variables. Land-use design choices are by nature usually discrete rather than continuous. The basic element of residential land use is the subdivision rather than the lot. Industrial land-use units tend to be industrial parks rather than individual factory sites, much less land acreage. While it is possible to round off the linear programming solution to satisfy these natural discrete levels, such a solution does not usually correspond with the associated discrete optimal combination. A second limitation of linear programming is the need for both a linear objective function and linear constraints. The linear objective function is not a severe limitation, because the inaccuracies introduced by a linear approximation of costs are usually less than the errors of cost estimation. In the few instances where known nonlinear cost functions occur, such as in the plant capacities of areawide facilities for water supply or sewage treatment, the cost break may usually be satisfactorily approximated by a multivariable series of linear cost variables.

Nonlinear constraint relationships present a more serious problem. Certain design standards are inherently nonlinear, and a linear approximation sometimes provides an unsatisfactory substitute. When a design model is not able to provide satisfactorily for a design standard, it loses most of its usefulness.

Dynamic programming, another member of the mathematical programming family, has the potential for removing the two primary restrictions inherent in linear programming. Although dynamic programming may be used to solve the same land-use plan design problem, it is based on a different class of mathematical procedures, which are capable of handling discrete and nonlinear objective functions and constraint relationships.

Richard Bellman of the Rand Corporation was the originator of dynamic programming and has developed the theory and application of this multistage approach to decision making to a high degree in the last decade. A large number of classes of dynamic programming processes have been formulated for problems in production scheduling, rocket trajectories, and feedback control systems, but the class of process of primary interest in design is the allocation process.[5] In a dynamic programming model, the basic cost and design relationships are similar to those defined for the linear programming model, but the method of computation differs and permits the use of more complex and discrete relationships.

The Design Viewpoint in Urban Planning

The ultimate contribution of this paper will depend on its success, or the lack of it, in accomplishing at least a partial reorientation of land-use model development toward design. Although the importance of forecasting land-use development was indicated by the role of the Land Use Simulation Model briefly described earlier in this paper and detailed in another recent paper,[6] the dangers and limitations of nondesign-oriented models that are only remotely related to the synthesis of better urban and regional plans should be apparent.

The need for design models in urban planning is fortunately accompanied by greater possibilities for their success. Industrial applications of mathematical models in normative functions such as production scheduling and optimal product design have been conspicuously more successful than attempts to simulate human behavioral patterns in a market. Quite simply, it is much easier to use a model to tell people what they *should do* than to explain *what they are doing*. Given the fantastic complexity of the modern metropolis, would it not be well to emphasize model development in areas that promise both a significant contribution and a high probability of success?

The image of design in urban planning as a remnant of a bygone age of the "city beautiful" must be replaced by a new design concept based on the creative synthesis of complex plans using all the tools provided by modern technology.

Postscript: Commentary
on Five Years of Development Experience

The original concept of a Land Use Plan Design Model was originated in the summer of 1964 at the Southeastern Wisconsin Regional Planning Commission (SEWRPC) by Kenneth J. Schlager and was further developed in detail for the publication of the foregoing original paper in the JAIP in May of 1965. This original paper stirred enough interest to serve as the basis for a research proposal to the Department of Housing and Urban Development. The proposal resulted in a research grant to SEWRPC under the Urban Planning Research and Demonstration program with the project designation of Wisconsin PD-1. This project has proceeded through two phases and is currently at the beginning of a third and concluding phase. This commentary will relate some of the experience gained during this research program and reflect some thoughts on the future potential and limitations of urban design models.

In summary, the purpose of Phase I of Wisconsin PD-1, which began in

LAND-USE PLAN DESIGN 65

October of 1966 and ended in January of 1968, was to develop a Land Use Plan Design Model and apply it to a small community as a test vehicle. Two important lessons were learned in Phase I. The first was learned early in Phase I and influenced the course of action. The second became apparent too late to have any effect on Phase I but became a primary determinant of the Phase II Program. These two were:

(1) Since the nature of urban design is such that it deals with discrete objects (schools, hospitals, shopping centers, etc.) rather than areas of land, the use of linear programming as the model algorithm became undesirable if not infeasible.
(2) The computer programs for reducing raw data to meaningful model inputs is as challenging a task as the computer program for the model itself.

The impact of the first lesson was felt early so that little time was spent with linear programming, and the model algorithm was formulated to deal directly with discrete elements designated as "modules" which were placed in geographic areas known as "cells" subject to certain constraints and with the objective of minimizing development and operating costs. The model algorithm, which used a steepest descent search approach, operated fairly satisfactorily in Phase I but its limitations became quite apparent with the larger scale applications of Phase II.

Data-reduction problems, the second lesson, were painfully obvious later in Phase I in which model input data was provided through a series of unrelated data processing programs. This piecemeal approach, with its clumsy inconvenience, served as the incentive for an integrated data-reduction program package in Phase II.

Phase II, which began in July of 1968 and ended in September of 1969, was concerned mainly with the application of the model on a larger scale to the development of a regional land-use plan. Since the SEWRPC is a regional planning agency and had previously developed a regional land-use plan by traditional methods, the plan developed by the model could be subject to some searching comparisons.

Since the Southeastern Wisconsin region is large in size (2,689 square miles), Phase II was dominated by data-reduction activities. With the experience of Phase I in mind, a great deal of effort was directed toward the development of an integrated data-reduction system. Integration was enlarged such that the data-reduction program and the model operating programs blended into one system with raw module, constraint, cost, and topographic data as inputs and a land-use plan as an output.

In Phase II with the data-reduction problem under control, the first opportunity arose to see the results of model operation with realistic input data. Although the results of these initial model runs were encouraging in that they resembled a plausible plan considering the goals of constraint observance and cost minimization, need for future improvement of the model were indicated in two areas:

(1) The model algorithm seemed slow in operation and did not provide a true optimal (or even near optimal) solution.
(2) The design constraints, which are intended to reflect the objectives of the design other than minimal cost, require a great deal of thought and study.

The original model algorithm assigns modules to areal cells in a series of binary partitions. The whole design area is first partitioned into two subareas, and each module is assigned to one of these two subareas based on constraint observance and cost minimization. Each subarea is in turn divided in half, and modules are assigned to each half again. This process continues until the smallest area is assigned: a single cell. This approach leads to "holistic" errors in that modules are assigned early in the process to a set of cells that later prove to be nonoptimal. Since such errors cannot be corrected, they result in permanent misallocation of modules contrary to an optimal plan. After a great deal of investigation of possible improvements in the present algorithm, a new approach to algorithm formulation seemed desirable.

The other problem concerning constraint formulation was less a mathematical problem than a value problem. Quite simply, the professed goals, objectives, and design criteria do not reflect the real goals, objectives, and design criteria. In the language of social psychology there is a "hidden agenda" of plan requirements. The problem is to uncover this hidden agenda of real design requirements and convert them into constraints for input to the model.

Results to date and the nature of existing problems indicated the need for a two-pronged attack to make the model a useful tool for planners, architects, and engineers:

(1) A program to document the existing model and associated data-reduction programs in the form of a User's Manual understandable by the practitioner such as the planner, architect, or engineer
(2) A research program to explore fundamental questions of algorithm operation and constraint formulation.

Fortunately, financial support has been obtained for both programs. A development program to document the present model with some minor improvements will be funded by the United States Department of Housing and Urban Development under the Wisconsin PD-1 Program to the Southeastern Wisconsin Regional Planning Commission. A second research-oriented program is being funded by the National Science Foundation through Marquette University. Together these programs have the potential of reducing the design model research to date to a system useful in the practical world of design.

Notes

1. *Review of Existing Land Use Forecasting Techniques,* Traffic Research Corporation, presented to the Boston Regional Planning Project, Toronto (1963).
2. Schlager, Kenneth J., "Simulation Models in Urban and Regional Planning," *Technical Record,* Southeastern Wisconsin Regional Planning Commission, Waukesha, Wisconsin, II, No. 1 (1964).
3. Alexander, Christopher, *Notes on the Synthesis of Form,* Harvard University Press, Cambridge, pp. 15–16 (1964).
4. *Ibid.,* pp. 74-75.
5. Bellman, Richard E., and Dreyfus, Stuart E., *Applied Dynamic Programming* Princeton University Press, Princeton (1962).
6. Schlager, *op. cit.*

5 Technique for Relating Transportation Improvements and Urban Development Patterns[a]

Daniel Brand
Brian Barber
Michael Jacobs

This paper describes a land-use forecasting model which embodies desirable features not heretofore available for use in planning transportation facilities. In the process of developing and calibrating the model, it was assumed that there are limited controls available at the regional scale for guiding the development of an urban area. One of these controls is the transportation system. It is hypothesized that there exists a partial ability to influence the development of a region by means of the transportation system. This is an ability which the planner should utilize, both for the promotion of a more desirable region in which to live, and for planning the transportation system in a more complete and efficient manner.

In the past, the required plan or forecast of the future pattern of land uses has normally been prepared somewhat independently of the planned transportation facilities. An important missing link in the overall urban plan-making process has been a systematic measurement of the effect that future transportation facilities themselves have in shaping the land-use pattern. This is an effect which generally leads to higher usage of transportation facilities than would otherwise be expected, since transportation facilities often attract land uses which require such facilities. It is, therefore, imperative that the planner and engineer plan transportation facilities to accommodate not only those land-use activities already in place and those expected owing to urban expansion, but also those activities which will be induced by the proposed facilities to redistribute themselves.

In this paper, attention is focused primarily on the information which the calibration of the EMPIRIC model reveals on the relative and absolute effect of transportation and community facility improvements on land-development patterns. Secondary attention is focused on some recent results of production forecasts with the model. The (production) EMPIRIC model, to date, has been structured with the equations estimated, for three data sets involving two

---
[a]This paper was sponsored by the Committee on Land Use Evaluation and is reprinted with permission from the Highway Research Board. Reprinted from *Highway Research Record*, No. 207, pages 53–67.

different urban regions. Production forecasts have been carried out for the two different urban regions for which the model was calibrated.

The remainder of this paper describes (1) the formulation of the EMPIRIC model, (2) the estimation of coefficients for the equations comprising the model, (3) generalized equations reflecting knowledge gained to date with the model on the forces underlying urban development patterns, and (4) some results of the forecasting with the EMPIRIC model.

Formulation of the Model

The EMPIRIC land-use forecasting model is a technique, programmed for the computer, which was designed for use in the planning process. It does not apply optimization techniques nor does it restrict freedom of choice; rather, it attempts to make planning a more meaningful procedure by forecasting one important consequence of a set of alternative policies and plans: namely, the future distribution of population, employment and other socioeconomic activities in the region.

The model was formulated such that it would satisfy several criteria, some of which were felt to be important theoretical constraints, and others of which were the operational realities of applying the model in the Eastern Massachusetts region. These criteria,[b] which are largely applicable to any North American metropolitan area, were the abilities:

(1) To recognize the simultaneous and interacting nature of metropolitan development
(2) To take as direct input, planned changes in the transportation system (both highway and transit)
(3) To output important categories of population, employment, and automobile ownership (i.e., the model must provide data for forecasting trip origins, destinations and modal splits)
(4) To provide forecasts for areas sufficiently small to allow meaningful forecasting of trip origins, destinations and modal splits
(5) To be applied recursively (in steps) over relatively short time intervals to allow inputting new values of staged construction of facilities (i.e., the model should produce information directly useful for public works programming).

Criteria of a second order were:

(1) The model should accept other important non-transportation policy

---

[b]This list is similar in many respects to the list of criteria presented by Lathrop and Hamburg (1969).

decisions as inputs. In effect, its output should be a systematic estimate of how a region would develop under the influence of regional growth rates and planning policies relative not only to transportation, but also to utilities, zoning, open space, etc.

(2) The model should allow for reasonable budget limits on operating costs of the model.

(3) Input and output to the model should be compatible with other needs; e.g., input transportation networks should be the same as those needed for traffic work.

The framework decided on for the EMPIRIC model consists of a set of simultaneous linear regression equations. That is, more than one output variable is contained in a single equation, and the relationships embodied in the model between the input and output variables are linear and additive. The simultaneous nature of the model (the coefficients of the equations are estimated using simultaneous regression techniques) is a major innovation, getting around the problem of having to decide which activities to locate or forecast first.

All variables in the equations are expressed as shares of regional totals, and the model forecasts changes in shares of activities, between base year and forecast year, in each of the zones or subregions into which the region is divided. Mathematically, a change in subregional share may be expressed as:

$$\frac{R_{ih}(t)}{\sum_{h-1}^{H} R_{ih}(t)} - \frac{R_{ih}(t-1)}{\sum_{h-1}^{H} R_{ih}(t-1)}$$

where R_{ih} is the level of activity i in zone h, H is the total number of zones in the region, (t) indicates the forecast year, and $(t-1)$ indicates the base year.

Data from two points in time are used to calibrate the model. The formulation of the variables enables both growths and declines of activity levels to be easily handled. Having forecasted changes in shares, the model adds these changes to the shares at the beginning of the forecast interval to obtain the new zonal shares, and then multiplies the new shares by regional totals at the end of the forecast interval to obtain the actual activity levels in each traffic zone. The regional totals are forecast independently of the model so that, with this formulation of output variables, the model is strictly a distributional model.

There are two classes of input variables used in the EMPIRIC model: policy variables, and nonpolicy variables. Policy variables may be manipulated or preset by planners, and therefore they enter the model as terminal or forecast year data. Examples are the transportation system (in the form of accessibilities) and sewage disposal and water supply service levels. Nonpolicy variables are base-year data, such as families-by-income categories and employment-by-industry categories. Also defined as nonpolicy variables are various measures of the capacity of a zone to house development of the various types of activities. These, however, could be used as policy variables by reserving land in zones in accordance with recreation and/or open space policies.

Estimation of Empiric Model Equations

To date, the EMPIRIC model has been calibrated for three data sets. Two of these data sets were for the 3.4 million population (in 1960) Eastern Massachusetts region (Figure 5-1). The first involved the region disaggregated into 626 traffic zones (i.e., observations for each variable), whereas the second divided the region into 97 subregions. The third data set divided the 400,000 population (in 1964) Southeastern Massachusetts Regional Planning District (Figure 5-2) into 71 land-use forecasting districts.

The regression analyses used to estimate the coefficients of the models were preceded by intensive theoretical studies as to the proper structure of the model. These studies, based on a priori reasoning as well as on knowledge gained from prototype EMPIRIC model development work (Hill, Brand, and Hansen, 1965), and the literature, resulted in initial or preliminary structuring of each model.

The theoretical studies were augmented by data-analysis techniques programmed as part of the EMPIRIC model, notably factor analysis, which provides insight into the proper grouping of data categories to form model variables that are as independent of one another as possible, and bivariate correlation analysis, which provides insights into the nature and strengths of the correlations or relationships between pairs of model variables. Using these analyses and the theoretical studies, coefficients for several models for each area (data set) were estimated, each successive model showing improvement over the preceding one. The improvements exhibited were not so much in the "goodness of fit" of the data, but in the stability, the conformance with theory, and the improved significance levels of the variables in the model. These factors are important criteria which must be met if the model is to be a valid and reliable forecasting tool.

The estimated coefficients for the most disaggregated version of the model will be described in detail here. This version of the model comprises a set of nine simultaneous equations, and forecasts four categories of population and five categories of employment for a set of 626 traffic zones. The categories are:

(1) Families with less than $5,000 annual income (1959 dollars)
(2) Families with between $5,000 and $9,999 annual income
(3) Families with between $10,000 and $14,999 annual income

TRANSPORTATION IMPROVEMENTS

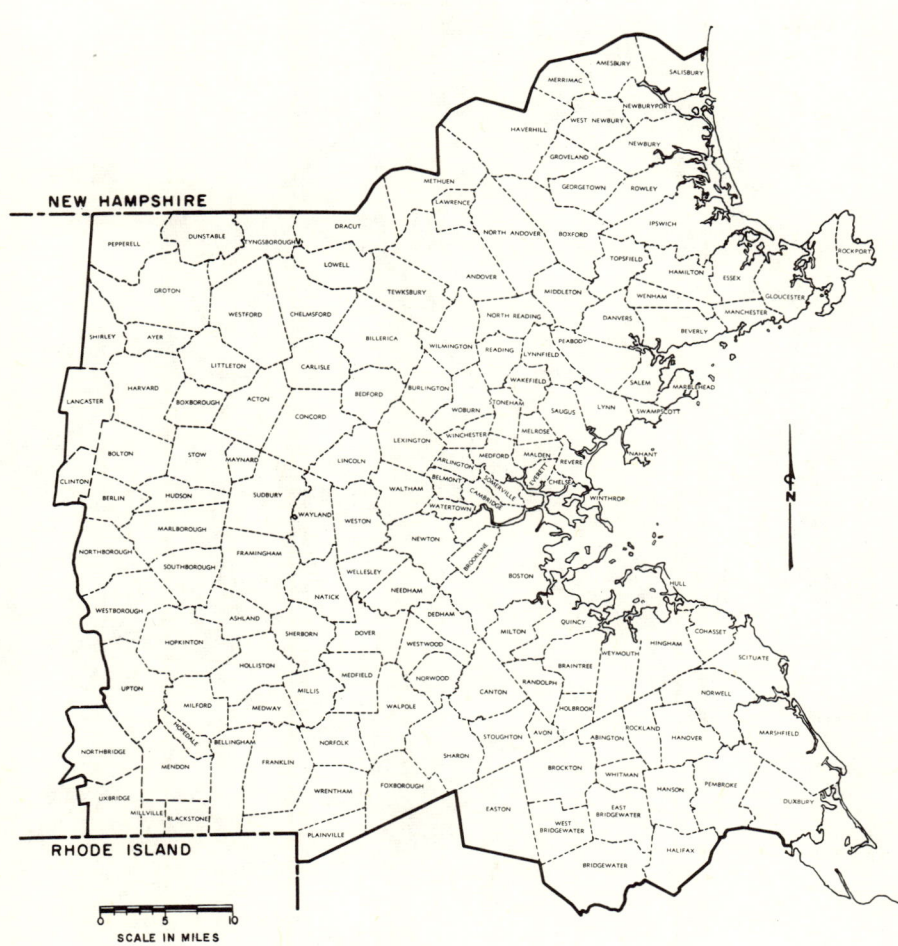

Figure 5-1. The Eastern Massachusetts Region

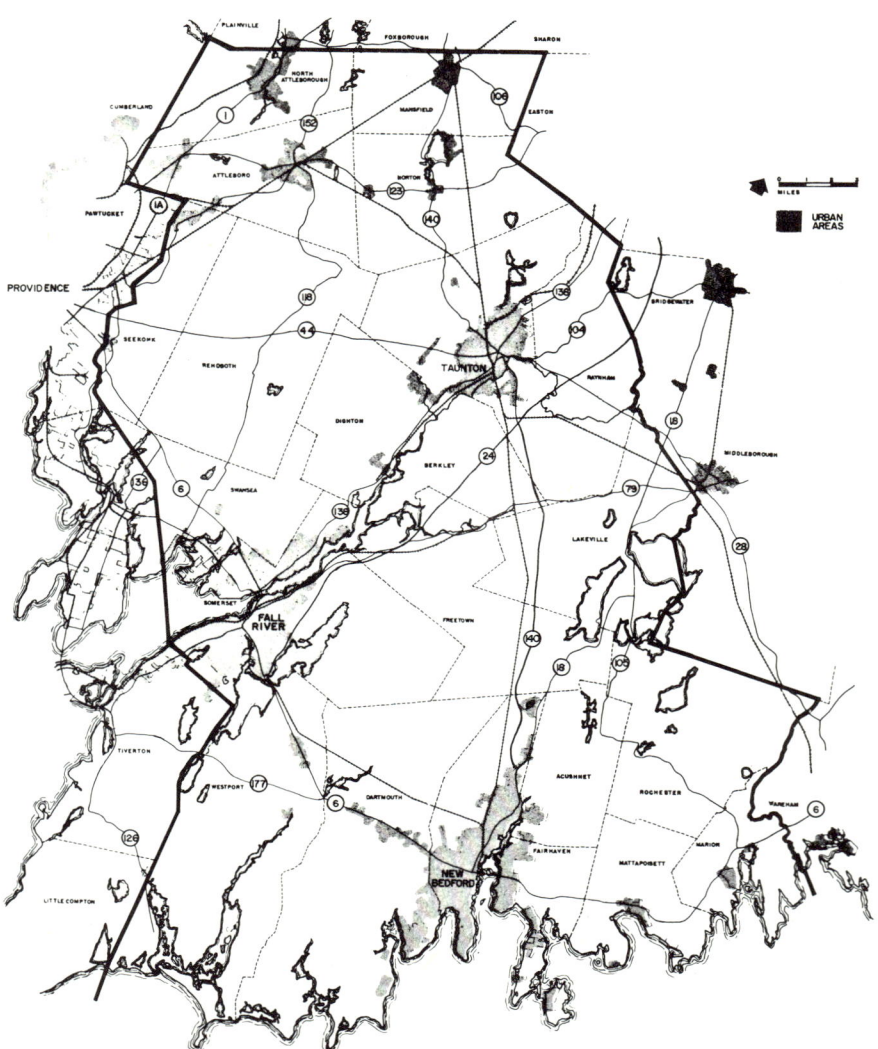

Figure 5-2. Southeastern Massachusetts Planning Region

(4) Families with greater than $14,999 annual income
(5) Manufacturing and construction employment (Standard Industrial Classification codes 15-39)
(6) Wholesale, transportation, communication, utilities, government, and other employment (SIC codes 01-14, 40-50, 91-99)
(7) Retail employment (SIC codes 52-59)
(8) Service employment (SIC codes 70-89)
(9) Finance, insurance, and real estate employment (SIC codes 60-67).

The estimated equations in this calibrated model are described in detail in the Appendix.

Data for two points in time (1950 and 1963) were used to calibrate this model. Due to insufficient data for the earlier year, the model was calibrated using data from 453 of the 626 traffic zones (representing about 80 percent of the 1960 regional population of about 3.4 million persons). Forecasting, however, is being done for all 626 zones.

The statistical significance of each of the variables in the equations of this model is measured with the t-test, which provides an index of the degree to which the effect of a variable upon an output variable is either random or systematic. The t values were computed, for all input and output variables, by the same programs which applied the regression techniques for the estimation of the coefficients in the equations. For 453 sampling points (i.e., traffic zones, a t value of 1.96 or greater is indicative of a variable which is significant to the 95 percent confidence level — a level which is felt to be a very stringent test of significance. Fifty-one of the 63 input and output variables in the nine equations of the model met this high standard. Of the other 12, ten are significant to a level of confidence of 75 percent or greater (the two exceptions being significant at the 56 percent and 58 percent levels).

The few variables which were significant to less than the 95 percent confidence level were still felt, therefore, to be statistically acceptable, and were retained in the final model structure because they, along with the other variables in the model, had regression coefficients whose signs and relative magnitudes satisfactorily expressed the hypothesized relationships between the variables.

An additional test of the model was its "goodness of fit" over the calibration period. That is, an indication of the model's reliability as a forecasting tool was obtained by using the calibrated model and the calibration base year (1950) data, and "forecasting" to the terminal year of the calibration period (1963) to see how well the model reproduced the activity growths occurring during the calibration interval. Statistical summaries were then prepared comparing observed and calculated (forecast) 1963 zonal values of the output variables.

These summaries include the root-mean-square (RMS) error, the RMS error ratio, and the coefficient of determination (R^2). The RMS error is computed in the following manner:

$$\text{RMS error} = \sqrt{\frac{\sum_{h=1}^{H}(O_{ih} - C_{ih})^2}{H}}$$

where O_{ih} is the observed value of variable i in zone h, C_{ih} is the calculated value of variable i in zone h, and H is the total number of zones in the region. Assuming normality, the observed value does not differ from the calculated value for about 67 percent of the zones by more than plus or minus the RMS error. The RMS error ratio is the ratio of the RMS error to the mean or arithmetic average of the observed output variables ($\overline{O}_i$).

The coefficient of determination (R^2) is computed as follows:

$$R^2 = \frac{\sum_{h=1}^{H}(O_{ih} - \overline{O}_i)^2 - \sum_{h=1}^{H}(O_{ih} - C_{ih})^2}{\sum_{h=1}^{H}(O_{ih} - \overline{O}_i)^2}.$$

As R^2 approaches unity, the reliability of the model is regarded to be quite high, and conversely, as R^2 approaches zero, the reliability is said to be quite low. These summaries, for the 453 traffic zones in the calibration area, are given in Table 5-1 for the nine equations in the final calibrated model. In addition, the corresponding statistics have been recomputed following the aggregation of the 453 traffic zones into 104 calibration analysis districts. This procedure was designed to provide some indication of the sensitivity of these reliability statistics to zonal aggregation.

It can be seen that the model fits the population data better than the employment data. This is to be expected, since a statistical model fits large numbers of small locating units (e.g., households) better than the "lumpier" activities which typify the employment locating units. The fit to the geographically small 453 zones appears highly satisfactory, and compares favorably with similar error measures calculated for home interview survey origin-destination data, and for various types of traffic models, e.g., gravity models. (Reliability Test Report, 1964.) In addition, the model in the Appendix appears quite sound from the standpoints of statistical significance (high t values), and logic (conformance with hypothesized relationships).

Table 5-1
Statistical Summaries of Observed vs. Calculated Population and Employment Levels

Category	453 Zones			104 Districts		
	RMS Error	RMS Error Ratio	R^2	RMS Error	RMS Error Ratio	R^2
Families, <$5,000	108	0.249	0.951	232	0.123	0.990
Families, $5,000–$9,999	209	0.269	0.906	685	0.203	0.950
Families, $10,000–$14,999	82	0.380	0.793	233	0.250	0.915
Families, >$15,000	61	0.578	0.826	150	0.328	0.946
Mfg. and construction employment	1,031	1.23	0.549	2,301	0.630	0.862
Wholesale, TCU[a] Govt., and other employment	412	0.782	0.876	969	0.422	0.982
Retail employment	310	0.781	0.860	846	0.490	0.949
Service employment	677	1.43	0.500	1,958	0.949	0.880
FIR[b] employment	224	1.33	0.953	260	0.352	0.997

[a] Transportation, communication and utilities.
[b] Finance, insurance, and real estate.

Generalized Land-Use Forecasting Equations

The true measure of the EMPIRIC model's worth as a forecasting and plan-making tool is in the empirical and logical reliability of the regression coefficients. Because the variables are formulated as zonal shares or changes in zonal shares, these coefficients may be interpreted as indicators of the relative effects of the variables in influencing relative growths or declines of an output variable at the zonal level. The sign of the coefficient (positive or negative) indicates whether the variable induces or hinders the growth in zonal share of the output variable, while the magnitude of the coefficient indicates the importance of this influence relative to the influence of the other variables in the equation on the growths of the output variables. Coefficient stability, therefore, becomes an important indicator of the success achieved in producing true relationships in the model; relationships from which one may learn about influencing the shape of metropolitan development, and, consequently, the usage of transportation facilities.

Two types of coefficient stability may be described. The first is coefficient stability as successive model structures are estimated in the model calibration process using a single data set. The coefficients in the model described in the Appendix behaved extremely well in this regard over the successive equation estimations. (Calibration Report, December, 1966.) In the few instances when coefficients in the final model exhibited appreciable changes from the corresponding coefficients in earlier models, it was almost always attributable to a problem of collinearity between independent variables in the earlier models. The situation was remedied by the deletion in the final model of all but one of the related independent variables, or by the substitution of a single variable for the complete set of collinear independent variables.

The second type of coefficient stability pertains to the similarity of the relationships expressed by the coefficients, as different data sets for the same region or for different regions are used to estimate the same structural equations. The three calibrations of the EMPIRIC model just described did not use the same structural equations because of the purposes for which the models were developed, and because of the differences in the data available for calibration. It is hoped that future work will allow the estimation of the same EMPIRIC model structural equations for different data sets.

Nevertheless, the three models all distributed classes of population and employment to relatively large numbers of small areas. And the types of independent variables used in each model were similar. The results indicate that there is enough coefficient similarity between corresponding input and output variables for the differing data sets and areas to warrant an attempt to generalize the results of the three models. In recording these results, it is recognized that there should indeed be different relationships between variables with differing zone sizes. Also, different urban areas have different regional growth rates and different compositions of activities comprising the urban development pattern. In fact, if the coefficient set were completely stable it would not be necessary to recalibrate the model for different zone systems and areas.

The generalized equations are written out completely below. The following notation is employed:

(Δ) = change in subregional share over the time interval
(t) = subregional share at the end of the time interval
$(t = 1)$ = subregional share at the beginning of the time interval

(All variables are formulated as shares or as changes in shares.)

POPL, POPM, and POPU = lower-, middle-, and upper-income population
MFG, RTL, SVC, and OTH = manufacturing, retail, service, and other employment
UTIL = measure of utilities service
CAPP, CAPM, and CAPR = measures of the capacity and propensity of a zone to house new population (i.e., residential), manufacturing, and retail development (the measures are defined in the Appendix)
VACC and QACC = measures of vehicle (automobile) and transit accessibility (accessibility is defined in the Appendix).

The magnitudes of the coefficients are indicated as s, m, or b — small, medium, and big (<0.1, 0.1 to 0.4, and >0.4).

The equations follow:

(Δ) POPL = b (Δ) POPM − m (Δ) POPU + s (Δ) SVC + m $(t - 1)$ POPL − s $(t - 1)$ POPU + s (t) UTIL − m (Δ) VACC

(Δ) POPM = − s (Δ) POPL + m (Δ) POPU + s (Δ) RTL + s (Δ) SVC − m $(t - 1)$ POPM + m (t) UTIL + m (Δ) VACC + s (Δ) QACC

(Δ) POPU = − m (Δ) POPL + m (Δ) POPM − m $(t - 1)$ POPU + m (t) UTIL + s $(t - 1)$ CAPP − m (Δ) VACC + s (Δ) QACC

(Δ) MFG = − m (Δ) POPM − b (Δ) POPU + m (Δ) OTH − b $(t - 1)$ MFG + m (Δ) CAPM + m (t) VACC + m (Δ) QACC

(Δ) RTL = m (Δ) OTH − s $(t - 1)$ POPU − m $(t - 1)$ RTL + m $(t - 1)$ CAPR + m (Δ) VACC

(Δ) SVC = − s (Δ) OTH − m $(t - 1)$ SVC + m (Δ) UTIL + m (t) VACC + m (Δ) QACC

(Δ) OTH = m (Δ) MFG + s (Δ) RTL − m $(t - 1)$ OTH + s (Δ) QACC

It must be reemphasized that these equations are for discussion and theory building purposes only, and are abstracted from only three models calibrated for two areas: the relatively slow-growing Eastern and Southeastern Massachusetts regions.

The equations generalize the interrelationships among activities in this type of area for this scale of zonal disaggregation (i.e., for an average zonal population of from about 5,000 to about 35,000), and for this type of model (linear and share). Each of the equations describes hypothesized relationships designed to explain the growth of a particular output activity. For example, the first equation states that growth of lower-income population in a zone is induced by a simultaneous growth of middle-income population but hindered by the growth of and presence of (at the beginning of the time interval) upper-income population. It is also induced by the simultaneous growth of service employment, by the presence at the beginning of the time interval of low-income population (the ghetto effect), and by the presence at the end of the time interval of utilities services. It is hindered by the (relative) growth of vehicle accessibility of the zone (since they compete for more accessible land with higher-income groups, as explained later).

An examination of the equations indicates that the accessibility variables are the most important of the policy variables for forecasting the location of population and employment. However, the nonpolicy variables, over which the planner has no direct control, are generally stronger determinants of locational patterns than are the policy variables. In particular, growths in the various population-by-income groupings are strongly related to growths in the adjacent population-by-income groupings. It is also observed that in the employment equations among the strongest variables are one or more of the other output variables. These observations provide evidence of the realism of this type of simultaneous model.

In all equations, one of the more important determinants of growth is the "lagged" variable, i.e., the value of the output variable at the beginning of the forecast interval. In every instance but one, the lagged variable carries a medium or large negative sign. The single exception is important in that it is in the (first) equation for the low-income population. In only that instance does the presence of the (same) activity at the beginning of the time interval induce increased growth in the zone in the regional share of the activity. This is striking statistical evidence of the increasing ghettoism of the low-income family, about which there is much discussion today.

Many of the coefficients capture other relationships worthy of examination. In the low-income population equation again, the medium-sized negative coefficient modifying growth in vehicle accessibility indicates that these low-income families do not have the resources to take their full share of the advantages of improvements in the regional highway system. However, it may also be noted that the highest income group (in the third equation) exhibits the same medium-sized negative sign for this variable. This appears to indicate that they would rather pay increased transportation costs to enjoy the other residential amenities which they desire. The very large middle-income group, on the other hand (in the second equation), exhibits the concern for improved highways with which we are familiar.

It is also of interest to note that the middle- and high-income groups take advantage in a small but noticeable way of transit improvements, which in this case were rapid transit and commuter railroad service changes.

The position of the accessibility variables as the most influential of the policy variables is especially significant because there seems to be considerably greater control at the regional level over the transportation system than over any of the other policy variables relating to the development and physical arrangement of land patterns. This is partly because most land development policies are determined at the local level by the citizens of the localities affected. Transportation policies, on the other hand, cannot be so isolated at the local level. The function of transportation is to connect places (which may have differing transportation desires), and major transportation policies must be decided on a broader (e.g., regional) level. At best, planners can plan and promote transportation improvements which reinforce development decisions made at the local level.

Forecasting with the EMPIRIC Model

The capabilities of the EMPIRIC land-use forecasting model to manipulate data, to reproduce significant parts of the environment, and to quickly simulate complex relationships between the forces which shape the environment, provide the model with the ability to predict the future distribution of land-use activities with varying sets of input public works policies. This ability is essential for providing information for judging alternative plans, i.e., for determining (1) how well each plan functions, (2) how well each plan achieves its desired set of values, and (3) whether a particular programming (scheduling) strategy has been successful. A means of using the model in conjunction with travel forecasting techniques for evaluating alternative transportation policies and programs is outlined as follows:

(1) The model is calibrated (i.e., the equations structured and the coefficients estimated) using data from two historical time points; say, time t and time $t + x$, where time t is x years earlier than time $t + x$. (The x-year forecasting interval would normally be about 5 or 10 years.)

(2) Estimates of regional growth for an x-year period would be made for each activity to be predicted, and regional forecasts of these activities would be made for time $t + 2x$.

(3) The land-use model would be applied for an x-year forecast from time $t + x$ to time $t + 2x$. The input data required for forecasting would include

base year (time $t + x$) values of activity levels, and base year and forecast year (time $t + 2x$) travel times (the latter times being based on the anticipated or proposed completion of new transportation facilities and the closure of old facilities). Also input would be base year and forecast year values of other policy variables, such as utilities service.

(4) The traffic model would be applied to forecast for time $t + 2x$, traffic flows, times and costs, based on the predicted land-use pattern and the travel facilities scheduled for completion at time $t + 2x$.

(5) The procedure outlined in Steps 3 and 4 would be repeated if the travel times and costs found in 4 differed substantially from final year values used in 3.

(6) The procedures outlined in Steps 2 through 5 would be repeated for successive x-year periods, using activity levels estimates by the land-use model at the end of each period as starting levels for forecasting the next period. This step would be continued until the final target year had been reached.

This process thus provides a systematic representation of the anticipated sequential stages of development of a region under the influence of a set of public policies relating to the transportation system, utilities service, etc. Repeating the process for different sets of policies will produce different anticipated development patterns. The planners and decision-makers can study these various patterns, analyze their relative merits and costs, and can more knowledgeably make decisions as to which sets of policies will be most effective in furthering the social and economic goals of the region. Especially valuable would be the exploration of alternative public works programming strategies. This process allows the program to be developed as an integral part of, and at the same time as, the overall plan.

At this writing, the EMPIRIC model has been used to make four sets of production forecasts at the 97 subregion level for the Eastern Massachusetts region and one set of forecasts at the 71 district level for the Southeastern Massachusetts region.

Subregion Forecast Results

For the purpose of exploring patterns of urban growth which are considered feasible for the future development of the Eastern Massachusetts region, an application of the 97 subregion EMPIRIC model was made. Forecasts were prepared for four regional growth alternatives. Each alternative pursued different basic physical objectives for structuring future urban growth. The alternatives are called (1) the composite plan, (2) the radial corridor plan, (3) the spread city plan, and (4) the nucleated plan. In this application the EMPIRIC model is viewed as a design tool; i.e., the designer is able to determine the consequences of selected programs. This in turn enables him to choose which program (set and schedule of actions) to propose for implementation or to subject to more detailed analysis.

Values for each of the policy variables were altered in this model application. For each of the four plans, appropriate "test" future highway, transit, water and sewer networks were designed. There were differences between the test networks only for the period 1975 to 1990 owing to the region's strong commitment to the 1975 program for highway and transit networks. Identical regional "control" totals of population and employment were used for each plan. These are listed in Table 5-2.

Table 5-2
Future Regional Control Totals (in Thousands)

Year	Population	Mfg. Employment	Non-Mfg. Employment
1963	3,540.5	426.8	870.0
1975	3,924.0	433.5	1,073.2
1990	4,733.0	478.7	1,322.4

Forecast results for 1990 showed an average difference between the highest and lowest subregional values among the four plans of 9 percent for population, 42 percent for manufacturing employment and 13 percent for nonmanufacturing employment. The range of differences between the high and low 1990 forecasts was 1 percent to 46 percent for population, with 14 of the 97 subregions having differences over 15 percent. The corresponding figures for manufacturing employment were from 2 percent to 500 percent with 11 subregions over 50 percent, and for nonmanufacturing employment, from 1 percent to 89 percent with 7 subregions over 30 percent. However, certain patterns are common to each of the four forecasts. First, the regional core area continues to decline although at a slower rate than during the model calibration period 1950-1963. Second, each geographic sector retains an almost constant share of regional population and employment. Third, change in share by ring is greater than change in share by sector as would be expected (growth is moving outward from the regional center or core).

By identifying and comparing subregions in which only the highway or transit network input data have been changed, it is possible to measure the impact of transportation facilities. It appears in some cases that good highway connections will result in 10 to 15 percent more population than poorer highway connections. Similar observations are possible with respect to employment. Many such observations would have to be made and investigated before any verified generalizations could be made. Sufficient differences existed between plans to warrant exploration of alternatives at a more detailed level (i.e., with the 626 traffic zone EMPIRIC model).

That sufficient differences occurred was not surprising. The hypothesis that the design of the transportation system plays a large and important role in the shaping of metropolitan development was borne out by a test carried out with a prototype version of the EMPIRIC model. (Reliability Test Report, 1964). This model was used to simulate the effect on the locational pattern of population and employment in the Eastern Massachusetts region of two different design policies of transportation facilities over the 1950-1960 decade. The first design policy simulated was exactly that which took place in the region between 1950 and 1960 insofar as highway and mass transportation improvements or closures were concerned. The second simulated design policy was that no changes were made in the highway and mass transportation systems between 1950 and 1960.

The major transportation improvements consisted of radial expressway sections plus Route 128, a major circumferential expressway which passes through a tier of suburban communities. The simulated policy of transportation improvements resulted in expected increases in population and employment in the third and fourth tiers or rings of subregions, relative to results with the simulated policy of no transportation improvements. However, it is interesting to note that relative increases in population and employment were also obtained in the older core cities of Boston, Cambridge, and Somerville, due to the new radial expressways and the extension of the rapid transit system to the periphery of Newton (i.e., to Route 128).

Conclusions

From the results obtained thus far with the three versions of the EMPIRIC land-use forecasting model, several observations may be drawn. The model has in each instance been satisfactorily calibrated in terms of logical relationships expressed by the variables and their coefficients (i.e., conformance with hypotheses), high statistical significance (as measured with t values), good fit with the data, and stability of the coefficients within each model (as observed by tracing variables through the successively estimated models).

The model thus far has been successfully used for forecasting to relatively large numbers of zones in two instances: (1) with the 97 subregion version calibrated for the (Boston) Metropolitan Area Planning Council, and (2) with the 71 district version calibrated for the Southeastern Massachusetts Regional Planning District. It is expected that the model will be able to successfully forecast to very large numbers of zones, as will be soon tested when forecasts are made using the 626 zone version of the model calibrated for the Eastern Massachusetts Regional Planning Project.

In addition, it appears that the model is properly sensitive to varying public policy inputs. The four sets of forecasts produced with the 97 subregion version of the model were intended to reflect widely ranging transportation policies, and the results displayed substantial and logical differences in the forecast values of population and employment. It is felt that this is in large part due to the fact that the model deals primarily with growths of activities rather than with absolute levels of activities at one point in time.

While these substantial findings have been made from the research and development work completed to date, further research into and with the EMPIRIC model would be useful. Moreover, future calibrations and applications of the model are warranted. Such calibrations and applications, with data from other metropolitan areas, would contribute to a better understanding of land-use development patterns in urban areas.

There are at least five major areas of research. First, the questions of coefficient stability could be investigated. Second, possibilities for designing optimal sets of inputs (e.g., accessibility variables) to produce desired plans could be undertaken through mathematical reformulation of the model. Third, the potential for developing programs for public investment using the staging capabilities of the model could be investigated. Fourth, further application of the model as a design tool is worth exploring. Fifth, the possibility of joining the EMPIRIC computer programming system to a plan evaluation system should be investigated. Such a joint or tandem system would be extremely desirable since it would increase our capacity for exploration of alternative policies and programs.

Finally, a more intensive analysis of the forecast results produced by the (Boston) Metropolitan Area Planning Council may yield more support for generalizations of the type attempted in this paper.

References

Bolan, Richard S., Hansen, Willard B., Irwin, Neal A., and Dieter, Karl H., "Planning Applications of a Simulation Model," paper presented to the New England Section of the Regional Science Association, Boston College (October, 1963).

Calibration Report: EMPIRIC Land Use Forecasting Model, 97 Subregion Version, presented by Traffic Research Corporation to the Commonwealth of Massachusetts, Metropolitan Area Planning Council (November, 1966).

Calibration Report: EMPIRIC Land Use Forecasting Model for 626 Traffic Zones, presented by Traffic Research Corporation to the Eastern Massachusetts Regional Planning Project (December, 1966).

Calibration Report: EMPIRIC Land Use Forecasting Model for 71 Forecasting Districts, presented by Traffic Research Corporation to the Southeastern Massachusetts Regional Planning District (January, 1967).

Hill, Donald M., "A Growth Allocation Model for the Boston Region," *Journal of the American Institute of Planners*, Vol. 31, No. 2, pp. 111-120 (May, 1965).

Hill, Donald M., and Brand, Daniel, "Methodology for Developing Activity Distribution Models by Linear Regression Analysis," Highway Research Record 126, pp. 66-78 (1966).

Hill, Donald M., Brand, Daniel, and Hansen, Willard B., "Prototype Development of a Statistical Land-Use Prediction Model for Greater Boston Region," Highway Research Record 114, pp. 51-70 (1965).

Irwin, Neal A., and Brand, Daniel, "Planning and Forecasting Metropolitan Development," *Traffic Quarterly* (October, 1965).

Lathrop, George T., and Hamburg, John R., "An Opportunity-Accessibility Model for Allocating Regional Growth," *Journal of the American Institute of Planners* (May, 1965).

Reliability Test Report: [Prototype] EMPIRIC Land Use Forecasting Model, presented by Traffic Research Corporation to the Eastern Massachusetts Regional Planning Project (January, 1964).

Seidman, David R., "The Present and Futures of Urban Land Use Models," paper presented to Fourth Annual Conference on Planning Information Systems and Programs, University of California, Berkeley (August, 1966).

Appendix:
The 626 Zone Eastern Massachusetts EMPIRIC Model

The following variables are used in the model:

Population variables: All income figures are given in terms of 1959 dollars.

$F_{<5k}$ = Number of families with an annual income less than $5,000
F_{5-10k} = Number of families with an annual income between $5,000 and $9,999
F_{10-15k} = Number of families with an annual income between $10,000 and $14,999
$F_{\geqslant 15k}$ = Number of families with an annual income equal to, or greater than, $15,000.

Employment variables: All employment variables are measured at the zone of employment.

$M \& C$ = Manufacturing and construction employment (SIC codes 15-39)
OTHER = Wholesale, transportation, communication, utilities, government and other employment (SIC codes 1-14, 40-50, 91-99)

TRANSPORTATION IMPROVEMENTS

RET = Retail employment (SIC codes 52-59)
SVC = Service employment (SIC codes 70-89)
FIR = Finance, insurance and real estate employment (SIC codes 60-67).

Land developability variables: The nomenclature used to define these variables includes: *NAP* = net residential area; *NAM* = net manufacturing area; *NAR* = net retail area; *UA* = total used area of a zone = *NAP* + *NAM* + *NAR* + other developed area; and *GA* = gross area = *UA* + developable area.

CI POP = Capacity or land developability index for population = (*NAP/GA*) (*GA* - *UA*)
CI MFG = Capacity or land developability index for manufacturing = (*NAM/GA*) (*GA* - *UA*)
CI RET = Capacity or land developability index for retail = (*NAR/GA*) (*GA* - *UA*).

Utilities service variables:

WATER = Index, from 1 through 7, of water supply service, multiplied by *UA*
SEWER = Index, from 1 through 5, of sewage disposal service, multiplied by *UA*.

Accessibility variables: The accessibility of zone *g* to activity *i* is equal to

$$\sum_{h=1}^{H} R_{ih} e^{-tgh}$$

where R_{ih} is the quantity of activity *i* in zone *h*, *H* is the total number of zones, *e* is the base of natural logarithms, t_{gh} is the travel time between zones *g* and *h*, and β (the beta factor) is an empirically derived factor. All accessibilities were then multiplied by *UA* for use in the model.

VACC TF = Vehicle accessibility of a zone to total families
QACC TF = Transit accessibility of a zone to total families
$VACCF_{\geq 10}$ = Vehicle accessibility of a zone to total families with an annual income equal to, or greater than, $10,000 (1959 dollars)
$QACCF_{<10}$ = Transit accessibility of a zone to families with an annual income less than $10,000 (1959 dollars)
VACC TE = Vehicle accessibility of a zone to total employment
QACC TE = Transit accessibility of a zone to total employment
VACCM & C = Vehicle accessibility of a zone to manufacturing and construction employment

VACCR & S = Vehicle accessibility of a zone to retail and service employment

Variables measured at the forecast year are preceded by (*t*). Variables measured at the base year are preceded by (*t* - 1). Variables representing changes between the base year and forecast year are preceded by Δ. All (*t*) and (*t* - 1) variables are formulated as subregional shares. The "Δ" variables are formulated as changes in subregional shares. The number in parentheses following the accessibility variables indicates the value of the beta factor used for the calculation of that accessibility. The model, then, is comprised of the following equations:

Equation 1: $\Delta F_{<5k} = 0.637 \Delta F_{5-10k} - 0.295 \Delta F_{10-15k} + 0.018 \Delta SVC + 0.133(t - 1) F_{<5k} - 0.109(t - 1) F_{10-15k} + 0.044(t - 1) WATER - 0.298 \Delta VACC\ TE\ (0.05) - 0.068(t - 1) VACC\ TE\ (0.15).$

Equation 2: $\Delta F_{5-10k} = 0.530 \Delta F_{<5k} + 0.337 \Delta F_{10-15k} + 0.022 \Delta RET + 0.060 \Delta SVC - 0.101(t - 1) F_{5-10k} + 0.036(t - 1) SVC + 0.044(t) SEWER + 0.025(t - 1) CI\ POP + 0.302 \Delta VACC\ TE\ (0.05) + 0.114 \Delta QACC\ TE\ (0.005).$

Equation 3: $\Delta F_{10-15k} = -0.125 \Delta F_{<5k} + 0.637 \Delta F_{5-10k} + 0.294 \Delta F_{\geq 15k} - 0.224(t - 1) F_{10-15k} + 0.196(t - 1) SEWER + 0.145 \Delta SEWER.$

Equation 4: $\Delta F_{\geq 15k} = -0.282 \Delta F_{5-10k} + 0.603 \Delta F_{10-15k} - 0.278(t - 1) F_{\geq 15k} + 0.145(t - 1) WATER + 0.118(t - 1) SEWER + 0.046(t - 1) CI\ POP - 0.384 \Delta VACCF_{\geq 10}\ (0.15) + 0.093 \Delta QACC\ TE\ (0.15).$

Equation 5: $\Delta M\ \&\ C = 0.220 \Delta OTHER - 0.302(t - 1) M\ \&\ C - 0.015(t - 1) FIR + 0.138(t - 1) CI\ MFG + 0.278 \Delta QACCF_{<10}(0.05) + 0.121(t - 1) VACC\ TF\ (0.05).$

Equation 6: $\Delta OTHER = 0.456 \Delta M\ \&\ C + 0.081 \Delta RET - 0.132 \Delta FIR + 0.106(t - 1) M\ \&\ C - 0.194(t - 1) OTHER - 0.414 \Delta VACC\ TE\ (0.15) + 0.095(t - 1) QACC\ TF\ (0.05).$

Equation 7: $\Delta RET = 0.440 \Delta OTHER - 0.117(t - 1) F_{\geq 15k} + 0.126(t - 1) OTHER - 0.363(t - 1) RET + 0.165(t - 1) CI\ RET + 0.213 \Delta VACC\ TF\ (0.15) - 0.064(t - 1) QACC\ TF\ (0.05).$

Equation 8: $\Delta SVC = -0.252 \Delta OTHER - 0.510(t - 1) SVC + 0.022(t - 1) FIR + 0.620 \Delta WATER + 0.240 \Delta SEWER + 0.564 \Delta QACC\ TF\ (0.05) + 0.390(t - 1) VACC\ TF\ (0.05).$

Equation 9: $\Delta FIR = 0.614 \Delta OTHER + 0.020(t - 1) SVC - 0.159(t - 1) FIR + 0.110(t - 1) QACC\ TF\ (0.05).$

The 626 Zone Eastern Massachusetts EMPIRIC Submodel

In addition to the nine output variables contained in the model, there were four additional variables for which forecasts were desired: total population (*POP*); automobile ownership (*AUTOS*); school enrollment in grades K-8 (*SCHOOL, K-8*); and school enrollment in grades 9-12 (*SCHOOL, 9-12*). These variables were not included in the main model owing either to their being highly correlated with other output variables, or to suitable data being available for only one of the calibration time points.

These variables, consequently, were incorporated into a submodel which was calibrated using data from only one point in time (1963). The equations comprising the submodel are written out below. The notation is the same as that used earlier for describing the main model structure, with the additional variables *TF* (total number of families) and *MED FI* (median family income in terms of 1959 dollars multiplied by *TF*).

Equation 1: $(t) POP = 0.944 \ (t) \ TF + 0.016 \ (t) \ WATER + 0.034 \ (t) \ QACC \ TE \ (0.15)$.

Equation 2: $(t) AUTOS = 0.871 \ (t) \ MED \ FI + 0.164 \ (t) \ WATER - 0.042 \ (t) \ QACC \ TF \ (0.15)$.

Equation 3: $(t) SCHOOL, K-8 = 0.918 \ (t) \ TF + 0.154 \ (t) \ WATER - 0.065 \ (t) \ QACC \ TF \ (0.15)$.

Equation 4: $(t) SCHOOL, 9-12 = 0.874 \ (t) \ TF + 0.095 \ (t) \ SEWER + 0.037 \ (t) \ QACC \ TF \ (0.15)$.

The submodel is forecast following forecasts with the main model. These latter forecasts are used to derive $(t) \ TF$ and $(t) \ MED \ FI$ for use in the submodel. The other input variables required for submodel forecasting (utility service and accessibilities) represent policy variables.

The reliability check performed on the submodel (i.e., the comparison of observed with "forecast" 1963 values) yielded the following results:

Category	453 Zones			104 Districts		
	RMS Error	RMS Error Ratio	R^2	RMS Error	RMS Error Ratio	R_2
Total population	643	0.104	0.984	2,477	0.092	0.991
Automobile ownership	410	0.229	0.915	1,179	0.151	0.963
School enrollment, K-8	211	0.220	0.929	632	0.151	0.969
School enrollment, 9-12	71	0.211	0.939	239	0.164	0.966

6

Application of a Land-Use Allocation Model for Franklin County, Ohio[a]

William C. Habig

The model discussed in this chapter has been developed to fit an operational situation in which the Midohio Regional Planning Commission (hereinafter referred to as the "RPC") is not faced with a problem of growth projections but with one of allocation. The RPC has regional growth projections and has designed this model to project where such growth will occur within Franklin County. This land-use allocation model has been fully documented in a report[a] prepared for the RPC by CONSAD Research Corporation as a consultant on part of a HUD-financed 701 planning program. This paper will point out interrelationships of this model to the transportation planning program which uses some of its outputs as inputs to other models.

One might logically ask why the RPC is doing such detailed work as allocating regional growth to small areas. Franklin County has been divided into 765 geographic areas called traffic zones as a result of the 1962 Highway Act which required comprehensive transportation studies. Many of the methods used in such planning required very detailed data projections for traffic zones.

The major elements of the plan deal with land use, community facilities, water and sewer facilities, and transportation. The application of this model bridges the gap between them. The transportation planning process places very stringent requirements on any output the allocation model produces. The preceding paper by Schlager mentions inventories and their inherent problems. The RPC is guilty of shortcomings in this area because serious problems with the O & D Survey greatly delayed getting out of the inventory phase. The RPC now is at the stage of beginning to use calibrated transportation models. One of these models (trip generation) is used to estimate the number of trips that are produced by individual traffic zones and it is the one that required detailed inputs from the land-use allocation model. For example, knowledge is needed of what kind of dwelling units will be built in a zone between 1975 and 1985 or of the number of persons who will work in the downtown area. These data can then be translated into trip attractions. So this is one major use of the model; i.e., to provide inputs for the transportation planning process. This paper will

---

[a]"A Land Use Allocation Model for Franklin County, Ohio," by CONSAD Research Corporation, William C. Habig and Richard I. Haller – Regional Planning Commission, Franklin County Regional Planning Commission, Columbus, Ohio (1969).

92   APPLICATION OF URBAN STRUCTURE MODELS

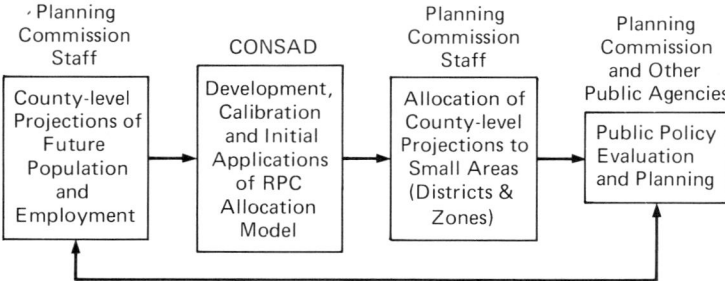

Figure 6-1. The Model's Place Within RPC's Planning Function.

also discuss other uses after presenting the model's structure as well as the use made in testing several types of policies in pursuit of a final plan. This latter use is illustrated by Figure 6-1.

The Model's Operation

The model is purely an allocation technique. Countywide development projections prepared three years ago are used as inputs. The initial application consisted of short-run allocations to the years 1970 and 1975 starting from the 1964 base year. The model allocates regional growth projections to 37 "districts." It also has a routine that can prorate a district's growth to its component zones, but this is often done manually.

The model had to do three basic things: allocate exogenous forecasts of county-wide growth to districts, use available data, and be sensitive to the kind of alternative public policies that would be used in evaluating future land-use alternatives. Its output requirements were five-year projections of certain variables: dwelling units by seven income classes, employment by three sectors (commercial, industrial, and public), land-use acres in terms of an employment sector or a residential type, labor force, and auto availability (number of automobiles based at the home).

Because of the restrictions of data and intended use, the model has been developed with the capability of producing district and zonal forecasts for each of several time periods based largely upon district data. The best way to accomplish this is by a two-phase allocation of regional growth to subareas of the county.

The first phase is the allocation of exogenously projected (1) households to place of residence and (2) employment opportunities by industry type to place of employment. These allocations are made by district, permitting the use of a relatively full data set including items indicating changes in population,

LAND-USE ALLOCATION

employment, and public policy and facility patterns between 1954 and 1964. The forecasts of employment and residence calculated for each district are then, in the second phase, allocated among the contained zones.

Because time series data are available at the district level, and because estimates of the impacts of alternative policies are desired, district forecasts are forecasts of change. The base year of each forecasting period provides some stability within the system, thereby preventing radical variations over time just as investments of efforts and finances impart stability to the activities and facilities of the region over time.

The region-to-districts sybsystem is composed of a set of simultaneous equations expressing the relationship between observed characteristics of each district and the relative attraction of the district for the regional growth of population and employment. These equations are of the following general form:

$$A_d^k = f(A_{d \cdot t-1}^k; A_d^{1-n}; AC_{d \cdot t-1}^{1-n}; HC_{d \cdot t-1}; SS_{d \cdot t-1}; + C)$$

where

$A_{d \cdot t-1}^k$ = size of activity type k in district d at time $t-1$

A_d^{1-n} = net change in some other activities $(1, 2, \ldots, n)$ in district d at time t

$AC_{d \cdot t-1}^{1-n}$ = accessibility of district d to regional distributions of some other activities $(1, 2, \ldots, n)$ at time $t-1$

$HC_{d \cdot t-1}^k$ = residual residential holding capacity of district d at time $t-1$

$SS_{d \cdot t-1}$ = index of sewer service in district d at time $t-1$

C = constant.

A second submodel then distributes the estimated change of each district to contained zones according to the relative ranking of each such zone in the value of selected state variables such as base-year population and employment levels and available holding capacity.

In addition to the District and Zone Dwelling Unit and Employment Submodels, the general structure of the RPC model system comprises two computerized submodels and three computerized supporting routines. The place of each of these elements within the system is indicated in Figure 6-2.

The function of the first and third supporting routines indicated is to translate quantified statements of existing and/or future public policy into

94   APPLICATION OF URBAN STRUCTURE MODELS

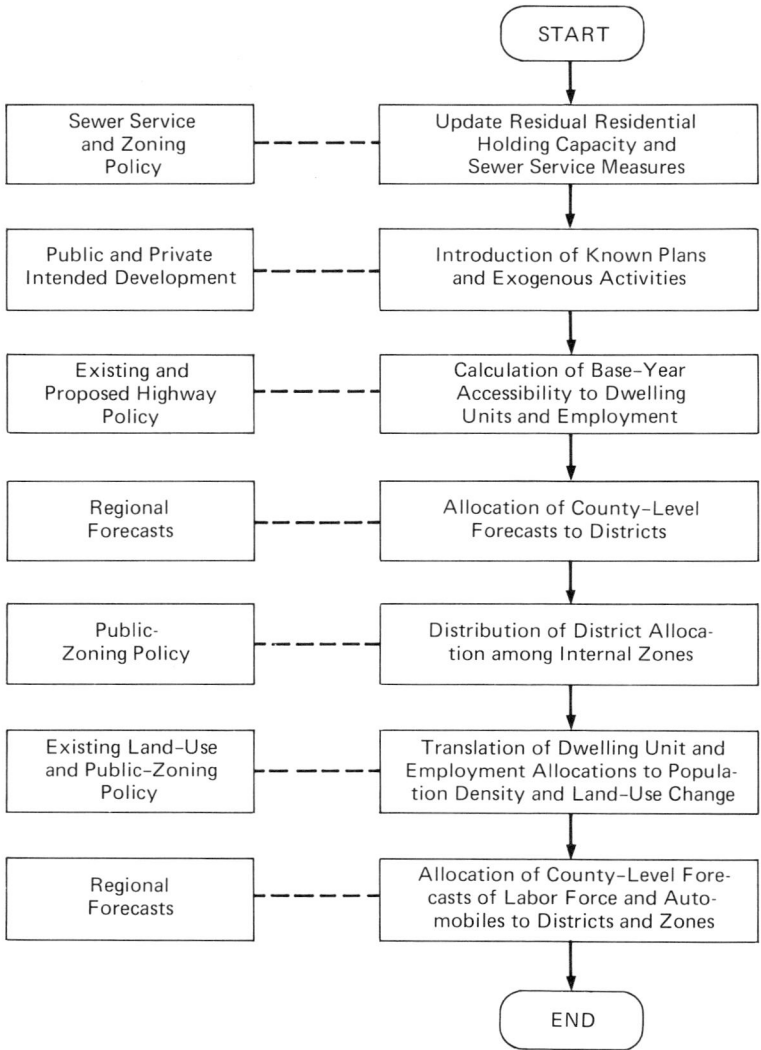

Figure 6-2. General Structure of the Model.

variables to be used in the district and zone submodels while the second routine ("known plans") accepts available exogenous estimates of changes in population, employment, and land use.

Subsequent to the preparation of base year and policy data by the supporting routines, the District Allocation Submodel distributes exogenous county-level forecasts of net change in dwelling units (by income group) and employment

LAND-USE ALLOCATION   95

(by sector) to the districts. The output of this submodel then provides input to the Zonal Submodel which allocates the change predicted for each district to the zones contained within it. The zonal level change measures thus produced are then converted by the third submodel to changes in land use and population. Finally, the fourth submodel allocates the labor force and auto availability measures of the terminal year of the forecast period.

Data and Geographic Units

Sources of data consisted primarily of the 1950 and 1960 U.S. censuses and our own 1964 O & D Survey. The O & D Survey had two aspects: (1) a dwelling unit inventory which gave population, auto availability, labor force, some data on the number of persons over five years of age, and (2) the years in residence at that particular address. The basic variables extracted for use in the model were dwelling units, population, automobiles, and labor force. Table 6-1 indicates those data which were available. It was necessary to develop additional data files (Tables 6-2 and 6-3) to have both cross-sectional and time series data sets. The time series was 10 years between a 1954 land-use survey and the 1964 O & D Survey. Items such as dwelling units by income group, accessibility to dwelling units and employment (both of these measures used district-to-district travel time on the highway system), holding capacities of zones, State and Federal employment, and sewer service, as well as population in group quarters, were developed for this project.

Incomes were expressed in 1960 dollars. The income data are very crude and the RPC is very much interested in improving it. Accessibility to the 37 districts in the county was calculated by using highway network minimum travel times.

The data imposed serious limitations. The most serious is the aggregation of areal units. Since the model was developed on the basis of districts rather than, as hoped, on a traffic-zone basis, its structure is based upon only 37 large units of area. This is not an ideal situation. On the other hand, the 765 zonal areas are so fine that they present too much detail. The real solution to calibrating this allocation model is somewhere around the level of 200 to 300 areal units.

Policy Variables

The model structure assumes several external inputs besides countywide development forecasts. They have been called policy variables. It uses policy on sewer service areas to compute the holding capacity of land in conjunction with local zoning policies and the "known plans" of developers. Policy variables take several forms: accessibility of an area, holding capacity of an area, and availability of regional sewer and water service.

Accessibilities are calculated based upon highway networks; i.e., the travel

Table 6-1
Available Data Files

Item	Definition	Areal Unit	1954	1964
Total Population	All persons, includes military and educational institutions but not penal or mental institutions	District Zone	x	x x
Total Dwelling Units	Total number of units	District Zone	x x	x x
Median Dwelling Unit Income	Median for families and unrelated individuals (adjusted for group quarters)	District Zone		x x
Car Availability	Number of cars garaged at home	District Zone		x
Density	Dwelling units per net residential acre	District Zone		x
Labor Force	Total employed persons by place of residence	District Zone		x x
Employment by Place of Work	Total number of employees by selected categories	District Zone		x x
Floor Area of Selected Industrial Activities	Total square feet of each activity group	District Zone	x x	x x
Selected Land Use	Acres devoted to each selected activity group	District Zone	x x	x x
Zoning Inventory	The area (acres) of each zone and district regulated by each zoning classification in 1964	District Zone		x x
Highway Networks	Description of each link in network in 1954, 1959, and 1964	District Zone		x x

Table 6-2
Additional Data Files Developed by RPC

Item	Definition	Areal Unit	1954	1964
D.U.'s and Pop. in Group Quarters	Total D.U.'s and population in group quarters associated with major institutions	District Zone		x x
State and Federal Employment	Total state and federal employment	District Zone	x x	x x
Total Housing Unit Population	Residential population not including group quarters (1950, 1954, 1960, and 1964)	District Zone		x x
Railroad Service	Percent of an area capable of being served by railroad	District Zone		x x
Sewer Service	Percent of an area served by the centralized sewage system	District Zone	x x	x x
Employment by Place of Work	Total number of employees by selected categories	District Zone	x x	

Table 6-3
Additional Data Files Developed by CONSAD

Item	Definition	Areal Unit	1954	1964
Residual Residential Holding Capacity	Maximum number of additional dwelling units which can be accommodated under current zoning	District Zone	x x	x x
Total Dwelling Units	Total number (less group quarters)	District Zone	x x	
Dwelling Units by Income Category	Number of D.U.'s with earnings of 0–2, 2–4, 4–6, 6–8, 8–10, 10–15, and + $15,000 per year	District Zone	x x	x x
Accessibility to Income	The accessibility of each district to dwelling units in each income class and total dwelling units	District Zone	x	x
Accessibility to Employment	The accessibility of each district to employment in each sector and total	District Zone	x	x
District-to-District Travel Times	Minimum time from each district to each of other districts	District Zone	x	x

times between the districts. Holding capacity is either in terms of the existing development that has occurred since the base year, for example from 1964 to today, in terms of zoning categories, or the basic ability of an area to absorb development.

Sewer service did not turn out to be very significant in the model. The reason for this was that over the 1954-1964 model calibration period sewer service followed the development. It was not there on a regional basis prior to major development. If we were to recalibrate the model on a recent five-year period or from 1960 to 1970, we would find this to be very significant.

The Model Equations

The basic concept of the model has already been discussed. At this point it is appropriate to discuss some details about its equations.

The district allocation model has twelve simultaneous equations (Tables 6-4 through 6-15) and deals with net changes in income, dwelling units, and

Table 6-4
Dependent Variable: Net Change in Income Group 1

Independent Variable	Coefficient	Standard Error
Net Change in Income Group 3		
Net Change in Income Group 4		
Net Change in Income Group 5	-.37521	.15183
Net Change in Income Group 7		
Net Change in Total Dwelling Units	.13226	.02955
Net Change in Nonmanufacturing Employment		
Net Change in Manufacturing Employment		
Net Change in Commercial Employment		
Net Change in Local Public Employment		
Net Change in Total Employment		
Base-Year Nonmanufacturing Employment		
Base-Year Manufacturing Employment		
Base-Year Commercial Employment		
Base-Year Local Public Employment		
Accessibility to Income Group 1		
Accessibility to Income Group 4		
Accessibility to Income Group 5		
Accessibility to Income Group 6		
Accessibility to Income Group 7		
Accessibility to Total Dwelling Units		
Base-Year Residential Holding Capacity		
Base-Year Sewer Service	2.0826	.87483
Constant	-73.91658	

$R^2 = .56$ $F = 10.219$ Standard Error of Estimate = 143.619

employment. These equations were selected based upon regression analysis to determine the significance of the several possible independent variables. For example, Table 6-13 shows the equation used to estimate the net change in commercial employment. Commercial employment is a function of total employment, base-year commercial employment, sewer service, and a constant. Given the set of twelve such equations, the model uses a countywide forecast together with base-year data to compute the net changes. It also constrains many of the net changes that may occur so that they are less than or equal to the base-year situation.

The zonal allocation submodel is just a simple proration technique. It allocates the district net change to zones within it based upon each zone's present development constrained by its unused holding capacity.

The labor force and auto submodels were used primarily to develop inputs to the traffic generation models of the transportation study. Labor force is a very simple function of dwelling units whereas auto availability is a function of dwelling units in different income classes as well as the auto ownership rates for the income classes based upon several auto ownership categories.

Table 6-5
Dependent Variable: Net Change in Income Group 2

Independent Variable	Coefficient	Standard Error
Net Change in Income Group 3	.70686	.03319
Net Change in Income Group 4	−.25556	.03889
Net Change in Income Group 5		
Net Change in Income Group 7		
Net Change in Total Dwelling Units	.03609	.00732
Net Change in Nonmanufacturing Employment		
Net Change in Manufacturing Employment		
Net Change in Commercial Employment		
Net Change in Local Public Employment		
Net Change in Total Employment		
Base-Year Nonmanufacturing Employment		
Base-Year Manufacturing Employment		
Base-Year Commerical Employment		
Base-Year Local Public Employment		
Accessibility to Income Group 1		
Accessibility to Income Group 4		
Accessibility to Income Group 5		
Accessibility to Income Group 6		
Accessibility to Income Group 7		
Accessibility to Total Dwelling Units		
Base-Year Residential Holding Capacity		
Base-Year Sewer Service		
Constant	−34.57517	

$R^2 = .95$ $F = 124.880$ Standard Error of Estimate = 48.8519

Table 6-6
Dependent Variable: Net Change in Income Group 3

Independent Variable	Coefficient	Standard Error
Net Change in Income Group 3		
Net Change in Income Group 4	.44560	.04771
Net Change in Income Group 5		
Net Change in Income Group 7		
Net Change in Total Dwelling Units		
Net Change in Nonmanufacturing Employment		
Net Change in Manufacturing Employment		
Net Change in Commercial Employment		
Net Change in Local Public Employment		
Net Change in Total Employment		
Base-Year Nonmanufacturing Employment		
Base-Year Manufacturing Employment		
Base-Year Commercial Employment		
Base-Year Local Public Employment	-.07528	.02688
Accessibility to Income Group 1		
Accessibility to Income Group 4	-.50548	.03964
Accessibility to Income Group 5		
Accessibility to Income Group 6		
Accessibility to Income Group 7	.22851	.08350
Accessibility to Total Dwelling Units	.06456	.00770
Base-Year Residential Holding Capacity	-.00458	.00245
Base-Year Sewer Service	-.92384	.76180
Constant	87.32540	

$R^2 = .92$ $F = 47.564$ Standard Error of Estimate = 97.4657

Table 6-7
Dependent Variable: Net Change in Income Group 4

Independent Variable	Coefficient	Standard Error
Net Change in Income Group 3		
Net Change in Income Group 4		
Net Change in Income Group 5	.42641	.15498
Net Change in Income Group 7		
Net Change in Total Dwelling Units	.13469	.03388
Net Change in Nonmanufacturing Employment		
Net Change in Manufacturing Employment		
Net Change in Commercial Employment		
Net Change in Local Public Employment		
Net Change in Total Employment		
Base-Year Nonmanufacturing Employment		
Base-Year Manufacturing Employment		
Base-Year Commercial Employment		
Base-Year Local Public Employment		
Accessibility to Income Group 1		
Accessibility to Income Group 4		
Accessibility to Income Group 5		
Accessibility to Income Group 6		
Accessibility to Income Group 7	-.62297	.10419
Accessibility to Total Dwelling Units		
Base-Year Residential Holding Capacity		
Base-Year Sewer Service		
Constant	114.37964	

$R^2 = .93$ $F = 83.028$ Standard Error of Estimate = 124.2164

LAND-USE ALLOCATION

Table 6-8
Dependent Variable: Net Change in Income Group 5

Independent Variable	Coefficient	Standard Error
Net Change in Income Group 3		
Net Change in Income Group 4		
Net Change in Income Group 5		
Net Change in Income Group 7		
Net Change in Total Dwelling Units	.16759	.00817
Net Change in Industrial Employment	.08004	.01514
Net Change in Commercial Employment		
Net Change in Local Public Employment	−.23533	.02855
Net Change in Total Employment		
Base-Year Nonmanufacturing Employment		
Base-Year Manufacturing Employment		
Base-Year Commercial Employment		
Base-Year Local Public Employment		
Accessibility to Income Group 1		
Accessibility to Income Group 4		
Accessibility to Income Group 5		
Accessibility to Income Group 6		
Accessibility to Income Group 7		
Base-Year Residential Holding Capacity		
Base-Year Sewer Service	1.47963	.53811
Constant	−24.65666	

$R^2 = .98$ F = 136.330   Standard Error of Estimate = 86.8593

Table 6-9
Dependent Variable: Net Change in Income Group 6

Independent Variable	Coefficient	Standard Error
Net Change in Income Group 3		
Net Change in Income Group 4		
Net Change in Income Group 5		
Net Change in Income Group 7		
Net Change in Total Dwelling Units	.23124	.01191
Net Change in Nonmanufacturing Employment		
Net Change in Manufacturing Employment		
Net Change in Commercial Employment		
Net Change in Local Public Employment		
Net Change in Total Employment		
Base-Year Industrial Employment	.02320	.00798
Base-Year Commercial Employment		
Accessibility to Income Group 1		
Accessibility to Income Group 4	.59696	.06471
Accessibility to Income Group 5		
Accessibility to Income Group 6		
Accessibility to Income Group 7		
Accessibility to Total Dwelling Units		
Base-Year Residential Holding Capacity	.00511	.00146
Base-Year Sewer Service	1.84425	.85056
Constant	−158.46350	

$R^2 = .98$ F = 216.762   Standard Error of Estimate = 119.9594

Table 6-10
Dependent Variable: Net Change in Income Group 7

Independent Variable	Coefficient	Standard Error
Net Change in Income Group 3		
Net Change in Income Group 4		
Net Change in Income Group 5		
Net Change in Income Group 7		
Net Change in Total Dwelling Units	.13468	.01728
Net Change in Nonmanufacturing Employment	-.18212	
Net Change in Manufacturing Employment		
Net Change in Commercial Employment		
Net Change in Local Public Employment		
Net Change in Total Employment		
Base-Year Nonmanufacturing Employment		
Base-Year Manufacturing Employment		
Base-Year Commercial Employment		
Base-Year Local Public Employment		
Accessibility to Income Group 1	-.06028	.02373
Accessibility to Income Group 4		
Accessibility to Income Group 5		
Accessibility to Income Group 6	.86736	.09124
Accessibility to Income Group 7		
Accessibility to Total Dwelling Units		
Base-Year Residential Holding Capacity		
Base-Year Sewer Service	.41683	1.15195
Constant	-57.01302	

$R^2 = .93$ $F = 81.207$ Standard Error of Estimate = 169.3134

Table 6-11
Dependent Variable: Net Change in Total Dwelling Units

Independent Variable	Coefficient	Standard Error
Net Change in Income Group 3		
Net Change in Income Group 4		
Net Change in Income Group 5		
Net Change in Income Group 7		
Net Change in Total Dwelling Units		
Net Change in Nonmanufacturing Employment		
Net Change in Manufacturing Employment		
Net Change in Commercial Employment	1.44383	.41440
Net Change in Local Public Employment		
Net Change in Total Employment	.42225	.13622
Base-Year Nonmanufacturing Employment		
Base-Year Manufacturing Employment		
Base-Year Commercial Employment	-.55603	.11241
Base-Year Local Public Employment	1.85434	.27448
Accessibility to Income Group 1		
Accessibility to Income Group 4		
Accessibility to Income Group 5	2.93082	.54498
Accessibility to Income Group 6		
Accessibility to Income Group 7		
Accessibility to Total Dwelling Units	-.16793	.04750
Base-Year Residential Holding Capacity	.04120	.02279
Base-Year Sewer Service		
Constant	-94.21538	

$R^2 = .85$ $F = 20.164$ Standard Error of Estimate = 931.6512

Table 6-12
Dependent Variable: Net Change in Industrial
(Manufacturing and Nonmanufacturing) Employment

Independent Variable	Coefficient	Standard Error
Net Change in Income Group 3		
Net Change in Income Group 4		
Net Change in Income Group 5		
Net Change in Income Group 7		
Net Change in Total Dwelling Units		
Net Change in Nonmanufacturing Employment		
Net Change in Manufacturing Employment		
Net Change in Commercial Employment	-.99885	.00357
Net Change in Local Public Employment	-.99630	.00674
Net Change in Total Employment	.99846	.00285
Base-Year Nonmanufacturing Employment		
Base-Year Manufacturing Employment		
Base-Year Commercial Employment		
Base-Year Local Public Employment		
Accessibility to Income Group 1		
Accessibility to Income Group 4		
Accessibility to Income Group 5		
Accessibility to Income Group 6		
Accessibility to Income Group 7		
Accessibility to Total Dwelling Units		
Base-Year Residential Holding Capacity		
Base-Year Sewer Service		
Constant	3.27533	

$R^2 = .999$ F = 25345   Standard Error of Estimate = 17.612

Table 6-13
Dependent Variable: Net Change in Commercial Employment

Independent Variable	Coefficient	Standard Error
Net Change in Income Group 3		
Net Change in Income Group 4		
Net Change in Income Group 5		
Net Change in Income Group 7		
Net Change in Total Dwelling Units		
Net Change in Nonmanufacturing Employment		
Net Change in Manufacturing Employment		
Net Change in Commercial Employment		
Net Change in Local Public Employment		
Net Change in Total Employment	.20710	.05087
Base-Year Nonmanufacturing Employment		
Base-Year Manufacturing Employment		
Base-Year Commercial Employment	.21530	.02009
Base-Year Local Public Employment		
Accessibility to Income Group 1		
Accessibility to Income Group 4		
Accessibility to Income Group 5		
Accessibility to Income Group 6		
Accessibility to Income Group 7		
Accessibility to Total Dwelling Units		
Base-Year Residential Holding Capacity		
Base-Year Sewer Service	-8.27660	3.07210
Constant	149.71998	

$R^2 = .93$ F = 111.547   Standard Error of Estimate = 440.7284

Table 6-14
Dependent Variable: Net Change in Local Public Employment[a]

Independent Variable	Coefficient	Standard Error
Net Change in Income Group 3		
Net Change in Income Group 4		
Net Change in Income Group 5		
Net Change in Income Group 7		
Net Change in Total Dwelling Units		
Net Change in Nonmanufacturing Employment		
Net Change in Manufacturing Employment		
Net Change in Commercial Employment		
Net Change in Local Public Employment		
Net Change in Total Employment	.13926	.03694
Base-Year Nonmanufacturing Employment		
Base-Year Manufacturing Employment		
Base-Year Commercial Employment		
Base-Year Local Public Employment	-.71003	.06678
Accessibility to Income Group 1		
Accessibility to Income Group 4		
Accessibility to Income Group 5		
Accessibility to Income Group 6		
Accessibility to Income Group 7		
Accessibility to Total Dwelling Units		
Base-Year Residential Holding Capacity	.01194	.01267
Base-Year Sewer Service	11.78378	3.54543
Constant	-71.17243	

$R^2 = .90$ F = 74.958   Standard Error of Estimate = 533.3618

[a]Excludes State and Federal employment which are exogenous.

Table 6-15
Dependent Variable: Net Change in Total Employment

Independent Variable	Coefficient	Standard Error
Net Change in Income Group 3		
Net Change in Income Group 4		
Net Change in Income Group 5		
Net Change in Income Group 7		
Net Change in Total Dwelling Units		
Net Change in Nonmanufacturing Employment		
Net Change in Manufacturing Employment		
Net Change in Commercial Employment		
Net Change in Local Public Employment		
Net Change in Total Employment		
Base-Year Nonmanufacturing Employment		
Base-Year Manufacturing Employment		
Base-Year Commercial Employment	.32757	.04903
Base-Year Local Public Employment	-.86582	.36855
Accessibility to Income Group 1		
Accessibility to Income Group 4		
Accessibility to Income Group 5		
Accessibility to Income Group 6		
Accessibility to Income Group 7		
Accessibility to Total Dwelling Units		
Base-Year Residential Holding Capacity	.01222	.03359
Base-Year Sewer Service		
Constant	878.76688	

$R^2 = .61$ F = 12.747   Standard Error of Estimate = 1414.5638

Problems With the Model

There are examples of things that pose problems which the model does not handle. Franklin County is undergoing a style shift in residential development toward the multifamily or high-density town house and apartment type developments and these are occurring on a larger and larger scale. For example, a developer proposed to take 610 acres in the northeast and develop it as 6,000 town houses and apartments from 1972 to 1986. He would do this around a golf course, and would have neighborhood shopping as well as recreational facilities both in the center and what he called village locations. If the model were run for this period it could never come up with anything like this development because the development violates many of the historical assumptions that went into development of the model.

This is the kind of thing that the model cannot allocate and which must be inserted manually, based upon knowledge of the area or development trends. Another example concerns major industries such as the Anheuser-Busch Brewery that attract an adjacent auxiliary industry — in this case the Continental Can Company, with a $2½ million plant. These things are difficult to build into the model. The model will allocate employment of certain types but may not get down to the detailed levels and concentrations needed.

Franklin County has a 250-acre automated rail yard being developed by Penn-Central. This is a very unusual happening and the model, of course, could not recognize it or allocate for it. The Penn-Central plans to abandon most of their other yards and concentrate all activities in this new location. This site happens to be about seven miles northwest of the downtown area in a totally undeveloped area. Penn-Central owns not only the 250 acres but about 1,300 acres around it, and has plans to develop it industrially.

Summary

At present, the model does certain things well and has several deficiencies. It is being used in the development of land-use alternatives, in evaluating population, and in coming out with a final land-use plan. This is in conjunction with transportation network development, using the model to test alternative policies. If it is decided to develop high-density corridors (such as in Chicago where they develop high-accessibility corridors with both transit and freeways), these areas might be able to tolerate more density. In other words, the model would be given a policy that this area has more holding capacity and the sewer service necessary to support it. On the other hand, if use or evaluation of a "sprawl" policy were wanted, the present development trends could be put in and the model would produce corresponding district allocations for review. This is the kind of use being planned for the model.

It is obvious that the RPC is just getting started in solving the problem of trying to come up with inputs to detailed traffic models. The matter of evaluating alternative land-use plans is greatly needed. It is questionable whether this model can do this nearly as well as would be liked, but it does provide a logical framework for experiment. On the other hand, the RPC has constrained itself in the sense that it is trying to allocate development for too small a set of areal units, i.e., the 765 traffic zones. For example, allocations of industrial employment are being made to small areas that really are not that fine. They are not as fine as the areas themselves. This is going to have an effect since these are used and chained together through trip distribution and traffic assignment models and then used to evaluate transportation plans.

The opportunity to develop and test a model of this type showed how difficult land-use modeling can be. The complexities of land development in Franklin County are such that it is difficult to keep track of present changes let alone future ones geographically. The model needs considerable refinement if it is ever to be used with confidence in allocating future growth.

Part II
New Concepts of
Urban Structure

The papers contained in Part II elaborate on the concept of urban structure. When viewed by various social science disciplines, urban structure will be defined in different fashions. The papers represent the views of the planner, geographer, sociologist, political scientist, and economist. In introducing these views, one is struck with the opportunities faced by the social science disciplines in introducing new dimensions to the analysis of urban structure and strengthening earlier modeling attempts. However, the limitations of discipline oriented research can also be detected and the need for interdisciplinary research efforts is reaffirmed.

Kaiser's paper discusses a model developed for simulating residential growth patterns. Casetti's model seeks to evaluate urban land values with an urban spatial system. A sociologist's view of urban structure is reviewed by Schwirian. Cox, a political geographer, examines the political structure of an urban area as interpreted by voting patterns. Weicher views the fiscal structure of an urban area and particularly the suburban and central city fiscal fragmentation. Finally, Goldstein reviews means of representing urban structure by means of new computer mapping techniques.

7 Decision Agent Models: an Alternative Modeling Approach for Urban Residential Growth[a]

Edward J. Kaiser

Decision agent modeling represents an attempt to understand growth-induced change in urban residential structure, and the influence of public policy on such change, by studying and modeling the residential development process underlying the change. This approach grew out of earlier research into urban structure at the Center for Urban and Regional Studies in the 1958-1965 period during which F. Stuart Chapin, Jr., Shirley F. Weiss, and Thomas Donnelly developed, tested, and refined a "probabilistic model" for urban residential growth. That model was based directly on multiple regression analysis. Residential land use was regressed on an array of factors describing the urbanscape. The factors were originally nominated by a panel of planners. In the last of four monographs discussing that model, Chapin and Weiss concluded:

If both the forecast and the policy-testing needs (of planners) are to be fulfilled, the overriding conclusion to be drawn . . . is the importance and the promise of subaggregating the residential development process . . . and substituting separate models for the producer and consumer stages in the process. (Chapin and Weiss, 1965, 33-34)

The decision agent modeling approach began with an attempt to identify critical decisions and decision makers in the development process and the factors that influenced them — particularly locational decisions and related factors. A series of interviews with development decision agents was conducted, mostly in North Carolina. Interviewed on the "producer" side were predevelopment landowners (Smith, 1967; Kaiser, Massie, Weiss, Smith, 1968), financiers (Fisher, 1966), attorneys, realtors (Carlson, 1967), and developers (Weiss, Smith, Kaiser, Kenney, 1966). Households were interviewed to represent the consumer side

---

[a]This paper is adapted from a presentation to the First Annual Conference of the Environmental Design Research Association, Chapel Hill, June, 1969. By and large, we have used a research team approach, so I am not just reporting my own work here but that of a number of faculty and student colleagues. Of these, Shirley F. Weiss has been the most consistent and it is under her research grants that much of the work on developer decisions, to be used as the prototype decision agent model in this paper, has been done. The research has been supported in part by the Environmental Engineering Policies and Urban Development Project, Public Health Service Research Grant UI 00128-07 from the Environmental Control Administration, and in part by the Residential Choice and Moving Behavior Project, National Science Foundation Research Grant, GS 2427.

of residential growth — including renters and owners, movers and nonmovers, blacks and nonblacks (Armiger, 1966; Butler, et al., 1968; Eldridge, 1967; Leaman, 1967; Weiss, Kenny, Steffens, 1966). Many of these interviews were tape recorded "in-depth" and open-ended; others were limited to precoded questionnaires.

The Residential Development Process

As a result of these exploratory "behavioral" investigations, we have conceptualized urban residential development as a land conversion process (Kaiser and Weiss, 1970). The conceptualization is illustrated in Figure 7-1. Nonurban land on the urban fringe is converted to urban residential use by going through a number of intermediate stages. We visualized the analogy of a chain of transitional stages necessary for land to fulfill its conversion to residential land use. A change of state in the conversion process requires a corresponding decision or combination of decisions on the part of one or more decision agents. Hence, we have a chain of decisions corresponding to the chain of intermediate states through which land must pass in order to acquire residential use.

Like any chain, the land conversion chain is no stronger than its weakest link. All of the decision links in the chain must be forged to complete the chain; any broken link breaks the chain. Based on our interviews, there are at least three really key decision agents involved directly in the process — the predevelopment landowner, the developer, and the consumer household. The financial intermediaries and public officials also play important roles, but in a much less direct manner. If public policy is to influence the transition of land, it will be by affecting this chain of decisions. To do this, public policy must affect the factors influencing decisions in the chain.

Three general types of factors seem to emerge consistently from our interviews and statistical analyses of transition decisions. They are contextual factors, property characteristics, and decision agent characteristics. Each of these three sets of factors influences each of the key decisions in the land conversion process in a unique manner. The contextual factors provide the macro environment for the decision, namely, the considerations which limit and determine the overall rate and type of change in the community and the general distribution of decision and property characteristics. The property and decision agent characteristics on the other hand describe the micro situation surrounding each decision. The property characteristics describe the property about which decisions are made. And the decision agent characteristics help explain the variation in decisional behavior among decision makers of the same type in the face of similar contextual and property characteristics affecting the decision.

Again referring to Figure 7-1 we see local public policy as an attempt to influence the residential evolution of land by affecting the contextual and/or

DECISION AGENT MODELS

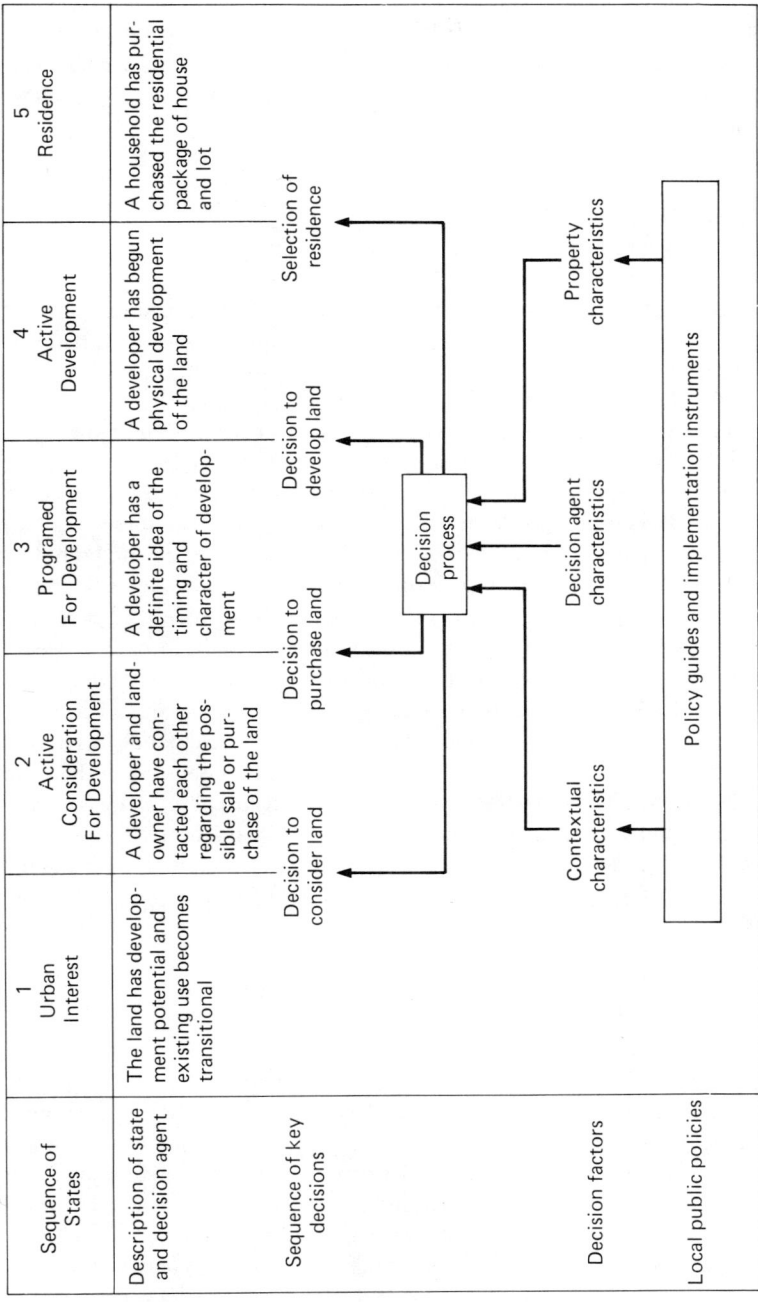

Figure 7-1. The Residential Land Conversion Process.

property characteristic factors in the key development decisions. Although public policy does not affect decisions through any direct influence over decision agent characteristics, the understanding of the role played by decision agent characteristics in determining the response of decisions to any land use policy proposal is crucial to the design of such policy.

A Linked Set of Operationalized Decision Agent Models

In an attempt to carry the concepts of the decision chain and the participating decision agents a step further toward an operational aid in the planning process, we have begun to think through a possible system of decision agent models. One such possible configuration of operational models based on the three key decision agents is sketched in Figure 7-2. A distribution of the supply of new single-family subdivision housing is estimated by a developer model, perhaps supplemented by a landowner model. Supplementing the estimated distribution of the supply of new housing is the supply of vacated existing housing units estimated by a residential mobility model based on the household's decision to move (not included in the conceptualization above, but related to it).

Over on the demand side, the mobility model also estimates the population of moving households who, along with immigrants and newly formed households, provide the population seeking housing from within the supply of new subdivisions and vacated housing. These supply estimation models and demand estimation models are linked together by a residential choice model, based on the household's residential choice decision, which allocates households to the supply of available housing. The output is visualized as a joint distribution of the spatial distribution of housing characteristics and household characteristics.

This modeling idea is still in the first stage of construction. The results of the work done so far on several separate parts are fairly encouraging even though success is modest.

The Developer Model Link in the Linked System of Models (Kaiser, 1969)

A brief description of the research involved in pursuing the single-family residential developer model link will serve as an example of one of the several links in such a system of models. The task of the developer-model link is to map the spatial pattern of the likelihood that developers would locate single-family residential subdivisions according to certain suppositions about public policy represented by the configuration of contextual and property characteristics in the model. The model is based on the concept that a developer's site selection

DECISION AGENT MODELS

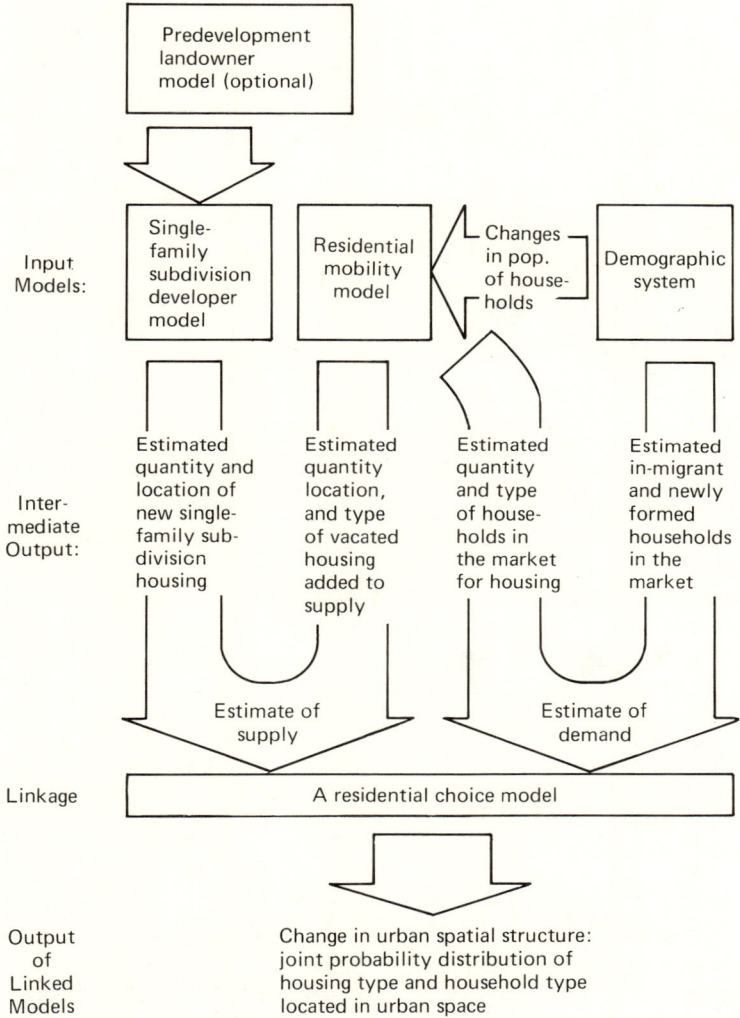

Figure 7-2. Linking Together Several Decision Agent Models.

is equivalent to the selection of an array of site characteristics. Some of these arrays will provide more desirable inputs into his residential production process than others. Locations having more desirable arrays of site characteristics will more likely attract a developer. (Whether that location also is likely to attract a household or be sold by the predevelopment landowner are other questions.) Figure 7-3 illustrates the list of variables suggested by earlier interviews as

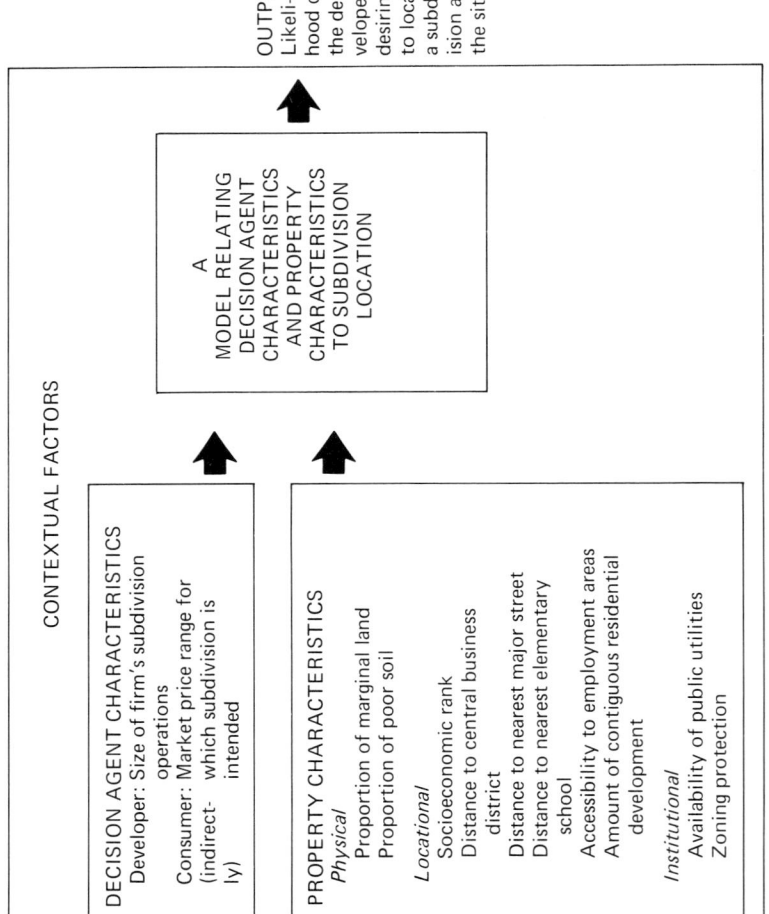

Figure 7-3. Elements in The Developer's Residential Subdivision Location Decision.

important to a developer's decision. Analysis of subdivision plat data from two North Carolina cities — Greensboro and Winston-Salem — provided the basis for calibrating a pilot version of a developer model based on discriminant functions.

The findings thus far suggest that such characteristics as zoning, socioeconomic prestige level of the location, and availability of public water and sewerage are the most significant variables. The amount of contiguous residential development and the accessibility to downtown, employment, elementary school, and the major street systems are also significantly related to developers' subdivision-location decisions and could probably be useful in an operational model. The physical characteristics of the land which were tested — proportion of marginal land due to excessive slope, subjectivity to flooding, or poor soil — do not appear to be important in the developers' locational decisions.

Our findings also suggest that at least two parallel model components be utilized in the single-family residential-subdivision developer model. One would produce the spatial pattern of likelihood of the location of large-developer subdivisions (those averaging over 100 lots per year in our study). The other would do the same for small developers (under 100 lots per year in our study). While both are influenced by site characteristics, large developers (at least in the study areas) are much more responsive to them than small developers.

The pilot version of the model was able to classify up to 81 percent of the large-developer decisions correctly in our sample as opposed to 66 percent of small-developer decisions. Further, the two almost appear to be looking for very different combinations of site characteristics. For example, small developers tend to choose sites farther from downtown, farther from an elementary school, farther from employment centers, and having fewer public utilities. Large developers tend to select the opposite kind of site.

The price market aimed for by the developer also influences his selection of property characteristics and hence the location of his subdivisions. Tests relating property characteristics to the price range of houses indicate that higher-priced subdivisions are more sensitive to socioeconomic prestige level of the site than lower-priced subdivisions, while middle- and lower-priced subdivisions are more sensitive to zoning, availability of public utilities, and amount of nearby development. The pilot version of the model was able to obtain a better record of classification for higher-priced subdivisions than for lower-priced subdivisions — 83 percent versus 67 percent. These findings suggest that the model can be calibrated separately for each of several price ranges.

There was statistical evidence in our studies that differences in location between developer types is greater than differences between price ranges. Combining price and developer distinctions enabled the discriminant model to achieve as high as a 95-percent correct classification. The differences between developer types hold even while controlling for price range of the subdivision. This lends further support to the idea of developing several parallel models — one to estimate large-developer, low-price subdivision locations; one for large-developer, high-price locations; one for small-developer, low-price locations; and one for small-developer, high-price locations.

Table 7-1 displays some of the results of preliminary tests of the discriminant model using data from Greensboro, North Carolina. It shows several prediction approaches and displays them in a way that will allow us to make a preliminary evaluation of the predictive capacity of the model. The first two rows show the percentage of cells classified correctly using discriminant analysis for the 1958-1960 and 1961-1963 periods, respectively. These percentages result from discriminant models that were calibrated on the same set of data for which the "prediction" is made. These can be considered as a kind of standard. That is, the percentages in the first two rows can be compared with the percentages classified correctly in the third row (which refers to the 1961-1963 period prediction using the model calibrated on the 1958-1960 data). The approach used to obtain the figures in Row 3 would be closer to the approach required in an actual predictive situation faced, for example, by an urban planner. By comparing these percentages to those of the second row, we may ascertain the loss in predictive ability due to using previously calibrated parameters instead of parameters calibrated on the actual 1961-1963 data. We can also compare Row 3 to Row 1; i.e., we can compare the 1961-1963 prediction using parameters calibrated on the 1958-1960 data to the 1958-1960 prediction using the parameters.

The table shows that the predictive capacity of the operational model in the 1961-1963 time period, using parameter coefficients calibrated in the 1958-1960 sample, ranged widely from a very unsatisfactory 51.7 percent for "small developer" subdivisions to a highly accurate 92.4 percent for the "large developer" subdivisions. This compares with the ranges of 55.4 to 92.7 percent and 66.2 to 92.4 percent for the 1958-1960 and 1961-1963 periods, respectively, when the model is used to predict for the same sample on which it was calibrated. Percentages correctly classified by the operational model in the 1961-1963 period were consistently a little lower than percentages obtained in the 1961-1963 sample. But, they were sometimes higher than those obtained in the 1958-1960 period. The fluctuation in predictive capacity from one dependent classification system to another is consistent through all three samples. For example, high-price subdivisions and large-developer subdivisions were more accurately classified than other types of subdivisions in all three approaches while small-developer subdivisions were less accurately classified in all three approaches.

It may be useful to add another input variable to the developer model — the likelihood of selling on the part of the landowners for any site being evaluated. Such an input could be generated by a separate predevelopment landowner model with which we have done some work (Kaiser, Massie, Weiss, Smith, 1968). However, in preliminary tests with a small sample, we have not yet been able to improve the performance of the developer model significantly by adding a landowner prefix model which supplies a likelihood of selling as an additional

Table 7-1
Comparison of Percentage of Sample Cells Classified Correctly by Discriminant Analysis as Opposed to the Operational Discriminant Model

Prediction Approaches	Unsubdivided Versus:			Unsubdivided Versus: Low-Price Subd.	Unsubdivided Versus: Medium-Price Subd.	Unsubdivided Versus: High-Price Subd.	Unsubdivided Versus: Small-Developer Subdivision			Unsubdivided Versus: Large-Developer Subdivision		
	Subdivided	Small-Developer Subdivision	Large-Developer Subdivisions				Low Price	Medium Price	High Price	Low Price	Medium Price	High Price
Discriminant analysis 1958–60 time period sample	62.6	55.4	77.9	69.8	60.5	78.7	65.4	NS	74.6	80.5	80.7	92.7
Discriminant analysis of the 1961–63 time period sample	68.2	66.2	81.2	66.9	72.1	83.2	NS	64.7	78.2	85.7	80.2	92.4
Operational discriminant model applied to the 1961–63 time period sample using discriminant function coefficients calibrated on 1958–60 sample	64.7	51.7	76.0	66.3	51.9	81.9	64.0	NS	77.9	77.5	74.9	92.4

NS = no variable was statistically significant at the .05 level in the discriminant analysis.

input to accompany the site characteristics described above. Nevertheless, the tests are not considered conclusive and further research effort in this direction is deemed desirable.

Concluding Remarks

Many of the limitations of this research should be obvious, but it may be useful to review some of them in order to place our discussion in the proper perspective. First of all, this type of model cannot be interpreted very literally as a prediction since it does not estimate the amount of growth nor allocate acres or other units of growth. Further, it is a relatively short-range model and makes no provision for iteration as it is now programmed. It produces a spatial distribution of likelihood or attraction for one type of development decision at a time, for one point in time, and does not yet allow "growing" a city over a substantial length of time by utilizing feedback from earlier time-period forecasts to affect later time periods, or by exogenously updating of site characteristics between time periods. The model is what could be called a policy impact model with some capacity to assess the impact of local governmental actions. It should be able to trace the impact of changes of policy-impacted property characteristics such as zoning, availability of water and sewerage, and accessibility for the planner or public policy maker. It traces this impact as a change in the probability of development process decisions being made — be they predevelopment land sales decisions, developers' subdivision location decisions, households decisions to move, or households selections of places of residence. Or, looking at its output in the form of a map, the model should be able to trace the impact of policy suppositions on the conceptual topography of the likelihood of a particular change of state of land.

The user of this type of model would have to recognize that the actual occurrence of development will deviate from the probable occurrence due to the many factors in the complex environment of decisions in the real world — factors that are not accounted for in the model. The researcher might concentrate on these deviations and try to explain them, as a fruitful research strategy. The planner in the field would probably get better pay-off by concentrating on experimentation with policy input values in order to trace spatial distribution consequences — tracing the impact of changes in the spatial distribution of input variables upon the development probabilities.

A second limitation is that the modeling approach is only a partial approach to planning models as opposed to a comprehensive one. It is partial in the sense that it does not estimate or allocate estimates of actual amounts of growth, as mentioned above. It is partial also in the sense that even the linked system focuses mainly on new single-family subdivision houses and does not include rental units, public units, or redevelopment of already built-up areas of the city. Further, it is partial in the sense that it focuses on spatial distribution and casts no insights as to the quality of residential growth. Lastly, its output is not directly related to objectives; the output consists only of a spatial distribution of the likelihood of a step in the development process and not an evaluation of that distribution.

A third area of qualification concerns the analysis that led to the model. There were some inconsistencies between observed associations and those expected on the basis of the literature and the earlier interviews that have not yet been satisfactorily explained. Also, the sample was limited in geographic area to two North Carolina cities for much of the "harder" data. This restricts generalization of the model and limits our understanding of the effect of contextual factors because there was insufficient variation in them. Even though each urban area would have to calibrate a model for itself anyway, the problem of a change in context is not avoided. If the planner wants to make any but marginal changes in the spatial distribution of the policy variables or if he wants to change the content of the policy, then he may actually be changing the contextual factors under which the model was originally calibrated, thereby invalidating the calibration. More study of the contextual factors is required to surmount this problem.

Still another limitation to the computerized model as it is now programmed is that experimentation is cumbersome for a planner interested in tracing implications of planning suppositions. Tracing the impact of a change in the spatial distribution of an input variable, say zoning, while holding others constant would require tedious coding and key punching to change values of the zoning variable for a number of sites. This difficulty might be alleviated by a computerized "graphic processing system." Such a system would provide a capability to reproduce maps of computer-stored data on a cathode-ray tube in such a way that the planner could experiment with the model by interacting with it and with the data in a very immediate and dynamic manner. He could call the input data onto the cathode-ray tube and utilize a light pen and a key punch to readily change the input. He could then send the new input to the computerized model, producing an alternative output map on the cathode-ray tube. This capability would make changing the inputs much less tedious and would allow almost immediate observation of the impact of the input change on the spatial distribution of development probabilities. Figure 7-4 attempts to diagram this interaction between man and machine.

In spite of these limitations, there are several reasons for continuing the decision agent approach to the study of residential growth. For one thing, it provides an alternative to the more common modeling approach of aggregating the many decisions involved in the residential process into a simpler relationship. This is not meant to be a criticism of other modeling efforts using the aggregative approach. It only suggests that an alternative approach has the possibility of leading to new insights that can supplement those insights already gained through aggregative models. For example, contrary to the assumptions and

NEW CONCEPTS OF URBAN STRUCTURE

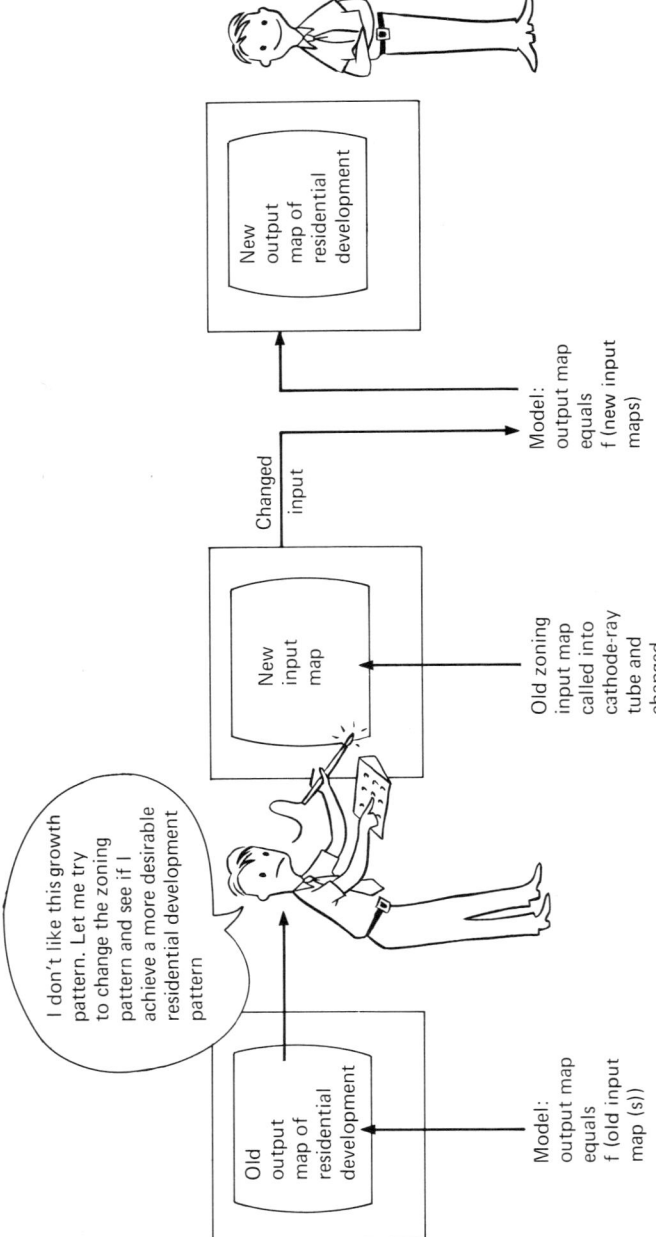

Figure 7-4. Illustration of Use of Graphic Processing System.

conclusions of many research and modeling efforts, a focus on the decision agents in the development process indicates, tentatively, that accessibility is of lesser importance than many other factors in explaining decisions to move, the selection of new dwelling units, and the location of subdivisions (Butler, Chapin, et al., 1968; Butler and Kaiser, 1969). And although property characteristics seem to be primary in the developer's locational decision, they seem to have little impact on a predevelopment landowner's tendency to sell.

We also feel that the insights provided by an emphasis on decisions, processes, and decision makers are especially suited to problem solving situations involving public policy making because, in the end, it is this processual complex of decisions that must be influenced in order to affect urban spatial structure. This approach can begin to suggest the ways in which different decision makers are affected by an array of policies. For example, some of our work suggests that tax policy could be an effective influence on predevelopment landowners, but that its effect upon a site depends on the contextual factor of rate of value appreciation in raw land real estate and on the wealth of the owner. And, even if it did encourage a sale, the tax policy would not necessarily make it more attractive to the developer — the next link in the chain (Kaiser and Weiss, 1967). The research suggests that mixes of policies, rather than single policies, are required, some of which are aimed at landowners, some at developers, and some at consumer households. Also, the arsenal may even have to be more specialized to account for differences among developers, among landowners, and among consumers.

References

Armiger, L. Earl, Jr., *Toward a Model of the Residential Location Decision Process: A Study of Recent and Prospective Buyers of New and Used Homes,* Thesis Series, No. 5, University of North Carolina, Chapel Hill (1966).

Study Team: Edgar W. Butler, F. Stuart Chapin, Jr., George C. Hemmens, Edward J. Kaiser, Michael A. Stegman, and Shirley F. Weiss, *Moving Behavior and Residential Choice: A National Survey,* National Cooperative Highway Research Program Report 81, Highway Research Board, Washington, D.C. National Research Council, National Academy of Sciences (1969).

Carlson, Eric D., *Operational Aspects of a Probabilistic Model for Residential Growth,* Thesis Series, No. 10, University of North Carolina, Chapel Hill (1968).

Chapin, F. Stuart, Jr., and Shirley F. Weiss, *Some Input Refinements for a Residential Model,* an Urban Studies Research Monograph, Center for Urban and Regional Studies, Institute for Research in Social Science, University of North Carolina, Chapel Hill, in cooperation with the Bureau of Public Roads, U.S. Department of Commerce (July 1965).

Eldridge, Mark T., *Explorations into Decision Factors in the Rental Housing Market,* Thesis Series, No. 9, University of North Carolina, Chapel Hill (1967).

Fisher, H. Benjamin, "Financial Intermediaries in the Development Decisions Seminar", unpublished research paper submitted to the Center for Urban and Regional Studies, Center for Urban and Regional Studies, Institute for Research in Social Science, University of North Carolina, Chapel Hill (September, 1966).

Kaiser, Edward J., *A Producer Model for Residential Growth: Analyzing and Predicting the Location of Residential Subdivisions,* An Urban Studies Research Monograph, Center for Urban and Regional Studies, Institute for Research in Social Science, University of North Carolina, Chapel Hill (1969).

Kaiser, Edward J., Ronald W. Massie, Shirley F. Weiss, and John E. Smith, "Predicting the Behavior of Predevelopment Landowners on the Urban Fringe", *Journal of the American Institute of Planners,* Vol. XXXIV, No. 5, pp. 328-333 (September 1968).

Kaiser, Edward J., and Shirley F. Weiss, "Public Policy and the Residential Development Process," *Journal of the American Institute of Planners,* Vol. XXXVI, No. 1, pp. 30-37 (January, 1970). Reprinted in *The Geography of the City,* A Collection of Readings for Beginning University Students, Oxford University Press, Toronto, 1971.

Leaman, Samuel H., *A Study of Housing Decisions by Negro Home Owners and Negro Renters,* Thesis Series, No. 8, University of North Carolina, Chapel Hill (1967).

Smith, John E., *Toward a Theory of Landowner Behavior on the Urban Periphery,* Thesis Series, No. 6, University of North Carolina, Chapel Hill (1967).

Weiss, Shirley F., Kenneth B. Kenney, and Roger C. Steffens, "Consumer Preferences in Residential Location: A Preliminary Investigation of the Home Purchase Decision," *Research Previews,* Vol. 13, No. 1, pp. 1-32 (March 1966).

Weiss, Shirley F., John E. Smith, Edward J. Kaiser, and Kenneth B. Kenney, *Residential Developer Decisions: A Focused View of the Urban Growth Process,* An Urban Studies Research Monograph, Center for Urban and Regional Studies, Institute for Research in Social Science, University of North Carolina, Chapel Hill (1966).

8 On the Derivation of Spatial Equilibrium Urban Land Value Functions

Emilio Casetti

Explicit spatial equilibrium[1] conditions may allow the derivation of urban land value functions consistent with assumptions on the behavior of relevant economic "actors" and on the structure of the space in which these actors operate. In this paper it is pointed out that these conditions provide a general method for extracting the implications of behavioral assumptions in a spatial context. A short statement of what is here called "spatial equilibrium method" will be followed by an application of the method to simplified settings similar to ones considered in the models of urban structure introduced by Alonso, Wingo, and Muth (Alonso 1960, 1964; Wingo 1961; Muth 1961, 1967, 1968, 1969).

The Spatial Equilibrium Method

Consider the class of models defining a space, "actors" operating on it, and a set of deterministic behavioral rules specifying in which circumstances the actors move into or out of the space or relocate within it, or acquire or change their attributes. These models consist of assumptions and propositions characterizing unambiguously space, actors, and behavioral rules, and therefore it identifies a "system".[2]

The spatial equilibrium states of this system require that no actor be motivated, in terms of his stated rules of behavior, to relocate into, out of, or within the systems space, or to change his attributes (Casetti, 1970). The distributions of attributes and actors within the model's space when a state of spatial equilibrium exists are defined as spatial equilibrium distributions.

The spatial equilibrium method calls for (1) determining from stated behavioral assumptions under which conditions a state of spatial equilibrium exists and (2) extracting from the assumptions and propositions constituting the model, augmented by the spatial equilibrium conditions, the spatial equilibrium distributions they imply. The method will be demonstrated using three sets of assumptions of increasing complexity embedded into a common background. These settings are in different degrees similar to the ones studied by Alonso, Wingo, and Muth. In all three of them (1) a homogeneous plane with all places of work located in a central point is assumed, (2) commuting between any two points on the plane is only related to their distance, (3) residential land is

123

privately owned and constitutes a constant fraction of the total land at any distance from the central location.

Throughout this paper distance from the central location and unit value of residential land will be respectively indicated by s and r.

A Setting à la Wingo

Let identical one-person households be the only "actors" in the plane. Each household faces locational costs C consisting of the sum of commuting costs C_T and residential land costs C_R:

$$C = C_T + C_R. \qquad (1)$$

The commuting costs are a function of distance, and incorporate gasoline costs and car depreciation as well as the value of time spent travelling:

$$C_T = C_T(s). \qquad (2)$$

The residential costs equal the quantity of land q consumed by a household times its unit price r:

$$C_R = qr. \qquad (3)$$

The quantity of land consumed by a household is function of the price of land:

$$q = q(r). \qquad (4)$$

Equations (1) through (4) imply that the locational costs associated with a residential site are a function of its distance from the central location and of its land values:

$$C = C(s,r) = C_T(s) + rq(r). \qquad (5)$$

Let the "actors" behavioral rules prescribe that the households minimize their locational costs. Then, they will relocate whenever by so doing they are able to reduce their locational costs. Therefore, a state of spatial equilibrium, in which no household has any reason to relocate, will exist only if the locational costs are identical throughout the urban area. Hence, the spatial equilibrium condition is that, within the urban area, the locational costs be equal to a given constant $\bar{\bar{C}}$ irrespective of distance from the central location:

$$C(s,\bar{\bar{r}}) = \bar{\bar{C}} \qquad s \geqslant 0. \qquad (6)$$

Equation (6) defines implicitly a function $\bar{\bar{r}}(s)$ indicating the spatial equilibrium land value at distance s.

The spatial equilibrium land value makes the locational costs of the households spatially invariant. If explicit $C_T(s)$ and $q(r)$ are given, $\bar{\bar{r}}(s)$ may be easily obtained. Let for instance

$$C_T(s) = ks \tag{7}$$

and

$$q(r) = ar^{-b}. \tag{8}$$

Then from Equations (5), (7), and (8) it follows that

$$C(s,r) = ks + ar^{1-b} \tag{9}$$

and by imposing the spatial equilibrium condition we have that

$$\bar{\bar{r}}(s) = ((\bar{\bar{C}} - ks)/a)^h \tag{10}$$

where

$$h = 1/(1-b).$$

A Setting à la Alonso

The setting to be now considered closely resembles the one discussed by Alonso in his well-known contribution on "Location and Land Use" (Alonso, 1964). Alonso's analysis however does not extend to the derivation of continuous function defining equilibrium land value surfaces. The following application of the spatial equilibrium method is based on Casetti's mathematical operationalization of Alonso's model (Casetti, 1971). Let the model's actors be households and landowners. Assume one-person households identical in preferences and income, and let their preferences be specified by an indifference map

$$u = u(z,q,s) \tag{11}$$

identifying the combinations of a composite good z, of quantity of residential land q, and of distance from the central locations that yield to a household the same utility level u. Commuting costs are proportional to distance. The households are confronted by a budget constraint stating that the sum of the outlays for the purchase of the composite good, for land rent, and for commuting must equal their income. Namely

$$y = pz + r(s)q + ks \qquad (12)$$

where p is the unit price of the composite good, $r(s)$ is the unit price of residential land at a distance s from the *CBD*, and k is the transportation cost per unit of distance. The households strive to maximize their utility subject to the condition that their budgets are not exceeded. The land owners aim at maximizing their rent. The allocation of the residential land to the households takes place by competitive bidding. Since the households maximize the level of satisfaction of their preferences, they will either relocate or change the mix of z and q they consume if by so doing their level of satisfaction u may be increased. The landowners maximize their lands' rents by allocating their properties to the highest bidder. The spatial equilibrium method calls for identifying from these behavioral rules the states of the systems in which the actors are not motivated to initiate any change in the status quo. Since the households in the model will relocate or change their consumption mix — namely, will change their s, z, and q — if by so doing they can increase their utility level u, a state of spatial equilibrium will exist only if (1) all households consume a mix of z and q that yield an optimal u, (2) the optimal utility level is spatially invariant over the urban area, and (3) the optimal utility level is identical to one attainable outside the urban area. If the utility level is not the highest that may be obtained by a suitable choice of z and q, a household will be prompted by its rules of behavior to change the consumption mix and consequently the spatial distribution of z and q. If the optimum utility level is not invariant over the urban space, (1) the less favored households will relocate into the better areas and in so doing will bid the rent down in the areas they leave and up in the areas they move to; (2) or the less favored landowners will raise the rents while the more favored landowners will lose tenants and will be forced to lower their rents. If the optimum utility level of the households in the urban area is not identical to the one attainable in other areas (urban or rural) in the system, households will move into or out of the urban area.

Hence, a state of spatial equilibrium requires that all households attain a utility level corresponding to an optimum mix of z and q, that this optimal utility level be spatially invariant over the entire urban area, and be equal to an exogeneously determined constant corresponding to the optimal utility level attainable "outside". These three points identify the required spatial equilibrium conditions.

In order to determine the spatial equilibrium land value surface defined by the assumptions in the earlier part of this section and by the corresponding spatial equilibrium conditions, (1) optimal values $\bar{q}$ and $\bar{z}$ are determined such that

$$u(\bar{z}, \bar{q}, s) = \text{maximum} \tag{13}$$

$$p\bar{z} + r(s)\bar{q} + ks = y \tag{14}$$

where

$$\bar{z} = \bar{z}(s) \tag{15}$$

$$\bar{q} = \bar{q}(s,r) ; \tag{16}$$

(2) then the optimal utility level $\bar{u}(s,r)$, corresponding to the optimal consumption mix is obtained,

$$\bar{u}(s,r) = u(\bar{z},\bar{q},s) ; \tag{17}$$

(3) and finally the spatial equilibrium condition is imposed that the optimal utility level be equal to an exogenously given constant $\bar{\bar{u}}$ throughout the urban area,

$$\bar{u}(s,\bar{\bar{r}}) = \bar{\bar{u}} \qquad s \geqslant 0. \tag{18}$$

The $\bar{\bar{r}} = \bar{\bar{r}}(s)$ identified by equation (18) is the required spatial equilibrium land value function.

For a demonstration of the method, assume

$$u = z^a q^b e^{-cs} \tag{19}$$

where $0 < a, b < 1$. Then the $\bar{z}$ and $\bar{q}$ yielding the required constrained maximum of u are

$$\bar{z} = a(y-ks)/pv \tag{20}$$

$$\bar{q} = b(y-ks)/rv \tag{21}$$

where $v = a + b$. The optimal utility level $\bar{u}(s,r)$ is

$$\bar{u}(s,r) = H(b/rv)^b (y-ks)^v e^{-cs} \tag{22}$$

where $H = (a/pv)^a$.

By setting $\bar{u}(s,r)$ of Equation (22) equal to an exogenously determined constant utility level $\bar{u}$, and by solving for r, the following spatial equilibrium land value function $\bar{r}(s)$ is obtained:

$$\bar{r}(s) = (b/v)((H/\bar{u})(y-ks)^v e^{-cs})^{1/b} \tag{23}$$

A Setting à la Muth

In the setting to be now analyzed the households choose an optimum mix of "quantity of housing" x, of a composite good z including everything but housing and of distance s from the central location. The variable x differs from the variable q employed in the previous analysis since it incorporates housing structures as well as residential land. Hence the households choose a mix including "housing" and "everything else but housing" rather than "quantity of residential land" and "everything else but land".

Housing is produced by producers of housing from land and nonland inputs, and is then rented to the households.

The "actors" are households, producers of housing, and owners of residential land. One-person households identical in preferences and income are assumed.

The preferences of the households are specified by an indifference map

$$u = u(z,x,s) \tag{24}$$

identifying combinations of the composite good z, of housing x, and of distance from the central locations yielding to a household the same utility level u. Commuting costs are proportional to distance travelled. The households are confronted by a budget constraint stating that the sum of the outlays for the purchase of the composite good, for housing, and for commuting must equal their income. Namely,

$$y = p_z z + p_x x + ks \tag{25}$$

where p_z, p_x are the unit prices of the composite good and of housing, k is commuting costs per unit of distance, and y is a household's income. The households strive to maximize their utility subject to the condition that their incomes are not exceeded.

All producers of housing are confronted by an identical production function

$$X = X(Q) \tag{26}$$

that specifies the quantity of housing produced on one unit of residential land X, from Q units of nonland inputs. Notice that while the x appearing in Equations (24) and (25) is the quantity of housing consumed by a household, the X of Equation (26) indicates quantity of housing on a unit of residential land. The "excess" profit of the producers of housing per unit of residential area π is

$$\pi = p_x X - wQ - r \qquad (27)$$

where w is the unit cost of the nonland inputs and r is the unit value of residential land. The producers of housing maximize their profits. The owners of land strive to obtain the highest price possible for the use of their land.

From the behavioral rules of the households, of the producers of housing, and of the land owners the following spatial equilibrium conditions may be derived. At equilibrium, (1) the households consume an optimal mix of housing and of composite good, so that no change in their consumption mix may improve their utility level; (2) the optimal utility level attainable by the households is constant throughout the urban area, so that no household may improve it by relocating within the urban area; (3) the optimal utility level attainable by the households within the urban area is identical to the one that may be attained outside it, so that no household may benefit by moving into or out of the urban area; (4) the quantity of housing on any residential site within the urban area corresponds to the combination of land and nonland inputs yielding a maximum excess profit so that no producer of housing has any incentive to produce any additional housing or to replace the existing one on the basis of a different input mix; and (5) no owner of any residential site may obtain a higher price for his land, which implies that the land values allow to the producers of housing a zero excess profit throughout the urban area.

If these conditions are met no household is motivated to change its consumption mix or location, and no producer of housing or owner of residential land is motivated to change the stock and location of housing or to force households to relocate, and therefore a state of spatial equilibrium will exist. In order to determine the spatial equilibrium housing value surface generated by Conditions 1 through 3, (1) optimal values $\bar{z}$ and $\bar{x}$ are determined such that

$$u(\bar{z}, \bar{x}, s) = \text{maximum} \qquad (28)$$

$$p_z \bar{r} + p_x \bar{x} + ks = y \qquad (29)$$

where

$$\bar{z} = \bar{z}(s) \qquad (30)$$

$$\bar{x} = \bar{x}(s, p_x) ; \qquad (31)$$

(2) then the optimal utility level $\bar{u}(s, p_x)$ corresponding to the optimal consumption mix is obtained,

$$\bar{u}(s, p_x) = u(\bar{z}, \bar{x}, s) ; \qquad (32)$$

(3) and finally the spatial equilibrium condition is imposed that the optimal utility level $\bar{u}$ be equal to an exogenously determined constant $\bar{\bar{u}}$ throughout the urban area,

$$\bar{u}(s, \bar{\bar{p}}_x) = \bar{\bar{u}} \qquad s \geqslant 0 . \qquad (33)$$

The $\bar{\bar{p}}_x = \bar{\bar{p}}_x(s)$ implicitly defined by Equation (33) identifies the required spatial equilibrium housing-value surface.

In order to determine the spatial equilibrium land value surface, (1) the optimal quantity of nonland inputs into the production of housing $\bar{Q}$ is determined such that

$$\pi(s, r) = \bar{\bar{p}}_x(s) \times (\bar{Q}) - w\bar{Q} - r(s) = \text{maximum}; \qquad (34)$$

(2) and then the maximum excess profit of the producer of housing is set equal to zero throughout the urban area,

$$\bar{\pi}(s, \bar{r}) = 0 \qquad s \geqslant 0 . \qquad (35)$$

The $\bar{\bar{r}} = \bar{\bar{r}}(s)$ implicitly defined by Equation (35) is the required spatial equilibrium land value function.

For a demonstration of this procedure, assume the following utility and production functions:

$$u = z^a x^b e^{-cs} \qquad (36)$$

and

$$X = hQ^n \qquad (37)$$

where $0 < a, b, n < 1$. The values of z and x that maximize u and satisfy the budget constraint of the households are

$$\bar{z} = a(y - ks)/vp_z \qquad (38)$$

$$\bar{x} = b(y - ks)/vp_x \qquad (39)$$

where $v = a + b$. The optimal utility level $\bar{u}(s,p_x)$ is

$$\bar{u}(s,p_x) = H(b/vp_x)^b (y - ks)^v e^{-cs} \qquad (40)$$

where $H = (a/vp_z)$. By setting the optimal utility level equal to a constant $\bar{\bar{u}}$, and solving for p_x, the spatial equilibrium housing value function $\bar{\bar{p}}_x(s)$ is obtained:

$$\bar{\bar{p}}_x(s) = (b/v)((H/\bar{\bar{u}})(y - ks)^v e^{-cs})^{1/b} . \qquad (41)$$

The nonland input that maximizes the profit of the producers of housing $\bar{Q}$ corresponding to the production function in Equation (37) is

$$\bar{Q} = (\bar{\bar{p}}_x hn/w)^{-m} \qquad (42)$$

where $m = 1/(1 - n)$. The optimum profit corresponding to $\bar{Q}$ is

$$\bar{\pi}(s,r) = W \bar{\bar{p}}_x^m - r \qquad (43)$$

where $W = (h/w^n)^m (n^{mn} - n^m)$. By imposing the condition that the optimal profits equal zero throughout the urban area, and solving for r, the spatial equilibrium land value function $\bar{\bar{r}}(s)$ may be obtained:

$$\bar{\bar{r}}(s) = W(\bar{\bar{p}}_x(s))^m . \qquad (44)$$

Conclusion

In this paper spatial equilibrium residential land value functions are derived in three settings of increasing complexity by what is here called the "spatial equilibrium method." The method is designed to extract the implications of behavioral assumptions in a spatial context. It calls for identifying under which conditions the entities of a model that are assumed to be capable of "decisions" are not motivated to initiate any changes in the status quo if they conform to the rules of behavior attributed to them. Spatial distributions of relevant variables are then derived from the initial assumptions augmented by the spatial equilibrium conditions. The generality of scope of the method is noted.

Notes

1. The expressions "spatial equilibrium" and "locational equilibrium" have been used in the literature mostly to denote competitive (and sometimes oligogolistic or monopolistic) market equilibrium in a variety of economic

contexts incorporating some form of space: Cf., for instance, the "Samuelson Enke problem" (Enke, 1951; Samuelson, 1952; Garrison, et al., 1959; Morrill and Garrison, 1960; and Takayama and Judge, two papers in 1964); the Hotelling problem (Isard, 1956, p. 161 ff.; Hotelling, 1929; Zeuthen 1933; Lerner and Singer, 1937; Smithies, two papers in 1941; and Ackley, 1942); the Tuhnen problem (Dunn, 1954); and the urban structure problem (Alonso, 1964; Muth, 1969; and Wingo, 1961).

Recently the competitive equilibrium framework has been extended to multiregional settings involving social and political, as well as economical "commodities" (Isard, et al., 1969). For a review and discussion of behavioral equilibrium within and without spatial settings, see Golledge, 1970.

The spatial equilibrium method discussed here may be viewed as generalization and formalization of some aspects of well known techniques and concepts.

2. Cf. Hall and Fagen, 1956; Von Bertalanffy, 1968; Handy and Lurtz, 1963.

References

Ackley, G., "Spatial Competition in a Discontinuous Market", *Quarterly Journal of Economics,* Vol. 56. pp. 212–230 (1942).

Alonso, W., "A Theory of the Urban Land Market", *Papers and Proceedings of the Regional Science Association,* Vol. 6. pp. 149–158 (1960).

Alonso, W., *Location and Land Use,* Harvard University Press, Cambridge (1964).

Bertalanffy, L. Von, *General System Theory,* G. Braziller, New York (1968).

Casetti, E., Equilibrium Land Values and Population Densities in an Urban Setting, *Economic Geography,* Vol. 47, pp. 16–20 (1971).

Dunn, E.S. Jr., *The Location of Agricultural Production,* University of Florida Press, Gainesville (1954).

Enke, S., Equilibrium among Spatially Separated Markets: Solution by Elictric Analogue", *Econometrica,* Vol. 19. pp. 40-47 (1951).

Garrison, W.L., Berry, B.J.L., Marble, D.F., Nystuen, J.D., and Morrill, R.L., *Studies of Highway Development and Geographic Change,* University of Washington Press, Seattle (1959).

Golledge, R., "Some Equilibrium Models of Consumers Behavior", *Economic Geography,* Vol. 46 pp. 417–424 of the *Supplement* containing the *Proceedings of the IGU Commission on Quantitative Methods* (1970)

Hall, A.D. and Fagen, R.E., "Definition of System", *General Systems,* Vol. 1. pp. 18–29 (1956).

Handy, R. and Kurtz, P., *General System Theory* in *A Current Appraisal of the Behavioral Sciences,* Behavioral Research Council, Great Barrington, pp. 137-141 (1963).

Hotelling, H., Stability in Competition, *Economic Journal,* Vol. 39, pp. 41-57 (1929).

Isard, W., *Location and Space Economy,* Wiley, New York (1956).

Isard, W., in association with T.E. Smith, P. Isard, T.H. Tung, and M. Dacey, *General Theory,* MIT Press, Cambridge (1969).

Lerner, A.P., and Singer, H.W., Some Notes on Duopoly and Spatial Competition, *Journal of Political Economy,* Vol. 45, pp. 145-186 (1937).

Morrill, R.L. and Garrison, W.L., "Projection of Interregional Patterns of Trade in Wheat and Flour", *Economic Geography,* Vol. 36, pp. 116-126 (1960).

Muth, R.F., "The Spatial Structure of the Housing Market", *Papers and Proceedings of the Regional Science Association,* Vol. 7, pp. 207-220 (1961).

Muth, R.F., "The Distribution of Population within Urban Areas", in *Determinants of Investment Behavior," pp. 271-299,* R. Ferber ed., National Bureau of Economic Research, New York (1967).

Muth, R.F., "Urban Residential Land and Housing Markets" in *Issues in Urban Economics,* pp. 285-333, H.S. Perloff and L. Wingo eds., John Hopkins Press, Baltimore (1968).

Muth, R.F., *Cities and Housing,* The University of Chicago Press, Chicago (1969).

Richardson, H.W., *Regional Economics,* Praeger, New York (1969).

Samuelson, P.A., "Spatial Equilibrium and Linear Programming", *American Economic Review,* Vol. 42, pp. 283-303 (1952).

Smithies, A., "Optimum Location in Spatial Competition", *Journal of Political Economy,* Vol. 44, pp. 423-439 (1941).

Smithies, A., "Monopolistic Price Policy in a Spatial Market", *Econometrica,* Vol. 9, pp. 63-73 (1941).

Takayama, T., and Judge, G.G., "Equilibrium among Spatially Separated Markets; A Reformulation", *Econometrica,* Vol. 32, pp. 510-524 (1964).

Takayama, T., and Judge, G.G., "Spatial Equilibrium and Quadratic Programming", *Journal of Farm Economics,* Vol. 46, pp. 67-93 (1964).

Wingo, L. Jr., "An Economic Model of the Utilization of Urban Land for Residential Purposes", *Papers and Proceedings of the Regional Science Association,* Vol. 7, pp. 191-205 (1961).

Wingo, L. Jr., *Transportation and Urban Land,* Resources for the Future, Inc., Washington, D.C. (1961).

Zeuthen, F., "Theoretical Remarks on Price Policy: Hotelling's Case with Variations", *Quarterly Journal of Economics,* Vol. 47, pp. 231-253 (1963).

Analytical Convergence in Ecological Research: Factorial Analysis, Gradient, and Sector Models

Kent P. Schwirian

Introduction

Two of the most basic trends in urban ecological research today are: (1) the analytical convergence of gradient, sector, and factor analytic models, and (2) the attempt to relate urban ecological differentiation to theories of societal development. The purpose of this paper is to assess and illustrate these trends. In doing so the discussion is organized around three topics: (1) the general nature of the trends, (2) some new, illustrative research findings on cities in Canada and Puerto Rico, and (3) the delineation of some problems in this type of analysis which are fundamental and common, but essentially unresolved. This paper is not meant to be a definitive treatise on current ecological research, but, rather, attempts to be somewhat provocative and suggestive of worthy areas for future discussion and research.

Convergence of Gradient, Sector, and Factor Analytic Models

While recent empirical investigations have merged the gradient, sector, and factor analytic models, the three differ in their initial orientations. Both the gradient model proposed by Burgess (1926) and the sector model espoused by Hoyte (1939) focus on the differentiated distribution of population and housing in urban space. According to their perspectives, the gross distributional pattern for any metropolis is a result of the interplay of socioeconomic forces of competition in the urban land market. In describing the process of residential site selection, Park emphasized the operation of the broader contextual forces as opposed to the current empirical and theoretical trends which focus on the calculus of the individual in the residential search process. In 1929 Park wrote:

The city is, in fact, a constellation of natural areas, each with its own characteristic milieu, and each performing its specific function in the urban economy as a whole ... The metropolis is, it seems, a great sifting and sorting mechanism, which, in ways that are not yet wholly understood, infallibly selects out of the population as a whole the individuals best suited to live in a particular region and a particular milieu.... The city grows by expansion, but it gets its character by the selection and segregation of its population, so that every individual finds, eventually, either the place where he can, or the place where he must live. (Park, 1952, p. 79.)

In addition to focusing upon the operation of the urban land market the gradient and sector models share other assumptions. Some of these were first suggested by Quinn (1940) as being implicit in the concentric zone or gradient model but they seem to apply to the sector model as well. They are: (1) the existence of social class gradations within the population, (2) a growing city, (3) an industrial-commercial urban economic base, (4) private ownership of property, (5) specialization in land use, (6) efficient, rapid, cheap transportation, (7) single centered city, (8) freedom of residential choice for the higher socio-economic strata.

Although the gradient and sector models share a preoccupation with the operation of the broader socioeconomic forces within the metropolis, the specific spatial configurations they propose differ markedly. While Burgess and Park argue that population and housing vary by zone with increasing distance from the city's center, Hoyte stresses the sectorial pattern in which population and housing differ more in terms of homogeneous wedges running from the city's center to the periphery than by distance gradient.

Another important difference between the gradient and sector model which is frequently overlooked is the relative attention to the process of change within each model. The sector model is much more specific about the processes of ecological change than is the gradient model. According to the gradient model, change is described in terms of the processes of invasion, succession, extension, and concentration in which one zone's land use and population type initially invades, and then succeeds, that in the next adjacent zone. Change is thus envisioned much like the result of dropping a pebble into a lake: a series of ripples radiate from the point of impact pushing into each other in their outward flow. Propositions for predicting change in the Burgess and Park model are somewhat vague and amorphous. More specific are the propositions of the sector model. Based upon his study of 142 American cities, Hoyte puts forth several hypotheses to account for urban sectorial change. These are:

"(1) High-grade residential growth tends to proceed from the given point of origin either along established lines of travel or toward another existing nucleus of building or trade areas.
(2) The zone of high rent tends toward high ground which is free from risk of floods and to spread along lake, bay, river, and ocean ports, where such waterfronts are not used by industry.
(3) High-rent residential districts tend to grow toward the section of the city that has free open country beyond the edges and away from "dead end" sections which are prevented from expanding by natural or artificial barriers.

(4) The higher-priced residential neighborhood tends to grow toward the homes of the community leaders.
(5) Sometimes movement trends of office buildings, banks, and stores pull the higher-priced residential neighborhoods in the same general direction.
(6) High-grade residential areas tend to develop along the fastest existing transportation lines.
(7) Deluxe apartment areas tend to be established near the business centers in old established residential areas.
(8) The growth of high-rent neighborhoods continues in the same direction for a long period of time.
(9) High-rent neighborhoods do not skip about at random in the process of movement; they follow a definite path in one or more sectors of the city.
(10) It is possible, under some conditions, for high-rent areas to "double back," or return toward the center of the city.
(11) High-rent areas tend to be adjoined by medium-rent areas, and sharp disjunctions in rental areas are not frequent." (As summarized in Thomlinson, 1969, pp. 146-147.)

The gradient and the sector model have had enormous impact upon urban sociology and urban geography, and the use and development of the models have been thoroughly reviewed recently by Mayer (1964), by Sjoberg (1965), and by Berry (1965) and their fine efforts will not be duplicated here.

While these two models initially appear to be antagonistic in their description of urban ecological structure, much recent research has found them to be more complementary than opposing. For example, in comparing the spatial distributions of two variables called "residential prestige" and "urbanization", Anderson and Egeland (1961) conclude that residential prestige is distributed sectorally while urbanization which is a measure of familial and housing patterns was distributed by gradient. A similar finding is reported by Schwirian and Matre in a study of 11 principal Canadian cities. The Canadian city data will be described more fully in a latter section of this paper. Other reseachers have found that when concentric zones and sectors are considered jointly, significant variations in demographic and housing variables are explained. Here I refer to such work as that of deVise who in a study of Chicago found that subareas formed by a combination of concentric zone and sector location had fairly uniform social and economic properties. (deVise, 1962.)

Thus, these two initially competing models have come to be used increasingly to supplement each other in the description of urban population distributions. Furthermore, a third model, factorial ecology, has been added to these other two in recent studies. The net effect of this combination has been a very comprehensive approach to ecological phenomena.

Factorial ecology has a much different initiating orientation from that of either the gradient or sector models. The term *factorial ecology* represents a series of differing approaches to urban ecological organization that mainly share on thing in common — their statistical techniques, which is factor analysis of urban subarea data. Berry and Rees (1969), distinguish between social area analysis and factorial ecology. Social area analysis studies are derived from the theoretical framework of Shevky (for a more recent restatement and development of the theory see Greer, 1962). The theory, in effect, asserts that the residential differentiation of urban populations in terms of social rank, familism, and ethnicity is a function of the degree of modernization of the society in which the city is located. The theory maintains that as a society modernizes or increases in "scale," the degree of social differentiation increases and this is reflected in increasing specialization of urban land use and population differentiation. The dimensions of life most sensitive to this change are viewed by the social area analysts to be social rank, family structure or life cycle patterns, and ethnicity. A fourth dimension, migrant status, has been suggested in a recent paper by Clignet and Sween (1969).

Thus, in small-scale societies or in societies that are less modern there is little social differentiation; that is, social rank is highly related to family form and both, in turn, are related to ethnicity and migrant status. These high correlations mean that differential population distribution in the city does not occur in their terms. In large-scale society where social differentiation has occurred, areal specialization in terms of these characteristics accompanies their growing independence. In terms of factor analysis, there is a separation of variables measuring social rank from those measuring familism and ethnicity and there is a separation of the familism (or life style) variables from those of ethnicity. Likewise, migrant status separates from the other dimensions in factor space. Thus, in a large-scale society at least three factors are needed to explain the interrelationships among the variables while in a small-scale society a fewer number of factors, perhaps one, is sufficient.

Factorial ecology differs from social area analysis in that factorial ecology is more inductive and includes a wider range of variables than does social area analysis although the social area analysis variables are usually included. In describing factorial ecology, Berry and Rees have recently written:

A data matrix is analyzed containing measurements on m variables for each of n units of observation (census tracts, wards . . .), with the intent of (1) identifying and summarizing the common patterns of variability of the m variables in a smaller number of independent dimensions r, that additively reproduce this common variance; and (2) examining the patterns of scores of each of the n observational units on each of the r dimensions. The dimensions isolated are an objective outcome of the analysis. (Berry and Rees, 1969, pp. 458-459.)

Since the inputs for factorial ecology are larger in number and of a wider variety of social and physical phenomena than are the inputs for social area analysis, the resulting number of factors extracted in factorial ecology usually exceeds that of social area analysis. Thus, factorial ecology usually identifies many more *dimensions* of urban social and physical organization. Thus, Sweetser (1969), in a study of Helsinki, has identified several ethnic factors; in Boston he has identified a nonwhite factor separate from other ethnic factors such as an Italian factor and an Irish factor. In a study of Copenhagen, Pedersen (1965) has identified — in addition to the usual factors found in such studies — a population growth factor and a mobility factor. In a study of Calcutta, Berry and Rees (1969) report such factors as literacy, high status Muslim, and a host of special land use configurations.

The discovery of factors unique to data inputs for specific cities make factorial ecology studies difficult to compare. Herein lies one of the largest methodological problems of this approach. Different inputs lead to different resulting factor structures. Social area analysis has escaped this problem to a great extent since the input variables are largely determined by the theoretical framework and not simply by what data are at hand. Thus, the tendency in social area analyses is to limit the factor analysis to aggregates of variables comparable between cities. However, unique configurations in the development of any one city are often missed. While the data inputs for the social area analysis studies are fairly comparable, the resulting factor structures are often quite varied. Berry and Rees have identified seven possible results just using the social area analysis variables and they present empirically discovered examples of each. (Berry and Rees, 1969, p. 468.)

With increasing frequency the gradient, sector, and factor analytic models are being used jointly in current research. There seems to be two major patterns for this analytic convergence. The first of these include investigations that calculate separate factor analyses of similar variables for different sectors and and zones within a single city. One of the current leading exponents of this line of analysis is Frank Sweetser. Sweetser's long-range goal is to develop a typology of cities classified in terms of their similar ecological configurations as measured by their factor structures. However, he argues, that before this goal can be achieved a number of procedural problems must be resolved. One of these involves the relative stability of ecological factors. In order to identify the factors common to all portions of one city, he advocates separate factor analyses for the different zones and sectors. From the results he identifies the factors common to the metropolis as a whole and sorts out those that are zone or sector unique. Once having identified the basic factors for a city they may then be compared to those from other cities. The cities are then classified as to similarity in basic factors. (Sweetser, 1969.)

The second pattern for this analytical convergence among the models may be seen in the work of Anderson and Egeland (1961), of Schwirian and Matre (1969), and Berry and Rees (1969). In each of these studies the major dimensions of ecological organization for a city are identified through factor analysis of a number of variables. Then, the spatial distribution of the factors in terms of gradients and sectors is determined. In a study of four U.S. cities, (Akron,

Dayton, Indianapolis, and Syracuse) Anderson and Egeland examined the distribution of the social area analysis indexes of social rank and familism (urbanization) by gradient and by sector. Rank and familism were identified as basic community dimensions in past factor analytic studies. As was mentioned previously, analysis of variance of the two indexes showed that social rank or prestige varied by sector in the cities while urbanization or familism varied by concentric zone. Schwirian and Matre present similar findings for a number of large Canadian cities. Likewise, Berry and Rees in their study of Calcutta first determined the major factors then fit a trend surface analysis to the factor scores. Once the surface had been established they were evaluated in terms of sectors and gradients.

In summary of the analytical convergence in current ecological research, the factorial, gradient, and sector models are coming to play unique and complementary roles. Factor analysis is generally used to identify basic dimensions of urban organization while the gradient and sector models are used to ascertain the spatial differentiation of these dimensions in relation to the city's center and to each other.

Relation of Urban Ecological Differentiation to Societal Development

The comparative interests of social scientists has produced a large number of studies of urban structure in a variety of societies. The growing mass of such materials is reflected in the recent flurry of summary reviews as found in such sources as Hauser and Schnore (1965) and in Breese (1969). Rather than accepting simple descriptive comparisons of U.S. and non-U.S. cities, urban ecologists are attempting to explain differences between U.S. and other cities in terms of theories of societal development.

Comparative studies of gradient and sector models have noted either reversal in patterns predicted on the basis of findings on U.S. cities (such as in Latin America) or the prevalence of multiple nucleation (as in some African or Asian cities). The difference between U.S. cities and the others are usually explained by some combination of the following three factors: (1) *Differences in Urban Function.* While U.S. cities are commercial-industrial centers, many of the nonwestern cities are primarily, or were at the time of location, primarily administrative centers. Thus, difference in primary function resulted in different land use patterns and differential population distributions within the city. Explanations of this type are most elaborately illustrated by Sjoberg's *Pre-Industrial City* (1960). (2) *Differences in Level of Transportation and Transportation Ownership Patterns.* Accordingly, the spread of the population in urban space is a direct function of mode of transportation and access to transportation of large segments of the population. In countries with a more restrictive transportation pattern than that of the United States, different forces work to sort the population thereby producing a different spatial pattern. (3) *Level of Technology at the Time of City Location.* Implied in this notion are two ideas. First, that the ecological pattern for a given city is largely determined by existing modes of transportation. And, second, that once such patterns are established, enormous inertia accompanies their change. Change when it comes, in most cases, is slow, disjunctive, disrupted, and piecemeal. Credence for this explanation has been given by Schnore's work (1965) on age of city as an ecological variable, and in the interest of other ecologists in so-called "historical residuals".

The vast number of studies of non-U.S. cities, then, leads to the conclusion that in terms of the gradient and sector model the differences between our cities and those abroad are a result of differences in societal modernization — that is, differences in level of industrialization and transportation technology, primary function, and age. Furthermore, many of these studies assert or imply that the non-U.S. cities are becoming more like the U.S. cities as they take on greater industrial and commercial functions.

To date no formal attempt has been made to tie the classical ecological models into a developmental theory of society even though such inferences abound in the literature. Perhaps the closest attempt at developing such a theory is that by Schnore in his review of the spatial structure of North and South American cities. He concludes that "What does emerge from this review is the possibility that (a) the Burgess concentric zone scheme, wrongly regarded as indigenous to the United States, and (b) the preindustrial pattern, erroneously identified as unique to Latin America, are *both special cases more adequately subsumed under a more general theory of residential land use in urban areas.*" (Schnore, 1965, p. 374.)

In the course of the discussion, Schnore speculates that there might well be a sequential pattern of ecological change as societies modernize. In the early pattern of city development, the "inverse gradient" characterizes the city in which the affluent population lives near the city's center and the lesser monied live toward the periphery. With growth, modernization, and aging, the central portions of the city become less attractive residentially and the upper class migrates toward the periphery. The vacated areas in the inner portions of the city become the targets for those urbanites who cannot survive in the stiffer competition for attractive fringe space. (For a discussion of the role of physical amenities in differential residential distributions, see Amato, 1969.) While this "theory" is intuitively appealing, no test of it has yet been made. Of course, longitudinal data would be required and for most cities of the world good small-area data for past years simply are not available.

While Schnore's speculation is far from a theory of ecological dynamics it does provide a foundation for future research endeavors and serves as a call for less descriptive cross-sectional studies and for more explanatory dynamic investigations.

Factorial ecology — specifically, social area analysis — has tied explanations of urban ecological structure to a much more specific theory of social change. As mentioned previously, when the degree of modernization within a society increases so too does the differentiation of the social system and the spatial segregation of population types. In low-scale societies there is sufficiently high correlations among the variables of social rank, familism, and ethnicity to prevent factorial separation of them, while in large-scale societies the correlations among the variables are reduced sufficiently to permit the separation of rank, familism, and ethnicity. Accordingly, it is inferred that as the scale of society changes so too does the degree of factor separation. Most studies, however, have *not* been longitudinal as required for test of the theory but have been cross-sectional comparisons of cities in different societies.

If the three factors of rank, familism, and ethnicity fail to separate, it is then argued that the society in which the cities are located is low on the scale of modernization. A recent example of this line of analysis is a study of Cairo by Abu-Lughod (1969). With data for both 1947 and 1960, Abu-Lughod reports that social rank and familism load on the same factor each year and that this combined factor accounts for approximately half of the total matrix variation. The failure of rank and familism to separate is attributed to the different degree of modernization in Egypt as compared to that in the U.S.

Perhaps an even greater contribution of the Abu-Lughod paper than its empirical findings on Cairo is its discussion of the conditions under which social rank and familism factors would appear for a given city and under which conditions the two factors would separate from each other. For a social rank vector to be identified the following conditions must be met: (1) that the effective ranking system in a city be related to the operational definition employed; and (2) that the ranking system be manifested in a pattern of residential segregation of persons of different ranks at a large enough scale to be picked up at the level of analysis (census tract, ward, etc.). For a familism factor to appear there must be: (1) variability in family types due to either "natural" causes such as those associated with stages in the life cycle or to other "social" causes such as those associated with other divisions in the society such as social rank or ethnicity; and (2) that subareas within the city be differentiated in attractiveness to different types of families. For familism and social rank factors to separate from each other, the following conditions must be met: (1) that there be no strong linkages between social rank and such familism variables as fertility, completed family size, and the propensity to remain within extended households; (2) that stages in the life cycle were clearly distinguished from one another with each stage being associated with a change in residence; (3) that sufficiently large subareas within the city offered, at all economic levels, highly specialized housing accommodations suited to families at particular stages in the life cycle; and (4) that cultural values permitting and favoring mobility to maximize housing efficiency are generally unencumbered by restrictive regulations or strong sentiments. (Abu-Lughod, 1969, pp. 108-109.)

The emergence of ethnicity as a factor differentiated from rank and familism has been described by Schwirian and Matre (1969, p. 5). For ethnicity to be separated from the other factors in a society there must be differential definitions, values, and behaviors characteristic of subpopulations differing in heritage, physical appearance, and/or philosophical or religious orientation. For ethnicity to separate from social rank and familism, there must be considerable variation in the residential location of ethnic groups at each level of social rank and at each stage in the life cycle.

By way of summary, it should be pointed out that the topic of social change is in vogue in the social sciences today and this interest is reflected in urban ecological research on the three models discussed in this paper. However, little longitudinal research has been conducted as a result of the scarcity of past urban subarea data. Inferences concerning change are restricted generally by the cross-sectional nature of the data. Let us hope that the interest of ecologists is not blunted by the lack of historical materials but that ecologists in the future will avail themselves of the baseline data collected in the recent past for some world cities and to be collected in the near future and that future studies will involve a longitudinal perspective.

In the following section of this paper the two trends discussed above will be illustrated with new data on Canadian and Puerto Rican cities.

The Ecological Structure of Canadian Cities

The tendency for the analytic convergence of factor, gradient, and sector models is illustrated in a recent study of the urban ecology of Canada by Schwirian and Matre (1969). The focus of this study is upon the 11 principal Canadian cities. The cities selected for investigation are Calgary, Edmonton, Hamilton, London, Montreal, Ottawa, Quebec, Toronto, Vancouver, Windsor, and Winnipeg. Two criteria were employed in identifying these cities: size of the central city and number of census tracts. The largest cities with over 20 tracts were included in the analysis.

The variables employed in the analysis are those predicted by the social area analysis theory: education and occupation as status indicators, fertility, female employment, housing type as indicators of familism (or urbanism), and language as the indicator of ethnicity or "segregation." In working with the three analytical models, the following propositions were tested for the Canadian cities:

(1) That the correlations among the variables will be explained by at least three factors which generally correspond to "social rank." "familism," and "ethnicity"
(2) That the spatial patterning of "social rank" will correspond to a sectoral distribution

(3) That the spatial patterning of "familism" will correspond to a gradient or zone distribution
(4) That the spatial patterning of ethnicity will not consistently fit either a gradient or sector distribution.

These propositions are based upon findings reported for U.S. cities (Shevky and Bell, 1955; Bell, 1955; Anderson and Bean, 1961; Anderson and Egeland, 1961; Van Arsdol, et al., 1958; and Ekstrom, 1968). We expect the findings on U.S. cities to be generalizable to Canada since the two societies are of comparable scale and, according to the theory of scale, the ecological structure of their cities should be similar.

The data for these cities are from the 1961 Canadian census. For each census tract in the 11 cities, indexes were calculated of the social area analysis variables. These indexes are:

(1) Occupation: The number of middle and upper status workers per 1,000 population in the labor force.

$$= 1{,}000 - \frac{\text{Primary} + \text{Craftsmen} + \text{Production Process and Related} + \text{Laborers}}{\text{Total Labor Force}} \times 1{,}000$$

(2) Education: Number of adults per 1,000 with a high school education or greater

$$= 1{,}000 - \frac{\text{Number of Persons with Less Than a High School Education}}{\text{Number of Persons Out of School}} \times 1{,}000$$

(3) Infertility: 1,000 − fertility ratio

$$= 1{,}000 - \frac{\text{Children 0-4 years}}{\text{Women 15 years} +} \times 1{,}000$$

(4) Women Labor Force Participation: Number of women per 1,000 women 15 years and older who are employed

$$= \frac{\text{Women in Labor Force}}{\text{Women 15 years} +} \times 1{,}000$$

(5) Multiple Dwelling Units: Number of multiple occupied dwelling units per 1,000 dwelling units

$$= 1{,}000 - \frac{\text{Single Detached Dwellings}}{\text{Multiple Dwelling Units}} \times 1{,}000$$

(6) Language: Number of persons per 1,000 who are conversant in languages in addition to or in place of English

$$= 1{,}000 - \frac{\text{Number of Persons Who Speak English Only}}{\text{Total Number of Persons}} \times 1{,}000$$

These indexes, with the exception of the language measure, are almost exact duplicates of indexes used in other social area analysis studies. To measure ethnicity in Canada, we selected the language variable since it reflects both the concentration of native-born, French-speaking peoples as well as the newer immigrants to Canada who have largely arrived since the end of the second world war. Had we included as ethnic variables place of birth, nation of origin, family heritage, and religion (all of which appear in the Canadian census), we would have discovered many unique ethnic patterns for the different cities. Thus, the span of the observed ethnic collage would parallel those of Boston and Helsinki discovered by Sweetser. However, our goal here is simply to discover if ethnicity in a broad sense is a separate dimension of ecological organization in Canada.

The first hypothesis tested is that for each city at least three factors are required to account for the variation in the correlation matrix and that these factors will correspond to "social rank", "familism", and "ethnicity". The findings from the separate factor analyses are in Table 9-1. For each city, five factors were extracted and in all cases the five collectively account for over 95 percent of the matrix variance. The factors in Table 1 are ordered under the general headings of social rank, familism, and ethnicity. The parentheses indicate which variables should be correlated highly with the factor. The starred loadings indicate the highest loading for each variable. The factor analysis results in the table are from an orthogonal rotation.

The data in Table 9-1 show that for all the cities a separate social rank factor emerges. In three cities, there are two social rank factors. In Edmonton, there is a slight tendency for education and occupation to become disassociated. However, Edmonton's Factor I and Factor II are very similar. The main difference is that education dominates Factor I while occupation dominates Factor II. In Toronto there are two status factors. However, Factor I includes fertility as well as the status variables. Factor II tends to be a unique occupation factor. In Vancouver the two-factor social rank pattern is similar to that of Edmonton in that one of the social rank factors is dominated by education while the other is largely an occupation vector. Furthermore, the data in Table 1 show that with the exception of Toronto, social rank is generally separate from the indicators of familism.

Inspection of the familism factors in the table indicates that in only Calgary and Hamilton is there a single familism vector on which all three indicators of familism load in excess of .300. In the other cities, the familism factors tend to be either one variable unique vectors or various combinations of pairs of variables. The instability of the familism factors for these cities differs from the findings of Van Arsdol, et al. for several U.S. cities which showed fairly strong familism

Table 9-1
Results of the Factor Analyses of the 11 Principal Canadian Cities[1]

Variables	Factors					
	Social Rank			Familism		Ethnicity
City	I	II	I	II	III	I
Calgary						
Occupation	(988)*		-026	016	008	015
Education	(950)*		-157	-170	-132	014
Infertility	-066		(432)	(889)*	128	051
Women L-F	-064		(945)*	(310)	072	033
Mult. Dwell.	-243		(642)*	(435)	(580)	-021
Language	023		028	012	-002	(999)*
Variance Explained	32%		25%	18%	6%	16%
Edmonton						
Occupation	(415)	(867)*	169	-169		-042
Education	(916)*	(341)	032	036		-137
Infertility	058	155	(904)*	(218)		328
Women L-F	036	-128	(207)	(920)*		276
Mult. Dwell.	-264	043	(248)	(364)		793*
Language	-007	-122	190	118		(942)*
Variance Explained	18%	15%	16%	18%		29%
Hamilton						
Occupation	(950)*		174	183	056	-082
Education	(978)*		-096	-077	024	-072
Infertility	068		(301)	(944)*	107	-029
Women L-F	182		(697)*	(315)	(608)	-112
Mult. Dwell.	-024		(969)*	(236)	053	029
Language	-107		-006	-012	-026	(994)*
Variance Explained	32%		26%	18%	6%	17%
London						
Occupation	(873)*		155	-029	244	356
Education	(943)*		-148	-208	126	-113
Infertility	017		(951)*	(230)	(-162)	123

	I	II	III	IV	V
Women L-F	-323	(212)	(379)	143	(-826)*
Multi. Dwell.	-217	(327)	(834)*	138	(-360)
Language	081	111	090	(980)*	-087
Variance Explained	30%	19%	16%	19%	15%
Montreal					
Occupation	(804)*	-184	-120	372	-249
Education	(930)*	-107	-120	128	-202
Infertility	344	(-336)	(148)	(853)*	-087
Women L-F	170	(-903)*	(151)	(286)	-228
Mult. Dwell.	-174	(-125)	(971)*	(096)	026
Language	-286	200	052	(083)	(931)*
Variance Explained	30%	17%	17%	16%	17%
Ottawa					
Occupation	(959)*	062	192	-026	-151
Education	(898)*	-026	165	234	-304
Infertility	042	(967)*	(-085)	(-234)	010
Women L-F	-128	(359)	(-317)	(-853)*	152
Mult. Dwell.	-338	(137)	(-806)*	(-379)	217
Language	-317	001	-200	-141	(916)*
Variance Explained	54%	25%	7%	3%	10%
Quebec					
Occupation	(863)*	-346	-033	253	-204
Education	(853)*	145	051	218	-402
Infertility	085	(-912)*	(271)	(217)	-156
Women L-F	295	(-198)	(064)	(962)*	-130
Mult. Dwell.	011	(-202)	(978)*	(010)	-000
Language	-407	178	008	-106	(887)*
Variance Explained	29%	18%	17%	17%	17%
Toronto					
Occupation	(639)	(715)*	149	130	-214
Education	(906)*	(161)	013	073	-263
Infertility	916*	169	(071)	(206)	-010
Women L-F	198	090	(257)	(939)*	059
Mult. Dwell.	036	075	(960)*	(240)	116
Language	-273	-107	133	061	(943)*
Variance Explained	36%	9%	17%	16%	17%

Table 9-1 (cont.)

Variables	Factors					
	Social Rank		Familism			Ethnicity
City	I	II	I	II	III	I
Vancouver						
Occupation	(958)*	(238)	-006	158		004
Education	(350)	(840)*	029	-260		-295
Infertility	224	280	(195)	(-891)*		077
Women L-F	020	077	(979)*	(-122)		-005
Multi. Dwell.	-084	-226	(646)*	(-519)		457
Language	-003	-168	054	-086		(977)*
Variance Explained	18%	15%	23%	20%		21%
Windsor						
Occupation	(888)*		322	272	086	114
Education	(900)*		063	090	-188	-359
Infertility	224		(910)*	(230)	(233)	-118
Women L-F	237		(230)	(907)*	(251)	-073
Multi. Dwell.	-114		(304)	(320)	(840)*	296
Language	-303		-119	-061	213	(919)*
Variance Explained	30%		18%	17%	15%	18%
Winnipeg						
Occupation	(907)*		-061	293	022	-104
Education	(916)*		-004	103	-148	-249
Infertility	352		(250)	(882)*	(173)	046
Women L-F	-042		(911)*	(223)	(281)	188
Multi. Dwell.	-080		(403)	(183)	(826)*	337
Language	-301		219	053	275	(884)*
Variance Explained	31%		18%	16%	15%	17%

[1] The parentheses indicate the variables predicted to load on the factor and the asterisk indicates the highest loading for a given variable. The decimal points have been omitted.

factors. However, other studies of U.S. cities have failed to find a single familism factor (see Ekstrom, 1968). Within the social area framework the familism dimension has proved to be somewhat troublesome from both empirical and logical points of view. In an early review of social area analysis, Duncan (1955) soundly criticized the dimension for its lack of undimensionality. Some subsequent studies including this one seem to support Duncan's position.

In all 11 cities, language separates from the other two factors, thereby supporting the notion that ethnicity is an independent dimension of urban organization. Only in Edmonton and Vancouver do we find a familism variable correlating with language. A supplementary investigation indicated that in both cities the comparatively high correlation of multiple dwelling units with language is a function of a concentration of both ethnic group members and multiple dwelling units near the city center. In Vancouver the ethnic group is the Asiatic while in Edmonton it is Ukrainian.

It also should be pointed out in regard to ethnicity that while the language variable generally disassociates in factor space from the status variables, for a number of eastern Canadian cities, where the concentration of French-speaking peoples is the greatest, there is a tendency for a low negative, correlation to exist between language and the status vector. The loadings for language on the status factor for these cities is: Montreal, $-.286$; Ottawa, $-.317$; Quebec, $-.407$; Toronto, $-.273$; Windsor, $-.303$; and Winnipeg, $-.301$.

In summary of the factor analyses for the Canadian cities, it may be stated that social rank and ethnicity are fairly independent of each other, and that each is fairly independent of the familism indicators. However, the familism variable is multidimensional and in most of the cities we find a separation of infertility, women in the labor force, and multiple dwelling units from each other. Each seems to represent a different "aspect" of familism and gross statements about "familism" in these cities would be inappropriate.

The next hypotheses tested on the Canadian city data involve the spatial distribution of the variables. Since the social rank factor seems to be general across the cities, a single measure of rank is investigated. This single measure is a simple sum of the education and occupation indexes. Since "familism" proved to be multidimensional, a separate analysis is conducted for each of the indicators. On the basis of other studies it is hypothesized that social rank is distributed spatially by sector while the familism variables are distributed by gradient. The ethnic variable is not expected to be distributed in either sectors or gradients. The two-way analysis of variance model is used to test these propositions.

For each city, 16 census tracts were selected for investigation. Each city was divided into 12 sectors of 30 degrees each. From these, only sectors that contained census tracts extending from the city's center to the periphery were retained for analysis. Thus, those sectors containing natural features such as rivers that halt the progression of the tracts were excluded. Four sectors were randomly selected from those eligible. Within each of the randomly selected sectors, four tracts were chosen for investigation: one next to the CBD; one one-third of the way out; one two-thirds of the way out; and one at the city's periphery. In each city the 16 tracts were classified by sector and by distance gradient and a two-way analysis of variance was calculated for each of the indexes. The results of this portion of the analysis are in Table 9-2. The values in the table are the percentages of the sum of squares explained by the two classifications for each of the variables in each city.

Inspection of Table 9-2 indicates that in most cases social rank is distributed by sector rather than gradient. The two largest exceptions to this are Edmonton and Windsor. In Edmonton, approximately 51 percent of the sum of squares is explained by gradient and about 32 percent by sector. It should be noted in the factor analysis of Edmonton that occupation and education tended to separate into different vectors. A separate analysis by sector and gradient was performed for these two aspects of status for Edmonton and it was found that occupation was distributed by sector while education was distributed by gradient.

The failure of sectors to be important in Windsor is largely a function of the shape of the city. The city is bounded on north and west by the Detroit River. The incorporation limits of the city roughly parallel the river at a distance of only two to five census tracts in width. This results in a ribbon-shaped city with development in only a few sectors. Thus, major variations can only exist by distance gradient.

Further inspection of Table 9-2 indicates considerable variation in the spatial patterning of the familism variables. The multiple-dwelling-unit variable in all but one city (Calgary) is distributed in the predicted gradient fashion. The variable of women in the labor force is distributed by gradient in six cities. Infertility is distributed by gradient in only five cities. Thus, the gradient pattern holds only for the housing element of familism.

The distribution of the language variable in the 11 cities shows considerable variation. The sector pattern is significant for Hamilton, Ottawa, and Quebec while the gradient pattern is significant for Edmonton, Toronto, and Winnipeg. For the remaining cities neither the gradient nor the sector model describes a statistically significant percentage of the variance in the distribution of the language indicator. This lack of consistency supports the proposition which states, in effect, that there is considerable difference between city variation in the distribution of ethnic groups.

In summary of the Canadian city data, it may be stated that the emergent patterns of the social area analysis variables are generally as predicted for a "large-scale" society. Perhaps the greatest variation between Canadian and U.S. patterns is in familism. While *most* studies of American cities suggest that infertility, women working, and apartment dwelling all go together in a familism factor in Canada there is a decided tendency for these variables to have only low to moderate ecological correlations and that in physical space only the dwelling

Table 9-2
Percent of the Total Sum of Squares of Social Area Variables Explained by Sectors and by Distance for 11 Canadian Cities

City	Social Status		Infertility		Women L-F		Mult. Dwell.		Language	
	Sector	Distance	Sector	Distance	Sector	Distance	Sector	Distance	Sector	Distance
Calgary	44.7	17.1	24.0*	61.0*	39.7	26.2	37.8	25.9	17.5	22.7
Edmonton	31.7*	50.8*	3.4	85.3*	4.5	86.4*	1.6	80.9*	13.0	62.0*
Hamilton	64.8*	0.8	27.0	38.7	25.1*	61.7*	8.9	83.0*	71.6*	15.0
London	62.0*	5.0	46.9*	24.5	2.0	71.2*	3.1	82.2*	36.3	23.2
Montreal	52.8*	19.5	16.0	60.7*	13.8*	78.5*	21.7	49.5*	50.0	9.9
Ottawa	22.6	29.3	35.1	24.9	9.6	74.2*	19.8	50.3*	81.5*	8.4
Quebec	67.4*	0.5	26.2*	60.9*	28.7	14.2	4.4	64.8*	93.2*	0.6
Toronto	62.8*	11.2	69.2*	12.7	39.9	14.8	6.1	71.8*	16.2	72.9*
Vancouver	35.1	15.6	61.0*	4.7	22.6	24.1	5.2	76.5*	17.2	39.4
Windsor	18.0	34.8	3.6	6.3	32.6	30.4	31.5*	61.1*	28.4	18.2
Winnipeg	68.6*	5.6	24.6	54.3*	6.5	76.3*	7.9	84.6*	17.6	49.1*

*Indicates that the percentage of the sum of squares is statistically significant beyond the .05 level. The test of significance is the two-way analysis of variance.

measure is distributed consistently by gradient. Infertility and women working are similarly distributed in less than half of the cities. The implication here is clear. Each of these familism dimensions should be considered as fairly independent aspects of urban spatial structure (for the Canadian cities at least). Perhaps if the ten U.S. cities studied by Van Arsdol and associates were restudied with more recent census data, similar disassociation among the familism variables would be manifest. If this were so, perhaps it would reflect an even greater variation in life style choice accompanying increase in societal scale than was envisioned by Shevky, Bell, and Greer.

The Ecological Structure of Puerto Rican Cities

The second major trend in the current ecological research discussed in the first section of this paper is for studies of urban ecological structure to be tied to theories of societal development. Within the social area framework, studies of such cities as Cairo have explained differences between U.S. cities and the one under investigaton in terms of differentials in societal modernization. Thus the failure of social rank to separate from familism in Cairo is seen to reflect the lesser degree of social differentiation in the U.A.R.'s total society as compared to that in the U.S. Such studies usually focus on only one city in these societies and the total urban ecological pattern is generalized from this pattern. The justification offered for this practice is usually that in the lesser developed nations it is the "primate" or largest city that is the apex of urban development and the nexus of social differentiation. If such a city does not reflect the ecological pattern of the industrial city then it is not likely that the lesser cities will reflect this pattern. While homogenous city structure may be true for societies at the low end of the scale of modernization, it is not necessarily true for the societies in the middle ranges of economic development and modernization. In modernizing societies there may well be considerable variability in pattern of urban structure. In fact, one indicator of the level of modernization of a nation might be the degree of difference between the primate city and secondary cities in urban patterns. The primate city would approximate the highly differentiated pattern of the industrial society while the secondary cities would reflect the lack of differentiation characteristic of the non-developed nation. This is a direct result of the fact that modernization is channeled through the existing metropolis. This large city is the society's contact with the outside world and is, therefore, the most sensitive to the influences of crosscultural forces.

One society well toward the middle of the modernization scale is Puerto Rico. In a recent study of Puerto Rico's principal cities, Schwirian and Smith (1969) have found considerable difference between the ecological structure of the primate city, San Juan, and the secondary and more isolated urban centers of

Ponce and Mayaguez. Using 1960 census data, the usual social area indexes of occupation, education, infertility, women working and multiple dwelling units were calculated for each census tract in the three metropolitan areas. To measure ethnicity the relative concentration of foreign born in the tract was determined (the actual index is the number of foreign born per 1,000 persons in the tract). The data for each of the three cities were subject to a factor analysis with an orthogonal rotation. The results are presented in Table 9-3. While six factors were extracted for each city, the factors presented are those which explain 2 or more percent of the variance.

The hypothesis tested here is that at least three factors account for the interrelationships among the social area variables and that these factors correspond to "social rank", "familism", and "ethnicity". The theory of scale leads us to temper this proposition somewhat. Since the level of modernization in Puerto Rico is not equal to that of the United States or Canada, we would not expect as great a factorial separation of the social area variables for Puerto Rican cities as found for U.S. and Canadian cities. Yet we expect a greater factorial separation of the variables for the Puerto Rican cities than found in cities of lesser developed societies such as the U.A.R.

The data in Table 9-3 show that our expectations are supported for Puerto Rico's principal and primate city, San Juan, but is not supported for the secondary secondary and more isolated centers of Ponce and Mayaguez. San Juan's Factor I corresponds to the "social rank" vector found in previous cities, although women working and foreign born correlate in the magnitude of .3 and .4. Given Puerto Rico's lesser degree of modernization as compared to that of the U.S. and Canada it is not surprising that these two variables vary to some extent with rank. Factors II, III, and V are the familism vectors. It should be noted that the three measures of familism do not all correlate highly with one factor. This is similar to the result for the Canadian cities. Finally, foreign born separates from rank and familism as predicted by the social area model.

In both Ponce and Mayaguez the three dimensions of rank, familism, and ethnicity do not separate as they do in San Juan. In Ponce, Factor I is a general factor with high correlations of the rank variables of infertility, women working, and foreign born. This one factor explains about 45 percent of the variance. The remaining factors in Ponce are dominated by single variables. In Mayaguez the first two factors are general with substantial correlations of all variables on them. Together they explain about 80 percent of the variance. Factor III seems to be a unique multiple dwelling unit vector.

In summary of the Puerto Rican city data, it seems that San Juan's factorial pattern approximates those of cities in modern, industrial societies although the extent of differentiation among the indexes is not as great. This is explained by the theory of scale and Puerto Rico's lesser development as compared to that of the U.S. and Canada. The factorial structure of Ponce and Mayaguez are characteristic of cities in "low-scale" societies. It is suggested here that the differ-

Table 9-3
Results of Factor Analysis of Puerto Rican Cities Data

Variable	Factors				
City	I	II	III	IV	V
San Juan	(Social Rank)	(Infertility)	(Foreign Born)	(Dwelling)	(Women L-F)
Occupation	823*	280	340	012	276
Education	833*	258	294	-129	306
Infertility	278	899*	228	082	238
Women L-F	448	330	186	-163	793*
Mult. Dwell.	-040	056	070	992*	-079
Foreign Born	373	240	872*	139	154
Variance Explained	30%	19%	18%	18%	15%
Ponce	(General)	(Infertility)	(Dwelling)	(Foreign Born)	
Occupation	876*	277	-104	338	
Education	831*	321	-120	366	
Infertility	399	880*	-100	238	
Women L-F	910*	301	121	218	
Mult. Dwell.	-095	-070	991	-059	
Foreign Born	487	310	-103	810*	
Variance Explained	45%	19%	17%	17%	
Mayaguez	(General)	(General)	(Dwelling)		
Occupation	577	-767*	175		
Education	698*	-695	-056		
Infertility	378	-922	-026		
Women L-F	777*	-565	080		
Mult. Dwell.	058	-039	998*		
Foreign Born	926	-361	086		
Variance Explained	40%	40%	17%		

*Indicates the highest loading for a variable. Only factors are reported that explain at least 2 percent of the variance. The decimal points are omitted.

ences between San Juan and the other cities is a function of their different niches in the societal development process. San Juan is the Puerto Rican gateway to the world. Social change affects San Juan first and later diffuses to the other parts of the island. Thus, there is a lag in ecological change between San Juan and the other cities. The Puerto Rican government currently plans to build an international airport in the Ponce-Mayaguez section of the island. When this is operational and Ponce and Mayaguez become centers of modernization in their own right, there should be an acceleration in the similarity of ecological structure between the secondary cities and the primate city.

Some Issues in Ecological Analysis

The separate and combined use of the factorial, gradient, and sector models in current ecological research have indicated some issues that warrant further discussion. It is not the purpose of this section to resolve these issues but, rather, to indicate their scope, as follows.

(1) Areas Used in Ecological Investigations. Should urban ecologists focus upon the central city or should the whole metropolitan area be included in studies of urban subarea differentiation? Many ecologists assert that the metropolitan community is a functionally integrated whole. The recent work of Sweetser suggests that different ecological patterns might characterize cities and suburban areas and that combined analysis might obscure such differences. However, the full development of the ecological patterning can only be seen in the analysis of the total metropolitan area. One problem here in comparative urban research which uses official statistics collected by different national governments is that the type of "fringe" areas included within metropolitan boundaries are quite varied in properties between nations while "city" definitions yield more comparable socioecological systems.

(2) Number of Cities in Analyses. In the study of a society's urban ecological structure, how many cities should be included for analysis? There is considerable danger in generalizing about societal urban patterns on the basis of single-city studies. Research on various societies have shown significant differences in ecological patterning between cities within the same society. Van Arsdol, et al. have reported a north-south regional difference in the factorial structure of U.S. cities. Schwirian and Matre have found some differences in factorial patterns between cities in western and eastern Canada. And Schwirian and Smith report large differences in ecological patterning between San Juan and the secondary urban centers of Puerto Rico. Thus, from a theoretical standpoint, multiple-city analysis seems preferable to the single case study investigation. Studies of several cities at one time are more possible now than they were 5 or 10

years ago because of the increased efficiency of automatic data processing systems.

(3) Longitudinal vs. Cross-Sectional Studies. While ecologists today tend to be interested in relating differences in urban structure to theories of societal development, most studies are of a cross-sectional nature. Longitudinal analysis for many societies is hindered by the lack of good historical data. As national censuses improve and are regularized, there will be an increasing amount of data that in the future may be incorporated into longitudinal projects for testing temporal hypotheses. A good example of such longitudinal analysis is Robert Murdie's (1969) study of Toronto for the period 1951-1961.

(4) Operationalizations of the Concept of Scale or Modernization. Comparative ecological studies to date have only distinguished between gross differences in level of social scale or modernization. If eventually we are to test such theories rigorously, we must develop quantitative measures of level of societal modernization. There is a considerable literature on this topic by students of broader social and economic change that could be brought to bear here.

(5) "Ecological" vs. "Spatial" Zones. In an early paper, Quinn (1940) discussed one of the basic problems of the Burgess model which to this date is unresolved. This involves the delineation of zones or gradients from the center of the city. Spatial zones are simply those arbitrarily established by drawing circles around the city's center at set mileages. Quinn argues that a time-cost measure should be used that is ecologically meaningful. Zones that have an equal time-cost distance from the center of the city may actually differ in the miles from the same point. To date, most ecologists have used equal mileages rather than the time-cost criteria. However, studies should be undertaken to see if analytical distortions result from this arbitrary approach.

(6) Arbitrary vs. Functional Sectors. The theory of urban sector development specifies that the boundaries of urban sectors are functional or "meaningful" objects such as rivers, highways, or railroads. Most studies to date, however, use arbitrary sectors usually established by simply marking off a number of angles at the city's center and extending lines to the periphery. All areas that fall within that sector are included for analysis. While this operationalization of sectors is cheaper and more conservative of time it still is at variance with the basic notion of sector development. The degree to which this violation distorts empirical findings needs to be explored empirically as does the problem of concentric zonation.

Summary

In this paper, two of the more recent trends in ecological analysis have been discussed and illustrated with data from Canada and Puerto Rico. These trends are: the analytical convergence of factorial, gradient, and sector models; and the attempt to relate differences in urban ecological patterns to aggregate differences in levels of societal development. Finally, six basic unresolved problems in this type of analysis have been discussed. Through extensions of ecological analyses to cities in other countries as good urban subarea data become available, there is good promise that urban ecology will become a truly comparative and dynamic enterprise.

References

Amato, Peter W., "Environmental Quality and Locational Behavior in a Latin American City", *Urban Affairs Quarterly,* Vol. 5, pp. 83-101 (1969).

Abu-Lughod, Janet L. , "Testing the Theory of Social Area Analysis: The Ecology of Cairo, Egypt", *American Sociological Review,* Vol. 34, pp. 198-211 (1969).

Anderson, Theodore R., and Bean, L.L., "The Shevky-Bell Typology: A Confirmation of Results and a Reinterpretation", *Social Forces,* Vol. 40, pp. 119-124 (1961).

Anderson, Theodore R., and Egeland, Janice, "Spatial Aspects of Social Area Analysis", *American Sociological Review,* Vol. 26, pp. 392-399 (1961).

Bell, Wendell, "Economic, Family and Ethnic Status: An Empirical Test", *American Sociological Review,* Vol. 20, pp. 45-52 (1955).

Berry, Brian, "Research Frontiers in Urban Geography", in Philip M. Hauser and Leo F. Schnore eds., *The Study of Urbanization,* John Wiley and Sons, New York (1965).

Berry, Brian, and Rees, Philip H., "The Factorial Ecology of Calcutta", *American Journal of Sociology,* Vol. 74, pp. 445-491 (1969).

Burgess, E.W., "The Growth of the City" in R.E. Park, E.W. Burgess, and R.D. McKenzie eds., *The City,* University of Chicago Press, Chicago (1926).

Clignet, Remi and Sween, Joyce, "Accra and Abidjan: A Comparative Examination of the Theory of Increase in Scale", *Urban Affairs Quarterly,* Vol. 4, pp. 297-324 (1969).

deVise, P., "A Social Geography of Metropolitan Chicago", Northwestern Illinois Metropolitan Planning Commission, Chicago (1960).

Duncan, Otis Dudley, "A review of E. Shevky and W. Bell, Social Area Analysis", *American Journal of Sociology,* Vol. 61, pp. 84-85 (1955).

Ekstron, Charles, "Community Social Structure and Issue Differentiation: A Study in the Political Sociology of Welfare", *Sociological Focus 1,* No. 3, pp. 1-16 (1968).

Greer, Scott, *The Emerging City,* The Free Press, New York (1962).

Hoyte, Homer, *The Structure and Growth of Residential Neighborhoods in American Cities,* Federal Housing Administration, Washington (1939).

Mayer, Harold, "A Survey of Urban Geography", in Philip M. Hauser and Leo F. Schnore, eds., *The Study of Urbanization,* John Wiley and Sons, New York (1965).

Murdie, Robert A., "Factorial Ecology of Metropolitan Toronto, 1951-1961", Department of Geography Research Paper No. 116, The University of Chicago, Chicago (1969).

Park, Robert, *Human Communities,* The Free Press, Glencoe (1952).

Pedersen, P.O., "An Empirical Model of Urban Population Structure: A Factor Analytic Study of the Population Structure in Copenhagen" (mimeo) The Technical University of Denmark, Copenhagen (1965).

Quinn, James, "The Burgess Zonal Hypothesis and Its Critics", *American Sociological Review,* Vol. 5, pp. 210-218 (1940).

Schnore, Leo F., *The Urban Scene,* The Free Press, New York (1965).

Schwirian, Kent P., and Matre, Marc, "The Ecological Structure of Canadian Cities." Department of Sociology, The Ohio State University, Columbus (1969).

Schwirian, Kent P., and Smith, Ruth K., "Primacy, Modernization, and Urban Structure: The Ecology of Puerto Rican Cities", Working Paper in Human Ecology No. 5, Mershon Caribbean Seminar, The Ohio State University, Columbus (1969).

Shevky, E., and Bell, Wendell, *Social Area Analysis,* Stanford University Press, Palo Alto (1955).

Sjoberg, Gideon, "Theory and Research in Urban Sociology", in Philip M. Hauser and Leo F. Schnore, eds., *The Study of Urbanization.* John Wiley and Sons, New York (1965). *The Pre-Industrial City,* University of Chicago Press, Chicago (1960).

Sweetser, Frank, "Ecological Factors in Metropolitan Zones and Sectors", in Mattei Dogan and Stein Rokkan, *Quantitative Ecological Analysis in the Social Sciences,* Cambridge: The M.I.T. Press

Thomlinson, Ralph, *Urban Structure, The Social and Spatial Character of Cities,* Random House, New York (1969).

Van Arsdol, Maurice Jr., Camilleri, Santo, and Schmid, Calvin, "The Generality of Urban Social Area Analysis Indexes", *American Sociological Review,* Vol. 23, pp. 277-284 (1958).

10 The Neighborhood Effect in Urban Voting Response Surfaces[a]

Kevin R. Cox

Introduction

The impact of the neighborhood upon behavior is a dominant if conceptually unformalized theme in urban studies. The analysis of such neighborhood effects has been a concern of geographers[1] and recently, insofar as they have an expression in political behavior, of political sociologists.[2] Indeed there is a sufficiently large body of research and associated ideas to merit a closer scrutiny of the neighborhood effect upon urban voting distributions both from the conceptual and methodological viewpoints.

Two major objectives are pursued in this paper. First, I present a theoretical consideration of the neighborhood effect in urban voting behavior from the viewpoint of the spatial processes which generate it. Second I review existing methodology for studying the neighborhood effect and, on the basis of this review, develop a new methodology which, I believe, permits the examination of important facets of the neighborhood effect hitherto inadequately or improperly treated. The application of this methodology to date for the metropolitan area of Columbus, Ohio should also provide some clarification of the spatial expression of neighborhood effects in the urban voting response surface.

Such a rubric is likely to be of interest not only to the student of urban political behavior but also the "urbanist" in general. Not only is voting behavior an opinion likely to be formed by processes similar to those which generate other citizen opinions and behaviors of interest to the urbanist, but the treatment here is also concerned with a very fundamental operational problem of the urban student — using available ecological and survey data in the most fruitful and informative way possible.

The Conceptual Basis of the Neighborhood Effect

The individual voting decision can most economically be conceptualized as a function of two sets of variables, each having additive effects and interacting

---

[a]The research on which this paper is based is supported by the National Science Foundation; this support is gratefully acknowledged.

with the other to produce multiplicative effects. The first set of variables refers to the individual characteristics of the voter such as his income, previous voting record, and race. The second set of variables refers to aggregate properties of the social group which form the environment of the voter as a political actor — the social class structure of his local area, for example, or the racial balance. Frequently, of course, these aggregate characteristics are simply averages of the characteristics of individuals within the aggregates; thus the percent of the population which is Negro in an area can be conceptualized as the mean racial characteristic of the population of an area.

Given an individual level variable Sij for the ith person in the jth area and an aggregate level variable $\bar{S}j$ for the jth area, one can postulate the following in a regression format about the party preference of the ith person in the jth subarea:

$$Yij = a + b_1 \, Sij + b_2 \, \bar{S}_j + eij \qquad (1)$$

where Yij is the vote of the ith person in the jth subarea for party Y and eij is the residual. Of course, one can also conceive more elaborate equations where, for example, b_1 is a function of $\bar{S}j$. That type of equation, however, does not concern us here.[3] If in Equation (1), $b_2 \neq 0$ then we have a neighborhood effect: the spatial structural situation where, across areally defined groups of voters, the residual voting variance after the extraction of variance associated with individual level variables is correlated with some aggregate property or properties of those areally defined groups.

In past studies of neighborhood effects, the variable $\bar{S}j$ has been measured as either some social structural property across subareas of a city or as a proportion voting for a particular political party. For example, one of the earliest students of neighborhood effects, Herbert Tingsten, showed in an analysis of Swedish election statistics that working-class Swedes living in working-class districts were more likely to vote for candidates of Socialist parties than if they lived in middle-class districts.[4] A more recent study showed how middle-class Britishers living in highly Conservative constituencies are more likely to vote Conservative than if they live in strongholds of the opposition party,[5] a generalization that applied not only to constituencies within metropolitan areas. Whatever the neighborhood variable employed, however, the spatial structural phenomenon being described can be identified as a *neighborhood effect* in which an individual's voting behavior, after the extraction of variance associated with within-individual characteristics, is correlated with the behavior of his neighbors.

A perusal of the relevant literature suggests three hypotheses to account for the neighborhood effect: (1) differential party activity; (2) residential selectivity; and (3) distance biased interpersonal influence. Each hypothesis will be discussed and evaluated in turn.

One of the rationales Tingsten advanced to explain the greater working-class Socialist vote in working-class areas of Swedish cities was the greater activity by

Socialist parties in such districts.[6] This is an example of the differential party activity hypothesis as an explanation of the neighborhood effect. The notion is based upon two postulates which must be shown to be valid if we are to lend any credence to it: (1) that party organization affects voting in cities and (2) that party organization tends to be strong where the party itself gains a relatively high proportion of the vote, and weak where the party gains a relatively low proportion of the vote.

As far as the first postulate is concerned, there seems little doubt about its general veracity. Studies in Gary, Indiana,[7] and Detroit, Michigan,[8] for example, have both returned consistent results. In Gary, the amount of precinct committeeman contact with the electorate of the precinct appears to have had a positive impact upon the vote of the precinct committeeman's party. In the Detroit study, the competitive nature of such contacts was taken into account by comparing, for example, the vote in precincts with strong Democratic leadership and weak Republican leadership with precincts in which the obverse occurred.

Whether or not the strength of party organization is directly correlated with the strength of the party vote in a precinct, however, is more debatable. The study of Detroit, for example, showed very meager simple correlations between the strength of precinct leadership and the aggregate voting proportions for precincts. This is supported by another study at the county level which showed that "the correlation between party electoral strength and the extent of personal contact by the party organizations is virtually nil".[9]

Indeed, the lack of empirical support for this second postulate prompts one to inquire whether it is a reasonable one or not. In one sense it is, in that a political party will find it easier to recruit committeemen in those precincts in which it gains a preponderance of the vote. Not only are there more supporters of the party in such precincts but committee work is less personally punishing where the work is among the faithful rather than among the inconstant. In another sense, however, the postulate is much less rational. Given limited resources the marginal utility of a vote in a (literally) marginal constituency is much higher than in a safe constituency. There is some evidence, moreover, that this is how the parties see it and allocate their resources accordingly. In Gary, for example, it was found that patronage by the Democratic machine was distributed not through areas where the voters need it the most (i.e., in the heavily Negro, working-class, Democratic precincts) but in areas where the party needs it the most (i.e., in the marginal precincts).[10] It was demonstrated, moreover, that the patronized were highly effective party workers in the marginal constituencies, as one might expect given their stake in the party.

A second hypothesis advanced by Tingsten was to the effect that the clustering phenomenon observed in the voting of social strata in Swedish cities might be due to characterological differences between working-class people in working-class areas and working-class people in middle-class areas.[11] Thus it is conceivable that individuals with politically conservative sympathies are dissatisfied at living in working-class areas and are therefore liable to move to other areas. This appears to be a possibility in the explanation of some of the difference between Republican suburb and Democratic central city in the North American city,[12] but the issue has been so little researched that it cannot be discussed at any length.

A much more likely explanation, for reasons which will become clearer below, is a distance biased interpersonal influence process. Research on change in party preference over time suggests that personal influence is overwhelmingly responsible as a direct source of change. During a study of the 1940 Presidential election campaign it became apparent that only a minority of individuals in a community are directly influenced by the mass media and they in turn relay this influence in a two-step flow manner to friends and associates.[13] Such a personal influence hypothesis is consistent with a great many empirical generalizations in the political sociology literature. Husbands tend to vote like wives, for example, and workers like their fellow employees; we talk about a Catholic vote or a Negro vote and, presumably, personal influence has an important role in sensitizing the voter to his group affiliations and what they represent in terms of issue stands. Furthermore, the fact that neighborhood effects are usually intensified when political discussion is taken into account seems to lend credence to an interpersonal influence process.[14]

Such a process of interpersonal influence, however, can only produce a morphology with the type of spatial predictability associated with the neighborhood effect if it has locational correlates. Specifically it needs to be shown that the interpersonal influence producing change in voting behavior is decreasingly likely with increasing distance between a potential sender and a potential receiver of influence. Indeed, a distance decay in a wide variety of informal movements within cities now seems clear; marital contact studies, for example, have demonstrated the significance of short intervening distance for interpersonal contact[15] though the confounding effects of residential segregation are not always taken into account.[16]

While a distance bias may affect interpersonal contacts, the strength of the bias is likely to differ from one subpopulation to another. In spatial structural terms these variable biases are likely to be manifest in neighborhood effects at different geographical scales, the proportional variance of the neighborhood effect at a given scale reflecting the proportional significance of the individuals making contacts at the scale level. That such scale effects do exist is already evident in studies of neighborhood effects in the political sociology literature and in the work of Reynolds and Archer.[17]

Nevertheless we should exercise caution in our claims as to the scale at which this neighborhood effect operates. All the evidence suggests that politically effective interpersonal contact is confined to exceedingly short distances and is not a process which decays only slowly in its effectiveness with increasing distance. Some evidence on this has come from Kish who carried out a variance decomposition of party preferences across individuals aggregated successively in a nested hierarchical manner in dwellings, blocks, and precincts.[18] For the percent Republican vote, for example, 73 percent of the variance occurred at the level of households, 20 percent at the level of blocks, and only 11 percent at the level of precincts. This at least should serve as an adequate caveat to wild claims regarding the geographical scale of the process.

Previous Methodologies

Existent methodologies and feasible methodological innovations must be seen within the context not only of plausible spatial processes but also in terms of available data and sets of data collecting units for urban areas. Broadly two types of data may be available for a metropolitan area: (1) survey data referring to the voting behavior and social characteristics of a sample of individuals and (2) aggregate data describing social and political properties of aggregates of individuals in terms of means, medians, and other measures of central tendency. The aggregate data are much more frequently available and are descriptive of individuals aggregated by territorial units or areas. Clearly given the definition of neighborhood effect above, where survey data are available their utility for the analysis of neighborhood effects requires that the behavioral identity between a voter and voters in his neighborhood be defined. This might be expedited by a spatially clustered sample of individuals with major attention being devoted to the relative locational attributes of the individuals, but this is unlikely due to the predominantly spatially random survey research designs usually characteristic of voting survey research work in cities. More usually, therefore, it is required that certain relevant properties of the neighborhood be measured at the time of the interview or that the location of the individual in an aggregate data collecting unit be specified.

Previous approaches to modeling neighborhood effects in urban voting response surfaces can be classified into three groups: (1) contextual analysis, (2) contiguity analysis of residuals from regression, and (3) curve fitting. Each of these approaches will be defined and exemplified. They will then be evaluated in terms of the spatial processes which they are intended to model.

Contextual Analysis: Contextual analyses employ both survey data and aggregate data for a set of data collection units. Usually such analyses incorporate at least two explanatory variables: (1) an aggregate level variable; given the conceptual basis for the neighborhood effect outlined above this is usually intended to indicate more or less precisely the probability of random contact within the confines of an observational unit with an individual who will present a political viewpoint biased in a certain direction representative of that observational unit as a whole; and (2) an individual level variable such as social class or party identification or voluntary organization affiliation intended to index *either* the resistance of an individual to political communication *or* some contact bias leading to a propensity to vote one way or another independent of random contact probabilities. Given that the dependent variable is a vote for one party or another, regression models such as that suggested above can provide estimates of the independent effects of the two variables via standardized partial regression coefficients. In actual fact, in the literature there has been a tendency to neglect quantitative effect parameters in favor of subjective evaluations based on observation of frequency count tables.

A recent study by Segal and Meyer exemplifies the structure typical of neighborhood effect studies.[19] Using data for wards in several U.S. cities, Segal and Meyer examine in 2 x 2 tables the proportions voting Democratic in groups of lower socioeconomic level individuals, both in areas of low average socioeconomic status and of high average socioeconomic status, respectively; and in groups of upper socioeconomic level individuals in the same two types of area. The results show that the voting of lower-class individuals is less Democratic in middle-class areas than in lower-class areas; the converse applies, though less clearly, for middle-class individuals. The inference from such an empirical observation is that individuals are somehow affected in their voting behavior by the information dominant in their area of residence.

Contiguity Analysis of Residuals from Regression: A recent attempt to identify neighborhood effects in urban voting response surfaces was based upon a provocative idea suggested by Geary, a student of spatial auto-correlation (or what he termed contiguity phenomena).[20] Geary, writing in 1954, expressed the idea that in an analysis,

". . . if the dependent variables are found to be contiguous, the fact that the remainders after the removal of the effect of independent variables are found to lack contiguity constitutes a prima facie case for regarding the independent variables included as *completely* explaining the dependent variables. There are of course, other and perhaps better reasons for developing the regression aspects. If the theory is to be applied to problems of contagion (morbidity and mortality rates or numbers), one cannot regard the fact of contagion in the narrow sense (i.e., that the disease is being transmitted by contacts) as established, or use the (contiguity) ratio as the measure of the strength of contagion, unless one has removed causative factors (independent variables) which may themselves have the property of contiguity. Contagion can only be established from the remainders when the causative factors have been duly allowed for. For instance if a disease is known to vary according to social group it is clearly necessary to correct for this defect, which itself is very likely to be contiguous."[21]

The political geographers Reynolds and Archer have developed the idea of isomorphisms between, on the one hand, disease and a process of contagious infection and, on the other hand, party preference and a process of interpersonal influence respectively.[22] They suggest that in fact the disease does vary with social group and that if neighborhood effects are present they will be apparent in a spatial clustering of the residual variation from the regression of aggregate voting on the social characteristics of data collecting units. They applied this model to voting across subareas of Indianapolis and measured the clustering of residual variation with Dacey's contiguity ratio. Significant clustering was identified, suggesting the operation of a neighborhood effect.

Curve Fitting: A third and final approach also employs aggregate data alone and involves the fitting of theoretical curves to such data. This body of research is largely associated with the work of French sociologists.[23] Much of the original impetus, however, came from an elaboration of the relationships existing between ecological and individual data by American sociologists and statisticians.[24]

As a point of departure for evaluating such curve fitting efforts, consider the case where no neighborhood effect is involved. Let us assume that the probability p of voting for party Y is purely a function of whether or not one belongs to a social group X and that no other independent variables, such as neighborhood effects, are involved. Then:

$$y = xp + (1 - x)q, \qquad (2a)$$

where y = the proportion of the voters voting for party Y

x = the proportion of the voters belonging to group X
p = probability of a member of X voting for party Y
q = probability of a nonmember of X voting for party Y.

This equation can be converted into an equation linear in a and b in order to provide estimates of the probabilities p and q:

$$y = q + (p - q)x \qquad (2b)$$

$$y = a + bx \qquad (2c)$$

$$\hat{y} = a + bx + e, \qquad (2d)$$

where

$\hat{y}$ = the predicted proportion voting for party Y
$a = q$
$b = p - q$.

Clearly the validity of such a method of inferring individual transition probabilities from aggregate data in this way depends upon the validity of the assumptions that p and q are constant from one constituency to another; i.e., that the probability of voting for party Y is not affected by any property of the neighborhood or neighborhood population.

If alternative assumptions appear more valid (and this may be based on grounds of theory or on the unreasonableness of the probability estimates derived by a linear hypothesis) alternative nonlinear hypotheses may be tested. It may be reasonable, for example, to postulate that both p and q are functions of y; hence if $p = b_1 y + a_1$ and $q = b_2 y + a_2$ then $y = x(b_1 y + a_1) + (1-x)(b_2 y + a_2)$, a homographic function which, via least-squares regression, allows one to estimate values of p and q for each area of the city. Boudon also presents parabolic and logarithmic functions for estimating p and q for (e.g.) different areas of the city, and such functions would also be applied under appropriate theoretical expectations of non-linearity.[25]

All three methods attempt to partial out the effects of individual resistance to information flow (individual effects) and the spatially structured process of information flow itself (aggregate effects). All three methods, however, are characterized by serious deficiencies either inherent in the model itself or in the manner in which it has been applied in the past. On two evaluatory criteria the models appear particularly deficient: their attention to the scale of the neighborhood effect and their attention to the dynamics as well as to the statics of voting behavior. Each of these two criteria will be discussed in turn.

As far as the scale used is concerned, a major problem with the analysis of residuals approach to the neighborhood effect is that it describes the efficacy of the neighborhood effect at a geographical scale that is too large. As we noted from Kish, even the small precinct seems to be associated with very little of the variance in party choice when variance attributable to households and blocks has been extracted. Given the size of the data units which can be reasonably employed in neighborhood effect analysis (wards and precincts) it seems overly optimistic to look for some sort of between-area contagion process. Rather we would suggest that the process should be viewed as very largely a within-area phenomenon and that any clustering of residuals should be attributable to a spatial clustering of relevant within-individual or aggregate-level variables that have been overlooked in the research design.

A second criticism, which is more addressed to the manner in which the models have been applied rather than to the structure of the models themselves, concerns their overwhelming bias towards the statics of political behavior rather than to dynamics. The idea of a neighborhood effect implies some temporal change in voting, yet a concern with a behavioral change is not reflected in the operationalization of the models. This is unfortunate since a cross-sectional behavioral similarity of adjacent areas could have been produced by very different rates of change in adjacent areal units. Presumably a neighborhood effect implies that voters in neighboring areal units are subject to very similar forces and this similarity of stimuli should be reflected in a similarity of dynamics though not necessarily in a similarity of statics.

A New Methodology

As one of our goals in fashioning a more effective methodology for the study of neighborhood effects is to take more explicit account of dynamics, let us take as our point of departure the definition of transition probability matrices.[26] For successive pairs of elections it is possible to imagine a transition probability matrix for each territorial unit of the city describing rates of change from one party preference to another; these probabilities, P_{ij}, for the two-party situation are shown in Figure 10-1. Clearly if a neighborhood effect is operating we would expect the probabilities of such matrices to be related to aggregate properties of the territorial unit. Thus we would expect the probability P_{11} to be higher in territorial units with a higher proportional vote for Party 1 and lower in those units having a lower proportional vote for Party 1. If we had some method for

		Party Preference at t_2	
		1	2
Party Preference	1	P_{11}	P_{22}
at t_1	2	P_{21}	P_{22}

Figure 10-1. Transition Probability Matrix for Party Preference.

computing the transition probability matrices, therefore, we would be able to regress selected probabilities on territorial unit aggregate voting proportions and obtain a crude measure of neighborhood effect.

Data considerations, however, usually allow us only to compute transition probabilities for a city as a whole or for sizeable groups within the city. However the computation of such city-wide probabilities does provide one with a bench mark from which neighborhood effects can be quantitatively evaluated.[27] Assume for example that the transition probabilities $P_{11}, P_{12}, P_{21}, P_{22}$ have been computed for a pair of successive elections; then for each territorial unit of the city for which we have aggregate voting statistics at t_1 and t_2, we can compute a predicted vote for t_2 on the assumption that the transition probabilities are invariant from one territorial unit to another:[28]

$$\hat{Y}i_{t_2} = P_{21} + (P_{11} - P_{21})Yi_{t_1} , \quad (3)$$

where

$\hat{Y}i_{t_2}$ = the predicted percent of the voters voting for party Y in observation i at t_2

Yi_{t_1} = the percent of the voters voting for party Y in observation i at t_1

$P_{11} = P_{yy}, P_{21} = P_{xy}$, etc.

Clearly these predictions will be erroneous to the extent that the assumption of invariance is invalid. We can obtain a measure of the error or residuality for each observational unit by the following computation:

$$Dev.i_{t_2} = Yi_{t_2} - [P_{21} + (P_{11} - P_{21}) Yi_{t_1}] . \quad (4)$$

Such a residual voting proportion could be attributed to a variety of phenomena. Two, however, seem especially plausible: (1) a neighborhood effect by which the residual voting proportion for observation i at time t_2 is related to the actual voting proportion for observation i at time t_1 and (2) differential transition probabilities for social groups which cluster in space or for groups definable in terms of locational objectives and criteria. The first possibility will be examined by means of some data from the Columbus metropolitan area; examination of the second possibility will proceed by an examination of the residual variance.

Application of the Methodology

The aggregate and survey data chosen to illustrate this methodology refer to the wards of the Columbus metropolitan area and contiguous municipalities together with three of the more urbanized contiguous townships. The elections involved in the definition of voting dynamics are the Presidential elections of 1960 and 1964. The survey data were gathered in 1965 from a random sample of 604 residents in the Columbus metropolitan area.[29] Voting preferences for 1960 and 1964 were identified and the resultant transition probability matrix is shown in Figure 10-2. Clearly, the accuracy of the transition probabilities is a function of such factors as accuracy of respondent recall and sample representativeness. The probabilities do accord, however, with the general impression gained in national results of an appreciable swing to the Democrats.

NEIGHBORHOOD EFFECT IN VOTING

	t₂ D	t₂ R
t₁ D	.84	.16
t₁ R	.23	.77

Figure 10-2. Transition Probability Matrix for Party Preference 1960-64 in the Columbus Metropolitan Area.

These probabilities permit the prediction of 1964 voting proportions by the equation:

$$\hat{Y}i_{t_2} = 23.0 + (.84 - .23)\, Yi_{t_1}$$

Subtraction of $\hat{Y}i_{t_2}$ from Yi_{t_2} permits the identification of a residual value $Dev.i_{t_2}$. The relationship between these deviation values and the original Yi_{t_1} is not insubstantial: $R^2 = .25$. This suggests that indeed the transition probabilities do vary as a function of Yi_{t_1} and that in the highly Republican areas the strength of the Republican party was eroded much less than in the Democratic strongholds; while conversely in the Democratic strongholds the Democrats gained in their proportion of the total vote to a much greater extent than in areas where they were already weak. The value of the coefficient of determination, however, suggests that while a neighborhood effect would account for some of the variance of $Dev.i_{t_2}$, it would be far from exhaustive. As we suggested earlier, this residual variance might be attributable to locational or social group specific transition probabilities for the 1960-1964 elections, i.e., to short-term forces affecting different groups defined in locational or social terms. It is to a consideration of this residual variance that we now turn.

Figure 10-3 presents the residuals calculated from the expression $Dev.i_{t_2} - \hat{Dev}.i_{t_2}$ where $\hat{Dev}.i_{t_2} = -17.54 + .23\, Yi_{t_1}$. Particularly striking is the cluster of underestimated wards to the northeast of the city center: the residuals here are particularly high, exceeding two standard errors of the estimate in two observational units. Also drawn in on the residual map is the boundary of the area in which over 40 percent of the population is black; this can be taken as a definition of the ghetto area of the city.[30] Confirmation that Negroes did indeed vote for the Democratic party more than we might have expected in the 1964 election comes from a breakdown of the transition probabilities by race in Figure 10-4. Cell entries for blacks are relative meager but the message is clearcut and not surprising. Given a hypothetical constituency evenly balanced between Democrats and Republicans in 1960, according to these transition probability matrices,

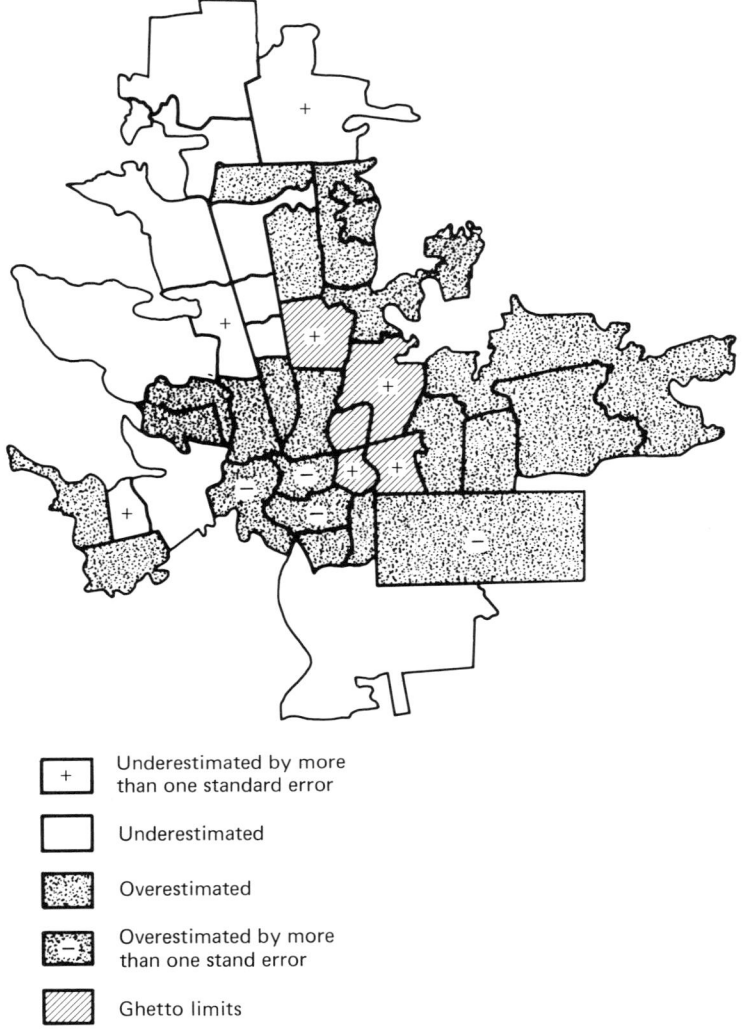

Figure 10-3. RESIDUALS $\text{Dev.i}_{t_2} - \hat{\text{Dev}}.i_{t_2}$

the aggregate Democratic vote in 1964 in a white constituency would be little different from what it was in 1960; in a black constituency, however, the Democratic vote would register a 66 percent increase!

Surrounding the black ghetto, on the other hand, is an area of overestimated wards suggesting the possibility of some type of locational conflict between these ghetto fringe areas and the ghetto itself. This receives further

	White			Black	
	D	R		D	R
D	.79	.21	D	1.00	.00
R	.20	.80	R	.66	.33

Figure 10-4. Transition Probability Matrices by Race.

plausibility from the fact that the highest negative residuals are found to the south and west of the ghetto, precisely in the area most subject to persistent black in-migration. This interpretation receives added force when one considers the issues of the 1964 Presidential campaign: especially significant were the issues of civil rights and open housing, pregnant with meaning for the ghetto and its white environs.

Implications

The model developed here has some rather interesting implications from both the conceptual and measurement viewpoints. Conceptually it should be possible to extend this type of analysis from the case in which the transition probabilities are defined for voting from one time period to another to the case in which "transition" takes place from a social category to a voting preference. This would be particularly useful, as all too frequently the only survey data available for a city refer to voting by demographic categories.

An analysis of some data for Paris is of interest in this respect. The voting data refer to the 1956 French elections. A sample survey in six arrondissements broadly representative of the 20 arrondissements of Paris permits the establishment of transition probabilities for "Ouvriers" and non-"Ouvriers" to the Communist party and to other parties respectively.[31] Computation of predicted and residual voting proportions for the arrondissements revealed a very strong neighborhood effect.[32] The coefficient of determination relating the predicted Communist vote to the actual Communist vote was a very high .97. The standard deviations were 1.6 and 8.6 respectively! Figure 10-5 presents a scatter plot of the actual Communist voting proportions against the actual "Ouvrier" proportions. (A regression line based on Paris-wide transition probabilities has been inserted to demonstrate the power of the neighborhood effect in this case.) Figure 10-6 is an analogous scatter plot for the Columbus case.

The implication for measurement which can be based on these ideas refers to the problem of computing area-wide transition probabilities on the basis of ecological regression. A number of social scientists have suggested that under certain circumstances it is possible to estimate transition probabilities in this way,

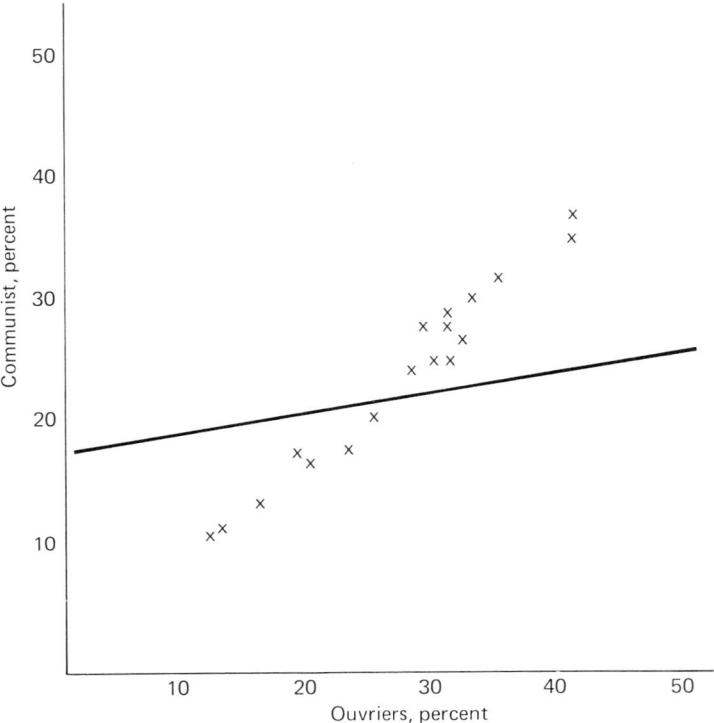

Figure 10-5. Scatter diagram and Regression Line Predicted on Basis of Citywide Transition Probabilities, city of Paris.

the notion being based on the identities defined in Equations (2a-2d). It should now be clear, however, that in many cases where it would be very useful to have area-wide transition probabilities, the ecological regression coefficients can be exceedingly misleading due to the neighborhood effect.[33] To underline this point, Figure 10-7 compares the transition probabilities for Columbus and Paris based on survey data and ecological regression, respectively. The absurdity of the Columbus entries for the ecological case, however, would of course be sufficient to arouse suspicion.

Summary and Conclusions

In this paper I have attempted to identify those processes most likely responsible for the neighborhood effect in voting response surfaces. Previous

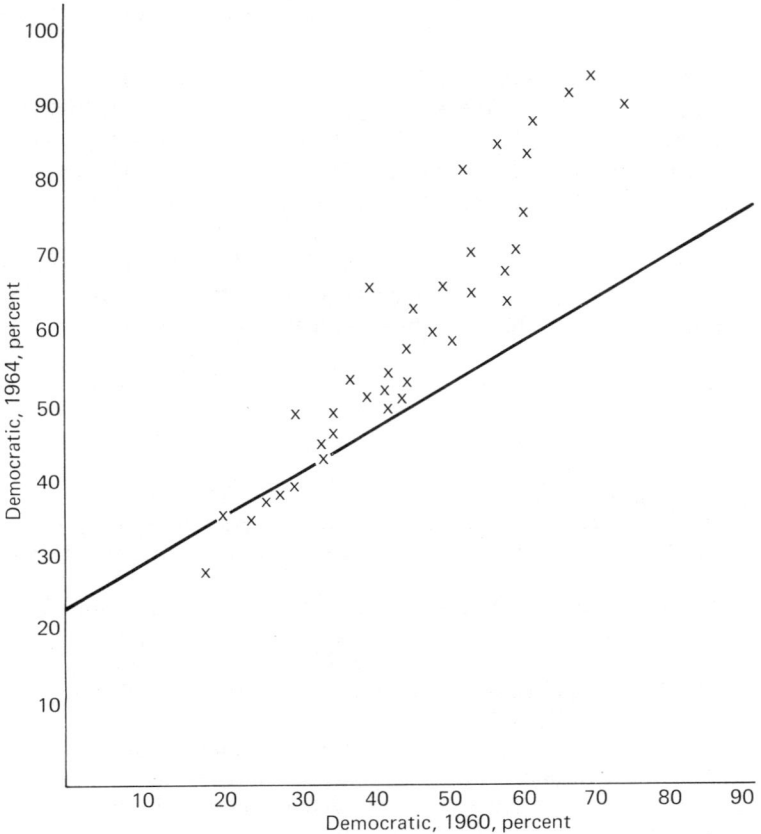

Figure 10-6. Scatter diagram and Regression Line Predicted on the Basis of Citywide Transition Probabilities, city of Columbus.

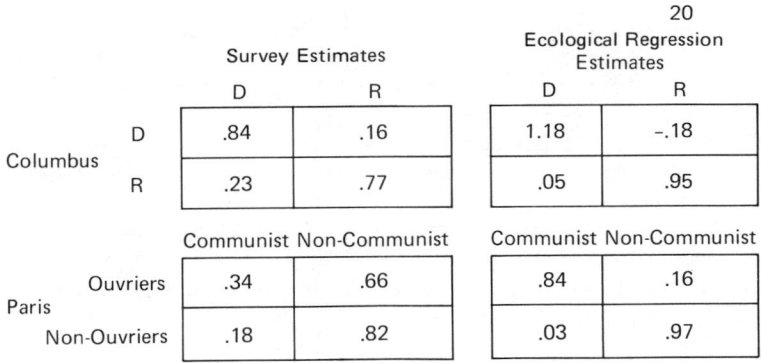

Figure 10-7. Transition Probability Matrices for Columbus and Paris Based on Survey and Ecological Regression Estimates.

173

methodologies aimed at measuring the neighborhood effect have been reviewed and evaluated. A new methodology paying attention to those issues of scale and voting dynamics ignored in previous methodologies was developed and applied to data for the Columbus metropolitan area. The methodology, however, should be of interest to others than the analyst of voting response surfaces. Spatial analysis in general exists in a state of tension between the need to come to conclusions about significantly large areas of geographic space and the data basis of relatively small samples of individuals. The methodology outlined here provides an additional strategy by which the tension can be resolved.

Notes

(1) Examples include:
   (a) Reynolds, David R., and Archer, J. Clark, "An Inquiry into the Spatial Basis of Electoral Geography", Department of Geography, University of Iowa, Discussion Paper, Series, No. 11.
   (b) Reynolds, David R., "A Friends–and–Neighbors Voting Model as a Spatial Interactional Model for Electoral Geography", in Kevin R. Cox and Reginal G. Golledge, eds., *Behavioral Problems in Geography: A Symposium,* Northwestern University, Department of Geography Publication No. 17 (1969).
   (c) Cox, Kevin R., "The Spatial Structuring of Information Flow and Partisan Attitudes", in Mattei Dogan and Stein Rokkan, eds., *Quantitative Ecological Analysis in the Social Sciences,* MIT Press, Cambridge (1969).
(2) Of particular interest are:
   (a) Putnam, Robert D., "Political Attitudes and the Local Community", *American Political Science Review,* Vol. 60, pp. 640–654 (1966).
   (b) Segal, David R., and Meyer, Marshall W., "The Social Context of Political Partisanship", in Dogan and Rokkan, *op. cit.* pp. 217–232.
   (c) Foladare, Irving S., "The Effect of Neighborhood on Voting Behavior," *Political Science Quarterly,* Vol. 83, No. 4, pp. 516–529 (December, 1968).
(3) For various manipulations of this basic equation see: Valkonen, Tapani "Individual and Structural Effects in Ecological Research", in Dogan and Rokkan, *op. cit.*
(4) Tingsten, Herbert, *Political Behavior: Studies in Election Statistics,* Chapter 3, Stockholm (1937).
(5) Butler, David, and Stokes, Donald E., *Political Change in Britain,* Chapter 6, London and New York (1969).
(6) Tingsten, *op. cit.*
(7) Rossi, Peter H., and Cutright, Phillips, "The Impact of Party Organization in an Industrial Setting", in M. Janowitz, ed., *Community Political Systems,* pp. 81–116, The Free Press, Glencoe (1961).

(8) Katz, Daniel, and Eldersveld, Samuel J., "The Impact of Local Party Activity upon the Electorate", *Public Opinion Quarterly,* Vol. 25 (Spring, 1961).
(9) Putnam, *op. cit.,* p. 643.
(10) Rossi and Cutright, *op. cit.,* p. 105.
(11) Tingsten, *op. cit.*
(12) Campbell, Angus, Converse, Philip E., Miller, Warren E., and Stokes, Donald E., *The American Voter,* pp. 453–472, Wiley, New York (1960).
(13) Lazarsfeld, Paul F., Berelson, Bernard, and Gaudet, Hazel, *The People's Choice,* Columbia University Press, New York (1948). Also see Katz, Elihu, and Lazarsfeld, Paul F., *Personal Influence,* The Free Press, Glencoe (1955).
(14) Putnam, *op. cit.,* and Cox (1969), *op. cit.*
(15) A number of these studies have been reviewed in Katz, Alvin M., and Hill, Reuben, "Residential Propinquity and Marital Selection: A Review of Theory, Method and Fact", *Marriage and Family Living,* Vol. 58, pp. 27–35 (February, 1958).
(16) Specifically this refers to the fact that within large cities residential segregation provides an individual with socially compatible contacts at short distances as well as least effort contacts in a minimum movement sense. An interesting study by Ramsy, however, has recently shown that physical distance and distance in social space have independent effects upon marital contact. See Ramsy, Natalie R., "Assortative Mating and the Structure of Cities", *American Sociological Review,* Vol. 31, No. 6 (December, 1966).
(17) Putnam, *op. cit.,* and Segal and Meyer, *op. cit.,* for example, came to different conclusions regarding the impact of the neighborhood upon members of voluntary organizations. Putnam working at the county level found a strong neighborhood effect while Segal and Meyer working at the ward level found a much weakened effect. Such results seem consistent with the idea that many voluntary organization memberships are in organizations within the county but outside the ward; Reynolds and Archer, *op. cit.,* have also identified different values for the neighborhood effect at different geographical scales.
(18) Kish, Leslie, "A Measure of Homogeneity in Areal Units", *Bulletin de l'Institut International de Statistique,* 33^e session, Paris (1961).
(19) Segal and Meyer, *op. cit.*
(20) Geary, R. C., "The Contiguity Ratio and Statistical Mapping", in B.J.L. Berry and D. F. Marble, eds., *Spatial Analysis,* pp. 461–478, Prentice Hall, New York (1968).
(21) Geary, *op. cit.,* pp. 461–462.
(22) Reynolds and Archer, *op. cit.*
(23) For example:
   (a) Klatzmann, Joseph, "Comportement électoral et classes sociales: étude du vote communiste et du vote Socialiste à Paris et dans la Seine," in Maurice Duverger et al., *Les Élections du 2 Janvier, 1956,* pp. 254–285, Librairie Armand Colin, Paris (1957).
   (b) Boudon, Raymond, *L'Analyse Mathématique Des Faits Sociaux,* Librairie Plon, Paris (1967).

(c) Boudon, Raymond, "Propriétés individuelles et propriétés collectives, un problème d'analyse ecologique," *Revue Francaise de Sociologie*, Vol. 5 (1963), pp. 275-299.

(24) Particularly important is a paper by Goodman, Leo, "Some Alternatives to Ecological Correlation", *American Journal of Sociology*, Vol. 64, pp. 610-625 (1959). Also published in Berry and Marble, *op. cit.*

(25) Boudon (1967), *op. cit.*, pp. 188-196.

(26) This section has gained considerable inspiration from a recent paper by Stokes, Donald E., "Ecological Regression as a Game with Nature" (mimeographed) (September, 1968). Though Stokes is more concerned with the possibilities and problems of inferring such matrices from ecological regressions his treatment does point out the possible confounding impact of neighborhood effects upon such inference.

(27) This methodology is similar to that discussed by Duncan, O. D., Duncan, B., and Cuzzort, R. P., *Statistical Geography*, The Free Press, pp. 111-128, Glencoe (1961).

(28) Implicit in this treatment is the assumption that there is an unchanging electorate between elections; this is admittedly a restrictive assumption but we have as yet no reason to believe that it critically falsifies the model's predictions.

(29) The survey was carried out by the author and Dr. John Orbell of the Department of Political Science, University of Oregon.

(30) Data on the Negro population are not available for wards. A computer program was written therefore to take the co-ordinates of the wards along with the co-ordinates and population data for census tracts and compute a ward percent Negro value on the basis of the figures for the four tracts nearest to the ward. The probable inaccuracy of the resultant estimates is recognized but so is the absence of a superior strategy! Details of the program may be obtained from the author.

(31) Stoetzel, Jean, and Hassner, Pierre, "Résultats d'un sondage dans le premier secteur de la Seine", in Maurice Duverger et al., *op. cit.*

(32) The relevant aggregate data were obtained from Klatzmann in Duverger et. al., *op. cit.*

(33) This is a point illuminated to great effect in Stokes, *op. cit.*

11 The Effect of Metropolitan Political Fragmentation on Central City Budgets

John C. Weicher[a]

Introduction

This study seeks to investigate the effect of suburbanization and metropolitan political fragmentation on the fiscal positions of local governments within the metropolitan area. It is particularly concerned with the effect of suburban population on central city expenditures and revenues, and with the effect of business activity in a city on the city's budget. It is argued that generally accepted notions on these subjects are inconsistent, and that previous scholarly research has been inadequate. A model is developed which does avoid the methodological shortcomings of the previous research, and tests the extents to which city expenditures or revenues are affected by the existence of suburban population and city business activity.

The results have interesting implications about the causes of current fiscal problems in metropolitan areas, particularly central cities, and about the direction of future research into these problems.

Prevailing notions about the relationship between the entities within a municipality and the municipality's fiscal situation, in the absence of any suburbs, run somewhat as follows: A city has two major components, business and population, which it taxes and to which it provides services. Business activities may be subdivided into "industry," meaning primarily manufacturing, and "commerce," usually meaning retailing; the nonmanufacturing and nonretailing activities of the Central Business District (CBD) may be explicitly mentioned separately, or implicitly included as part of "commerce."

Population may also be subdivided, usually into three groups on the basis of income: the rich, or well-to-do; those of middle income; and the poor. The city taxes and serves all entities within it; however, on balance the city receives more in taxes from business and the well-to-do than it spends in providing services to

---

[a]I am grateful to many of the participants at the conference for helpful comments on an earlier draft of this paper. I would also like to thank my colleagues, Ben E. Laden, Richard D. Porter, and Richard T. Stillson for their comments. Remaining errors, of course, are solely my own responsibility.

them, and spends more in serving poor residents than it receives in taxes from them. Put another way, the city redistributes income to its poor residents, from business and the well-to-do, and perhaps from the middle income group.

This pattern has been fragmented by suburbanization, creating fiscal problems for many municipalities. As suburbs have developed, industry, commerce, and the various population groups have tended to fall under separate political jurisdictions. As a result, municipalities within a metropolitan area have had widely unequal tax bases and expenditure needs. Central cities have lost substantial parts of the groups which are net revenue sources, and have been left with nearly all of the metropolitan area's poor. In particular, middle-income residents and manufacturing have left the central city for its suburbs. Overall, the central city has fewer rich residents, relative to its poor, than it used to, and still fewer middle-income residents. Concurrently, the central city has less business activity; the greatest decline has been in manufacturing, although retailing and CBD activities have also shown some tendency to disperse into the suburbs. The result of this pattern of movement, it is believed, is that central cities face a fiscal crisis: they have been left with the group which demands more in services than it can pay for, and have lost many of the entities which are net revenue sources.

However, the suburbs are not without problems. The groups which have left the central city have gone to the various suburbs in different proportions. Some suburbs consist entirely of well-to-do residents, with no business of any kind within their borders, while others may have a handful of residents together with a very large number of manufacturing plants; a wide variety of intermediate cases also exist.

The fiscal situations of the suburbs also vary. Suburbs consisting largely of businesses, or of well-to-do residents, are generally believed to be exceptionally, and perhaps unfairly, fortunate. On the other hand, "Many suburbs and small towns that have become mainly the abode of the resident-commuter have had their own financial crises, because the local property tax — the main source of local revenue — is an inadequate source of local finances if it has to be levied almost exclusively on residential property. Thus, suburbanization has, at times, added the problems of the 'unbalanced' suburban community to the plight of the metropolitan center. The former, in an attempt to create a sounder property tax base, has often offered special concessions to commerce and industry in an attempt to lure them away from the metropolitan center, thereby adding further to the latter's difficulties." (de Torres, 1967.)

These prevailing notions are frequently invoked in advocating public policies to deal with municipal problems, such as metropolitan government, or federal aid to local governments on an unconditional basis. Yet these notions about the ways in which city governments redistribute income have been subjected to very little in the way of rigorous analysis. Indeed, it is not difficult to show that they are mutually inconsistent, particularly when used to analyze the fiscal problems of municipalities within a single metropolitan area.

For example, middle-income families are regarded as desirable residents for central cities. They are desirable partly for political reasons, to promote political stability in the central city, but partly also in the belief that they may be taxed to provide services to poorer residents. (Fitch, 1964, p. 114). But, when this group leaves the central city for a homogeneous middle-income suburb, they are believed to be unable to pay for municipal services to themselves alone, unless industry is present to share the tax burden. (Fitch, 1964, p. 115). It is not clear what, if anything, has happened to change them from net sources of revenue in the central city to net recipients of subsidies in the suburbs.[1]

A second example of inconsistency may be seen in the argument by central cities that they are "exploited" by their suburbs, in that the central cities must provide services to nonresidents who do not pay taxes to the central city.[2] This claim conflicts with the notion that business establishments are net sources of revenue for municipal governments. If nonresidents enter the central city, they do so largely to make use of its business establishments, to work, shop, or entertain themselves. Therefore, by implication the central city has retained a larger share of its business establishments than of its population; presumably it can tax these businesses to provide services to its population.

To take an extreme illustration, if the central city has lost *only* population so that it is surrounded by purely "bedroom communities," then it has lost only some entities which do not "pay for themselves." It may still be possible that the city's fiscal situation is worsened, however, if the loss of tax revenue (in this case, through a loss in the residential property tax base) is greater than the decline in expenditures (which would include schools, and services provided to residential property, such as police and fire protection, sanitation, street maintenance, etc.). This is an empirical question, but it is surely possible that the sales tax revenue derived from suburbanites shopping in the city, or the property taxes paid by the businesses at which they shop and the factories at which they work, are greater than the expenditures on services which the city provides to them while they are in the city.

If, on the other hand, business establishments have followed residents to the suburbs, then the city can hardly claim that it is being exploited by the suburbs, which now contain both the residents and the business activity that serves them. If the residents involved were well-to-do or middle-income families which were net sources of revenue to the central city, then the city's financial plight may be worsened, but it is the former residents and businesses who are no longer being exploited by the city, rather than the city now being exploited by the suburbs.[3]

These examples demonstrate that the analysis of income redistribution between business and people is related to the analysis of redistribution between central city residents and suburbanites. The empirical work in this study will present results bearing on both types of redistribution. The question of the extent to which cities redistribute income among resident population groups is not discussed in this paper, but is deferred for future study.

Previous Research

The effect of political fragmentation on local government fiscal patterns has been investigated frequently in recent years, in a variety of contexts. The studies may be conveniently classified on the basis of the dependent variable chosen, which has been either local government expenditures or the local government tax base.

The former approach has been more common; there are a large and growing number of "expenditure function" studies, investigating the factors which affect intercity variations in local government expenditures.[4] Many have looked at the relationship between suburbanization of population and central city expenditures, usually finding that an increase in suburbanization (measured as the ratio of suburban population to SMA population) increases expenditures per capita by the central city. In the pioneering analysis of this relationship, Hawley claimed that these results "indicate that the size of the metropolitan population not included in the corporation limits of the metropolitan center represents a cost factor to the residents of the center. The latter are carrying the financial burden of an elaborate and costly service installation, i.e., the central city, which is used daily by a non-contributing population that in some instances is more than twice the size of the contributing population." (Hawley, 1956, pp. 781-782).

Brazer, Kee, Bahl, and Campbell and Sacks have also generated the same statistical results, but have not drawn Hawley's conclusion that central cities were being exploited by their suburbs. They have instead pointed out that it is necessary to investigate the revenues which central cities receive from suburbanites, as well as the expenditures the cities incur on account of the suburbanites. None have carried out such an investigation.[5]

Fewer studies have looked at the extent of business activity as a determinant of local government expenditures. The first study to include a variable to represent business activity (in this case, retail trade) is by Scott and Feder (1957). They used retail sales per capita as a proxy for "the general level of business activity in the city" (Scott and Feder, 1957, pp. 10-11) and found a positive and significant correlation, which they took to indicate "the existence of a close relationship between fiscal capacity and per capita government expenditures". (Scott and Feder, 1957, p. 1). Subsequently Brazer used a broader measure of business activity (the ratio of employment in manufacturing, trade and services to population) finding generally positive relationships which were not consistently significant (Brazer, 1959, p. 30); Bahl used measures of both central city retail trade and central city total employment, finding positive and generally significant effects on expenditures for both, with the retail trade coefficients more consistently significant. (Bahl, 1969, Ch. 3).

Unfortunately, the theoretical foundations of these studies are so defective that the results have no implications about either the extent of income redistribution between business and population or the question of exploitation between city and suburb. The reason is that local governments face a budget constraint which greatly affects their fiscal behavior. Generally, they are required to balance their budgets, at least for current operating expenditures; they cannot print money, of course, and have limited borrowing powers, particularly on current account. The budget constraint, which for most local governments is a legal as well as political necessity, requires that revenues approximately equal expenditures on an annual basis. (Local governments are not prohibited from running surpluses, but the recurrent fiscal crises confronting them suggest that they rarely manage to do so.) The budget constraint therefore implies that any factor which affects revenues of municipalities, will also affect expenditures, and vice versa. Indeed, in those studies which have used factors affecting revenues as independent variables in expenditure regressions, the revenue factors have usually been more significant than have been factors affecting expenditures directly, such as demographic characteristics.[6] This result has been noted before, but its significance has been overlooked: it completely vitiates the usefulness of the previous studies for our purposes.

The importance of the budget constraint, and the inadequacy of the previous research, can be demonstrated by means of a simple model of a municipal government. The model describes the process by which the city adjusts its budget in response to changes in population or business activity. It is assumed that the city starts in equilibrium, with expenditures equal to revenues; a change then occurs in either city or suburban population, or city business activity, which affects both the city's tax base and its expenditures. The city adjusts to the impact by altering either its tax rate or its expenditures, or both, so as to reach a new equilibrium with a balanced budget, satisfying the budget constraint.

Algebraically, the model can be written as follows:

$$W_0 = \alpha C_0 + \alpha' S_0 + \beta B_0 \qquad (1)$$

$$X_0 = aC_0 + a'S_0 + bB_0 \qquad (2)$$

$$t_0 = \frac{X_0}{W_0} \qquad (3)$$

$$R_0 = t_0 W_0 = X_0 \qquad (4)$$

where

W = tax base,
X = expenditures,
R = revenues,
t = tax rate,
C = central city population,
S = suburban population,
B = business activity.

(The subscript 0 refers to the initial level of the variables.)

Now let there be an increase in the number of entities to be taxed and served, in each category. The tax base will increase because of the greater number of entities which can be taxed, and the level of expenditures also will increase because of the greater number of entities to be served. However, the level of expenditures will also change for another reason: if expenditures and the tax base change in different proportions, then the city budget is out of balance, and the city must adjust either its expenditures or its tax rate, or both, to restore the balance. The new level of expenditures is thus greater than the old by an amount "a" for each new city resident, "a'" for each suburbanite, and "b" for each unit of business. This component of the new level of expenditures may be referred to as X_N. However, if the change in expenditures by the municipality, measured by $(X_N - X_0)$, differs from the change in its revenue, measured by $t_0(W_1 - W_0)$, the city no longer has a balanced budget. In reacting to the imbalance, the city may alter its expenditures; this change will be referred to as X_W. The sum of these changes represents the net change in the city's expenditures. Algebraically,

$$X_1 = X_{N1} + X_{W1}' \qquad (5)$$

where

$$X_{N1} = aC_1 + a'S_1 + bB_1 \qquad (6)$$

$$X_{W1} = d[t_0(W_1 - W_0) - (X_{N1} - X_0)] . \qquad (7)$$

(The subscript 1 refers to the new levels of the variables.)

In Equation (7), the terms in parentheses are the changes in the tax base and expenditures generated by the changes in population and business. The entire term in brackets represents the net change in the city's budget, given the initial tax rate. This term may conveniently be called "surplus" revenue; it may be either positive or negative. If it is positive, the city is "richer" as a result of the increased number of entities within it: it gets more in revenue, at the initial tax rate, than it spends in providing the initial level of services to the new entities. The parameter d is the fraction of the surplus revenue that the city spends on additional services; $(1 - d)$ is the fraction returned to individuals in the form of lower taxes.[7] The parameter d lies between 0 and 1, inclusive; if it is 0, the city chooses to keep the level of services constant, and lower taxes by the full amount of the surplus; if d is 1, the city chooses to keep the initial tax rate and spend all of the surplus on additional municipal services. At intermediate values, of course, the city both lowers taxes and raises expenditures.

In the new equilibrium, Equation (1) now becomes:

$$W = \alpha C_1 + \alpha' S_1 + \beta B_1 . \qquad (8)$$

Equation (7) can be simplified (since, from equation (4), $t_0 W_0 = X_0$) and then rewritten in terms of C, S, and B by substitution from Equations (8) and (6):

$$X_{W1} = d(t_0 \alpha C_1 + t_0 \alpha' S_1 \ t_0 \beta B_1 - aC_1 - a'S_1 - bB_1). \qquad (9)$$

Equation (5), the new level of expenditures, now becomes:

$$X_1 = [a + d(t_0 \alpha - a)] C_1 + [a' + d(t_0/\alpha' - a')] S_1 +$$
$$[b + d(t_0 \beta - b)] B_1, \qquad (10)$$

after collecting terms. The new tax rate is

$$t_1 = \frac{X_1}{W_1}. \qquad (11)$$

The coefficients in Equation (10) measure the effect of population or business on municipal expenditures.[8] The meaning of any of the coefficients is somewhat more complicated than the previous literature has suggested. For example, in regard to suburban population, a' is the amount by which expenditures change as the number of suburbanites changes, *ceteris paribus*; it is non-negative. The term in parentheses is the net effect of an increase in suburban population on the central city budget, given the initial tax rate. This term is positive if the central city receives more in revenue from suburbanites than it spends in serving them, and negative if the opposite is true. The sign of this term, taken by itself, therefore, measures whether the central city exploits, or is exploited by, its suburbs.

Unfortunately, however, the sign of the parenthetical term has no effect on the sign of the coefficient (the bracketed expression). The coefficient is always positive: since $0 \leqslant d \leqslant 1$, $b \geqslant db$; and dt_0 is positive.

The same analysis applies to the coefficient of business activity. The sign of the parenthetical term measures whether cities receive more in tax revenue than they spend in serving businesses; but whether it is positive or negative, the coefficient is positive.

The previous literature can be analyzed in terms of this model. While none of the studies have contained explicit models, they all appear to have estimated Equation (10) or some variant of it cross-sectionally.[9] In the context of this model, it is clear that Hawley is wrong in asserting that his results imply that suburbanites exploit the central city; also, Brazer, Kee and Bahl have misinterpreted the meaning of their results. They appear to believe that they have estimated a structural relationship between suburbanization and city expenditures; in fact, because of the budget constraint, they have estimated a reduced-form relationship which has no useful interpretation. A regression analysis of revenues, if carried out, would have almost the same results, since revenues and expenditures must be approximately equal; comparison of the results of expenditure and revenue analyses which they suggested, would therefore have no implications about the direction of exploitation.[10]

The same problem exists with regard to business activity. Scott and Feder appear to believe that $b = 0$; they refer to business activity as representing increased "fiscal capacity," with no mention of possible additional demands for expenditures. Brazer and Bahl, however, recognize that their coefficients include both expenditure and revenue effects (Brazer, 1959, p. 21; Bahl, 1969, p. 83); however, they have not realized the coefficient for business must be positive nor that the coefficients for business and suburban population have the identical form, and are therefore equally useless for analyzing the impact of political fragmentation on local government finance, or for determining the directions of income redistribution generated by municipal budgets.

The alternative approach in previous research has been to use the tax rate as the dependent variable. This approach has the virtue of being methodologically correct; it can be shown, using our model, that the change in the tax rate, given an increase in resident or suburban population or city business activity, depends on whether the entity "pays its own way." In the case of business activity, the change in the tax rate will be positive if the city spends more in serving the businesses than it receives in tax revenue from them at the initial tax rate, and negative if businesses are net sources of revenue.[11] The major problem with this approach is empirical; the data on the tax base (and therefore on the tax rate) are extremely poor. The tax base for most local governments largely consists of real property, the value of which is very difficult to measure. The commodity changes hands infrequently, so that there is no well-established market price for it. Instead, data on "value" are usually assessed values, representing more or less expert opinion as to what the property would sell for, if it were sold.

These assessed values are generally regarded as poor proxies for market value; the standard public finance texts point out that substantial inter-area and intra-area disparities exist. (Cf. Due, 1968, pp. 431-432). This can easily be verified by examining data on the ratios of assessed to sales value in the *Census of Governments* (Vol. II, 1967), showing substantial variation within an individual city, within its suburban area, between city and suburb, and between different metropolitan areas. These disparities greatly reduce the usefulness of the tax rate approach; it is very difficult to know whether the response of the tax rate to a change in population or business activity represents what actually happened to the tax base, or what the local assessor(s) thought should have happened.

Given the data problems, it is not surprising that there have been few empirical analyses. There have been five studies of the relationship between business activity and the local tax rate. Two (Isard and Coughlin, 1957; Groves and Riew, 1963) have been concerned with developing a method of analysis whereby local governments could estimate for themselves the fiscal impact of various kinds of growth, rather than with estimating actual impacts; the data in these studies have been primarily used for illustrative purposes, although all of the examples indicate that businesses (particularly manufacturing) are net sources of revenue for cities.

The empirical analyses have been confined to individual metropolitan areas. Margolis, studying San Francisco-Oakland, concluded that cities with concentrations of business activity (relative to population) had higher tax rates than "dormitory" cities; expenditures per capita were higher in the "business" cities, and real property values per capita were lower. Since the two central cities were "business" cities, with higher concentrations of business than most of their suburbs, Margolis concluded that the central cities were exploited by their suburbs. The results also imply that cities redistribute income from population to business establishments. (Margolis, 1957).

The other two studies (Brazer, 1964; Loewenstein, 1963) have challenged Margolis' conclusions. Margolis examined only the total expenditures of the municipal government; Brazer pointed out that this procedure caused school taxes and expenditures to be excluded, since school districts in California are independent units of government, having separate taxing and spending powers. (Brazer, 1964, p. 136). In a study of Detroit, Brazer found that property tax rates (including school and county taxes) were higher for "dormitory" suburbs than for "business" suburbs. While this result reverses Margolis' conclusions, it is not directly comparable, since Brazer did not present property tax rates for the municipalities alone, and neither he nor Margolis has amended the latter's results to include school systems. It is also true that San Francisco and Detroit are very different areas, and the results may be due to differences in tastes or other omitted factors.

Loewenstein investigated the effect of industry on tax revenues and local government expenditures in three suburban townships around Philadelphia; he concluded that in at least two cases, industrial development had increased revenues more than expenditures, largely because workers at the new plants did not move into the suburbs when the plants did, but chose to commute from greater distances. His conclusion is somewhat weakened by his choice of particular establishments: the plants chosen were generally large and frequently provided their own "municipal services," such as roads, sewers, and water. Loewenstein also assumed that there was no increase in expenditures on local government services as a result of increased commuting into the suburban areas, and that the presence of industry exerts no influence on the value of other property in the suburb. These assumptions raise the probability that his results would differ from those of Margolis, but they also reduce the usefulness of his analysis for comparative purposes.

With the possible exception of Margolis' work, there have been no direct investigations of the relationship of the central city tax rate to the *extent* of suburbanization. The intrametropolitan studies, of course, are not designed to shed any light on this question, there are only one or two central cities in each SMA, so that statistical analysis is impossible. A number of studies have concluded that central city tax rates are generally higher than suburban rates (Advisory Commission on Intergovernmental Relations, 1967, Vol. II), but they have not indicated how central city rates are affected by differences in the relative importance of suburban population. There have been no nationwide cross-sections using the tax rate approach; such a cross-section could generate a statistical test of the relationship, but would be subject to the data limitations to an even greater extent than the intra-metropolitan studies.

In summary, previous research on the fiscal effects of political fragmentation does not provide any clear or even probable answers. There is little empirical basis for asserting that central cities are exploited by their suburbs, or that businesses are net sources of revenue to local governments, which appear to be the prevailing opinions; nor is there much basis for asserting the opposite.

The Theoretical Model

While the analysis of total municipal expenditures does not generate a test of prevailing notions about the fiscal impact of political fragmentation, it is possible to disaggregate expenditures in order to develop a model which does generate such a test.[12]

This model rests on the assumption that, at least to some extent, population and business desire different services from the municipal government. In particular, some services are demanded only by city residents; these would include education, public libraries, and perhaps recreation. Other services are demanded by both city residents, suburbanites, and businesses; these would include police and fire protection, sanitation, streets, and water, for example.

These differences in the demand for particular services affect the amounts spent on the services. If the basic model developed in the preceding section is disaggregated into two sectors, sector Y consisting of services provided only to residents, and sector Z consisting of services provided to all three groups, then the initial situation in the city is as follows:

$$W_0 = \alpha C_0 + \alpha' S_0 + \beta T_0 + \gamma M_0 \qquad (12)$$

$$Y_0 = a_y C_0 \qquad (13)$$

$$Z_0 = a_z C_0 + a'_z S_0 + b_z T_0 + g_z M_0 \qquad (14)$$

EFFECT OF POLITICAL FRAGMENTATION

$$X_0 = Y_0 + Z_0 \tag{15}$$

$$t_0 = \frac{X_0}{W_0} \tag{16}$$

where

T = retail trade,
M = manufacturing,

in addition to the variables previously defined. "Business activity" is thus disaggregated into two components. The subscripts y and z in the expenditure regressions are used to distinguish the amounts spent to provide each kind of service to the particular entity, such as resident population.

Again, an increase in the number of entities to be taxed and served will affect both the tax base and the level of expenditures; and again the new level of expenditures has two components. This is true of each category of services. Algebraically,

$$Y_1 = Y_{N1} + Y_{W1} \tag{17}$$

$$Z_1 = Z_{N1} + Z_{W1}. \tag{18}$$

The components may be rewritten in the form of Equations (6) and (7):

$$Y_{N1} = a_y C_1 \tag{19}$$

$$Y_{W1} = d_y [t_0(W_1 - W_0) - (X_{N1} - X_0)] \tag{20}$$

$$Z_{N1} = a_z C_1 + a'_z S_1 + b_z T_1 + g_z M_1 \tag{21}$$

$$Z_{W1} = d_z [t_0(W_1 - W_0) - (X_{N1} - X_0)] \tag{22}$$

where

$$X_{N1} = Y_{N1} + Z_{N1}. \tag{23}$$

The bracketed terms in Equations (20) and (22) are identical, and also are identical to the bracketed term in Equation (7): the only differences between the right-hand sides are in the parameters d, d_y, and d_z. These parameters represent propensities to spend on public services out of the city's surplus revenue, after it has met the demands for additional services in *both* categories generated by the increased population and business.

As in the total expenditure model, the new tax base is a function of the increased number of entities to be taxed:

$$W_1 = \alpha C_1 + \alpha' S_1 + \beta T_1 + \gamma M_1 . \tag{24}$$

By a process of substitution similar to that used to derive Equation (10), Equations (17) and (18) can be written as:

$$Y_1 = [a_y + d_y(t_0 \alpha - a)] C_1 + d_y (t_0 \alpha' - a') S_1$$
$$+ d_y (t_0 \beta - b) T_1 + d_y (t_0 \gamma - g) M_1 \tag{25}$$

$$Z_1 = [a_z + d_z (t_0 \alpha - a)] C_1 + [a' + d_z (t_0 \alpha' - a')] S_1$$
$$+ [b + d_z (t_0 \beta - b)] T_1 + [g + d_z (t_0 \gamma - g)] M_1 \tag{26}$$

where

$$a = a_y + a_z ; \tag{27}$$

for the other coefficients, since $b_y = 0$ by assumption,

$$b = b_z . \tag{28}$$

Equations (25) and (26) imply that, for the purposes of testing the prevailing hypotheses, the analysis of municipal expenditures on services provided to nonresidents and businesses, as well as residents, is no more useful than the analysis of total municipal expenditures; however, the analysis of expenditures on services provided *only* to residents does generate a test.[13]

The effect of an increase in business activity on expenditures for Y, for example, is entirely due to the businesses' effect on surplus revenue; any increased expenditure on Y will come about because the businesses are a net source of revenue to the municipality, given the original tax rate. The sign of the coefficients of T_1 and M_1 will be positive if the prevailing hypotheses are true; while the sign of the coefficient of S_1 will be negative.

In the next section of the paper, Equation (25) will be estimated empirically; however, it is useful before doing so to extend the model to take into account the distribution of income within the city, in order to improve the specification of the model. Since the empirical work will analyze expenditures on education, it is also useful to include a measure of school enrollment as an independent variable, to allow for the fact that the service is provided to a specific subset of the city's population.

The central city population is conveniently divided into two groups, the rich and the poor. The city spends different amounts on providing services to members of the two groups, and raises different amounts of revenue from them, since the tax bases are different. Algebraically, the two-category model becomes:

$$W_0 = \alpha_R C_{RO} + \alpha_P C_{PO} + \alpha' S_0 + \beta T_0 + \gamma M_0 \tag{29}$$

$$Y_0 = a_{Ry} C_{Ro} + a_{Py} C_{P0} + eE_0 \tag{30}$$

$$Z_0 = a_{Rz} C_{R0} + a_{Pz} C_{P0} + a' S_0 + bT_0 + gM_0 . \tag{31}$$

(The subscripts R and P refer to the rich and poor residents, respectively. The variable E is public school enrollment.)

As population and business increase, the tax base and the level of expenditures change in the same manner already described, and the new equilibrium levels are:

$$W_1 = \alpha_R C_{R1} + \alpha_P C_{P1} + \alpha' S_1 + \beta T_1 + \gamma M_1 \tag{32}$$

$$Y_1 = [a_{Ry} + d_y (t_0 \alpha_R - a_R)] C_{R1} + [a_{Py} + d_y (t_0 \alpha_P - a_P)] C_{P1}$$
$$+ d_y (t_0 \alpha' - a') S_1 + d_y (t_0 \beta - b) T_1 + d_y (t_0 \gamma - g) M_1 + eE_1 \tag{33}$$

$$Z_1 = [a_{Rz} + d_z(t_0 \alpha_R - a_R)] C_{R1} + [a_{Pz} + d_z (t_0 \alpha_P - a_P)] C_{P1}$$
$$+ [a' + d_z(t_0 \alpha' - a')] S_1 + [b + d_z(t_0 \beta - b)] T_1$$
$$+ [g + d_z (t_0 \gamma - g)] M_1 . \tag{34}$$

In order to eliminate multicollinearity between C_{R1} and C_{P1} in the empirical estimation, when all variables are deflated by C_1, it is useful to rewrite Equations (33) and (34), utilizing the fact that $C_{R1} = C_1 - C_{P1}$. These equations then become:

$$Y_1 = [a_{Ry} + d_y (t_0 \alpha_R - a_R)] C_1 + [a_{Py} + d_y (t_0 \alpha_P - a_P)$$
$$- a_{Ry} - d_y (t_0 \alpha_R - a_P)] C_{P1} + d_y (t_0 \alpha' - a') S_1$$
$$+ d_y (t_0 \beta - b) T_1 + d_y (t_0 \gamma - g) M_1 + eE_1 \tag{35}$$

$$= [a_{Rz} + d_z (t_0 \alpha_R - a_R)] C_1 + [a_{Pz} + d_z (t_0 \alpha_P - a_P)$$
$$- a_{Rz} - d_z (t_0 \alpha_R - a_R)] C_{P1} + [a' + d_z (t_0 \alpha' - a')] S_1$$
$$+ [b + d_z (t_0 \beta - b)] T_1 + [g + d_z (t_0 \gamma - g)] M_1 . \tag{36}$$

Equations (35) and (36) will be estimated for certain services in the next section of this paper.[14]

It is probably unnecessary to point out that the model developed in this section is very crude. It clearly ignores important factors which affect the expenditures of cities. The independent variables employed are gross measures which obscure important differences between individual members of the same category: people have different incomes and tastes; individual manufacturing plants may have greatly differing demands for a particular service, depending on such factors as size of plant and the relative importance of land and labor in the production function; and so on. Other types of activity, such as central offices and government itself, also generate revenues or demand expenditures by the local government.

These limitations should of course be kept in mind in interpreting the empirical results in the next section.

Empirical Results

As previously mentioned, empirical estimation of municipal expenditure regression has generally been carried out using cross-sectional data, rather than time series. This applies to studies of both total expenditures and individual service categories. The reason is that data, particularly for independent variables, is much more readily available for cross sections. For dependent variables, some time-series data is available; the *Compendium of City Government Finances* has provided annual municipal expenditure data for large cities in the United States since 1949, and some data on education expenditures are published by several sources.[15] However, there are few independent variables for which annual estimates for individual cities are available, apart from population. More comprehensive data are available cross-sectionally, particularly from the *Census of Population and Housing*, the *Census of Business*, and the *Census of Manufactures*.

Given the greater availability and reliability of the cross-sectional data, this study will follow previous expenditure analyses in estimating cross-sectional expenditure regressions. If the model of the previous section is applied to a cross section of cities, it implies that the prevailing hypotheses may be tested by investigating whether cities with greater suburban population, retail trade, and manufacturing spend more on the services provided only to residents.

Rather than investigating the broad expenditure categories Y and Z, this study analyses expenditures on individual categories of services. Theoretically this is as acceptable for testing the prevailing hypotheses, while empirically it is far more desirable. Theoretically, it can be shown that disaggregation of Equation (35) into several individual categories of Y does not affect the interpretation of the coefficients of S_1, T_1, or M_1, which are the coefficients of particular interest.[16]

Empirically, it is highly preferable to disaggregate. Statistical analysis of total expenditure functions is rendered difficult by the fact that total expenditures and those for individual categories reported by different local governments depend to a great extent on the division of labor between state governments, counties, municipalities, and special districts; without adjusting for these differences, analysis of municipal expenditures tends to become analysis of local government structure.[17] Recognition of this problem has led more recent studies to focus on either individual categories of expenditures, or those which all cities under study appear to perform — the "common functions," to use Brazer's convenient term. However, as he said, "in its narrowest construction this would probably permit inclusion only of police and fire protection."[18]

The problem is particularly acute for the services included in Y. In accordance with the model developed in the previous section, the analysis is restricted to central cities of Standard Metropolitan Statistical areas. Among these, however, data on library expenditures are available only for the very largest cities, and some of these operate public libraries through special districts which are not coterminous with the central city. For parks and recreation, per capita central city expenditures in 1960 varied from 49 cents in Rockford, Illinois, to $77.27 in Atlantic City, New Jersey.[19]

Education appears likely to be the only service which is both provided only to people and performed by local governments throughout the country. Accordingly, the test of the competing hypotheses will be carried out using education expenditures as the variable Y.[20] To eliminate the effects of city size, Equation (35) is deflated by central city population, converting it to an estimation of school expenditures per capita.

It is then estimated by ordinary least-squares (t-ratios of coefficients appear in parentheses under the coefficients):

$$\frac{Y_1}{C_1} = 14.648 - 1.197 \frac{C_{P1}}{C_1} + .0409 \frac{S_1}{C_1}$$
$$(2.05) \quad (7.41) \qquad\qquad (5.23)$$

$$+ .00944 \frac{T_1}{C_1} - 0.322 \frac{M_1}{C_1} + 3.443 \frac{E_1}{C_1}$$
$$(2.60) \qquad\quad (2.07) \qquad\quad (17.66)$$

$$R^2 = .775 \qquad\qquad F = 113.1 \ . \tag{37}$$

The results in Equation (37) are mixed.[21] They support the prevailing hypothesis in the case of retail trade and refute it in the case of manufacturing. In terms of income redistribution, the results imply that cites spend more on serving manufacturing establishments than they receive in taxes from them;

and that cities spend less in serving retail stores than they receive in taxes from them.

The positive coefficient for suburban population implies that central cities exploit their suburbs. Since central cities do not provide schooling for the children of suburbanites, the coefficient measures only the surplus revenue that the central city receives from suburbanites. The positive coefficient refutes the prevailing hypothesis about the direction of exploitation.

It has previously been demonstrated in Footnote 16, above, that the analysis of expenditures on individual Z services is of little use in determining the directions of income redistribution within the metropolitan area. However, it is still worthwhile to estimate Equation (36), because the results in Equation (37) have implications for the signs to be expected in estimations of Equation (36). The coefficients of S_1/C_1 and T_1/C_1 should be positive; the coefficient of $M_1 C_1$ may have either sign.

Municipal expenditures on three services provided to both people and business are analyzed in Table 11-1. The services chosen are police protection, fire protection, and highways, services which seem likely to be provided on the most uniform basis by municipal governments in different parts of the country.[22] Expenditures are again deflated by central city population.

Ordinary least-squares analysis of Equation (36) for the three services produces the results shown in Table 11-1.[23]

The results in Table 11-1 are in general consistent with those predicted by the model in light of Equation (37), although there are discrepancies. The coefficients of T_1/C_1 are all positive and significant. The results for S_1/C_1 are less clearly consistent with those to be expected; the coefficients for police and

Table 11-1
Regression Analysis of Selected Municipal Expenditure Categories

Variable	Police Protection	Fire Protection	Highways
Constant	7.00028	6.14409	3.79130
	(3.31)	(4.31)	(3.14)
C_{P1}/C_1	−0.07986	−0.08747	−0.05411
	(1.49)	(2.41)	(1.77)
S_1/C_1	0.00530	0.00202	−0.01155
	(2.02)	(1.14)	(1.03)
T_1/C_1	0.00253	0.00219	0.00195
	(2.16)	(2.77)	(2.91)
M_1/C_1	0.05631	0.10647	0.07429
	(1.14)	(3.20)	(2.64)
R^2	.115	.195	.125
F	5.31	9.87	5.83

fire protection are positive, although only the former is significant, while the coefficient for highways is negative, even though insignificant. It may be that central cities provide no fire protection to suburbanites while the latter are in the central city, which might explain the lack of significance of this coefficient. The coefficient of highways, however, is simply at variance with the predicted coefficient.[24]

The results for M_1/C_1 are interesting primarily because of their different signs from that in Equation (37). Education expenditures are negatively related to manufacturing activity in the central city, while expenditures for other services are positively related to it. These results are consistent with those of Margolis and of Williams, *et al.*, but they are not consistent with what has been termed the prevailing hypothesis.

Summary and Conclusions

This study has investigated some of the directions of income redistribution generated within metropolitan areas by the taxing and spending policies of local governments. It has shown that, contrary to prevailing notions, cities appear to spend more on providing services to manufacturing plants than the cities receive in tax revenue from them. On the other hand, cities appear to receive more in tax revenue from retail stores than they spend in providing services to them. The results also imply that central cities are able to exploit suburbanites.

The results indicate that current beliefs about the causes of fiscal problems in central cities are at least in part mistaken. The loss of manufacturing to the suburbs has not, by itself, produced the fiscal crisis of our cities; further, the results suggest that suburbanization and political fragmentation have not created these problems. A possible implication of these results is that metropolitan government or some other form of area-wide cooperation will not reduce the fiscal problems of the cities; however, it is entirely possible that concentration of low-income residents within central cities has generated some of the problems,[25] so that bringing well-to-do and middle-income residents under the same government as the poor may relieve the fiscal pressures on cities, although bringing manufacturing activity back under the same government will not do so. Perhaps the fiscal problems of cities are generated simply by changing tastes for local government services, or by changes in the relative prices of these services, along the lines suggested by Baumol (1967).

It may be noticed that the coefficients of determination in Table 11-1 are rather low, even though the F-ratio is significant at the 1-percent level in each case. The low coefficients of determination are not in themselves particularly disconcerting; it is not the purpose of this study to "maximize R^2", but rather to investigate the effect of certain independent variables upon expenditures. However, it is obvious that variables which do affect municipal expenditures have been omitted from the model. It is possible that the variables actually may be proxies for some of the omitted variables, so that the results are in fact false.[26]

It is always necessary to bear this possibility in mind when interpreting the results of this study, and for that matter of any of the numerous expenditure studies already made. However, it is surely preferable to try to isolate specific variables whose effect on expenditures can be predicted on the basis of theory, rather than to engage in attempts at statistical explanation whose results are subject to any of several interpretations a posteriori.

The implications for future research clearly lie in the direction of further refinement of formal models. The crudeness of the models developed in this paper was discussed at the conclusion of "The Theoretical Model" section; desirable modifications, in addition to those discussed there, can easily be suggested. It would also be useful to try to extend the present analysis to additional services, particularly in the Y category. The wide variability in the assignment of functional responsibility for these services, as noted, makes this difficult, but perhaps more refined models can be developed to overcome this data problem.

The crudeness of the model, however, should not be allowed to obscure the fact that it *is* a model, capable of generating tests of competing hypotheses. In this respect, this study differs fundamentally from the mainstream of expenditure analyses in state and local finance, which have generally lacked any but the most rudimentary theoretical framework. They have tended to serve as a kind of guide for municipal officials and city planners, focussing their attention on the independent variables as affecting various classes of expenditures, rather than on the dependent variables as being affected by different factors. This approach is probably useful for some practical purposes, telling municipal policy makers that if certain things happen in a city (i.e., if the independent variables vary in certain ways), municipal expenditures will be increased, or decreased, in various categories; however, it does not illuminate the underlying structural relationships. One result is that notions such as the prevailing hypotheses are accepted without questioning, and used as guides to policy.

It seems clear that more attention should be directed to the formulation of specific models of urban fiscal structure, and less to the kind of wholly empirical analysis of expenditures that has been generally produced.

Notes

1. One hypothesis that has been offered is that new suburban municipalities incur heavy capital costs in establishing a municipal government. The validity of this hypothesis rests fundamentally on the existence of economies of scale. If metropolitan area population increases, both current and capital expenditures would be expected to increase, whether or not the new residents live in the central city or in suburbs. However, it is possible that

capital facilities can be provided more economically for larger populations, in which case suburbanization could increase the expenditures necessary to achieve a given level of municipal services. Most studies, however, find little if any evidence of economies of scale, at least when measured in expenditure terms.

    A second hypothesis is that the problem is psychological: middle income families move from apartments in central cities to owner-occupied houses in suburbs, and suddenly become aware of the property tax burden. In this case, the "problem" is not very interesting to an economist, if indeed it exists at all. (Fitch, 1964, p. 115, 124.)

2. For example, see "No Matter the Name, the Game's Still the Same," *The National Observer,* April 1, 1968, p. 1. Mayor Joseph L. Alioto of San Francisco, in proposing a 1% payroll tax on nonresident commuters, is quoted as saying: "The revenues the commuters bring into the city do not begin to match the cost to the city for added traffic policemen, parking complexes, transportation services, all the myriad other daily services . . . "

3. It is frequently argued that political fragmentation generates intra-metropolitan external diseconomies, and a suboptimal allocation of resources; examples include water and air pollution. This study does not touch on these problems; the services analyzed are not commonly believed to generate such externalities. This study is concerned only with the effect of political fragmentation on the city budget, not on the "social welfare function."

4. Different studies have used different measures of expenditures. The most common have been total municipal expenditures per capita, or total municipal current operating expenditures per capita (excluding capital outlays). All of the studies referred to in this section have used one or both of these measures. Another approach has been to analyze expenditures per capita on individual functions, such as police and fire protection, or groups of services. Studies using this approach will be discussed in Section IV. (Some studies have used both approaches and will be discussed in both sections.) A convenient summary of the more important "expenditure function" studies may be found in Hirsch (1968), pp. 498-501.

5. See Brazer (1959), pp. 57-58, Kee (1965), p. 347, Kee (1967), p. 210, and Bahl, (1969), p. 23. The only investigation of both expenditures and revenues of central cities is Feinberg (1965). He found that the decline of the city reduced its revenues, particularly from the property tax, but also reduced expenditures. His method of analysis, relying only on correlation coefficients, provided no way of measuring the relative changes of expenditures and revenues, although he seems to believe that the decrease in revenues was greater.

6. E.g., Brazer (1959), Campbell and Sacks (1967), and Bahl (1969). Kee (1965) finds the same phenomenon for categories other than education. Bollens and Schmandt (1965), p. 366, have also commented on the relative importance of the revenue factors.

7. This approach to municipal expenditures is somewhat analogous to the

standard theory of consumer demand. For example, Lipsey and Steiner (*Economics,* 1966, pp. 71–73) list six factors affecting market demand: tastes, the size of the population, the level of income of the average household, the distribution of income, the price of the commodity, and the prices of substitutes and complements. The above formulation of municipal expenditures (best defined as quantity times price) concentrates on two of these factors: the size of the "population" (including suburbanites and businesses) and the average level of wealth, rather than income, since wealth is probably the best measure of the tax base. The distribution of income will be introduced into the model in a subsequent formulation. Tastes, and the prices of substitutes and complements, are ignored in the simple model presented in this paper; a more complete model undoubtedly should attempt to take them into account.

8. The assumption that the coefficients "a," "a'," and "b" do not change as more entities are served implies constant returns to scale, if expenditures are regarded as a proxy for output. This assumption is made for expository convenience; the model would not be changed in any important way by assuming increasing or decreasing returns to scale. It is also possible that the services may be pure "public goods," so that the marginal cost of providing the services to additional persons or businesses is zero; in this case the only effect on expenditures arises through the increased revenue generated. However, there is little basis for arguing a priori that the more important services, in a financial sense, such as police and fire protection, sanitation, and education, are pure public goods. "General control" (including the mayor and city council) may be a public good, but this is a relatively small part of municipal expenditures, amounting to 5.1 percent in 1960.

9. Given the available data, time–series analyses are far more difficult. If the model is interpreted cross–sectionally, then equation (10) implies that cities with more business activity, *ceteris paribus,* may spend more on public services than "bedroom" cities, whether or not the additional business activity brings in more revenue to the city treasury than it costs the city to provide services to it.

10. The only study to take explicit account of the budget constraint is Gramlich (1969), who incorporated it into a model of the entire state and local government sector as part of the Federal Reserve Board–MIT macroeconomic model. He found that state and local governments did in fact react to the budget constraint, concluding that, "the budget constraint comes through . . . strongly . . . it is quite important statistically, and it profoundly alters the state and local response to external shocks." (Gramlich, 1969, p. 181). Gramlich's results are especially noteworthy because he was working with quarterly data, while the usual statutory budget constraint is either annual or biennial.

11. Formal proof of this statement is omitted, in the interests of conserving space; the simplest approach is to examine the difference between t_1 and t_0 in response to a change in any independent variable.

12. It will be convenient in the remainder of this paper to refer to the hypotheses that central cities are exploited by suburban residents, and that

businesses are net sources of revenue to the cities in which they are located, as the "prevailing hypotheses" about the fiscal impact of suburbanization and business activity, respectively.

13. The previous literature does not shed much light on the hypotheses under study. A number of studies have investigated the determinants of local government expenditures on individual categories of services, including several of the categories that would be included in Y. However, almost none of these have used any measures of business activity among their independent variables. In a study of Philadelphia suburbs, Williams *et al.* (1965) have come closer to testing the hypothesis than has anyone else. They divided suburbs into "Industrial and Commercial Centers" and "Residential" (the latter again subdivided by density), and found that: Industrial and Commercial Centers spend more than the other types of suburbs for each function, with the exception of planning, libraries, and refuse disposal. In the next chapter, school expenditures will also be seen to be lower for the Centers. Thus, for the Industrial and Commercial Centers, services which relate to residential amenities and to home and school environment receive somewhat less emphasis than the industrial and commercial property servicing functions such as servicing of streets, and fire and police protection" (Williams *et al.*, 1965, p. 112).

However, the analysis in support of this conclusion consists entirely of a simple comparison of mean per capita expenditures of each group of suburbs, with no attempt to determine if the means are significantly different between the groups. Further, no evidence is in fact presented in the next (or any other) chapter about the school expenditures of these groups of suburbs, although there are several more statements to the effect that school expenditures for the industrial suburbs are lower.

There have been three other relevant studies. Brazer (1959) found no significant relationship between "Employment per 100 of Population in Manufacturing, Trade and Services," and noncapital recreation expenditures per capita for any of several sets of cities; he also found no significant relationship between the same independent variable and education expenditures for the 40 largest cities, the only group for which education expenditure data were available to him. Brazer's results, taken at face value, imply that there is no income redistribution, but rather that the city engages in benefit taxation of businesses, which "get what they pay for" from the municipal government.

More recently, Bahl (1969), in amplifying on Brazer's work, has found a positive and generally significant relationship between per capita retail sales and per capita expenditures on parks for 198 central cities in 1960. He also found that the ratio of city employment to city population had no effect on parks expenditures, and that the percentage of city employment engaged in manufacturing in manufacturing had a negative effect. Bahl's work is of interest in that it is the first to separate "business" into retail trade and manufacturing; however, he does not look at the possible implications of his results in regard to the prevailing hypothesis.

Davis (1965) found a positive relationship between per capita industrial property and education expenditures in school districts around Pittsburgh. However, he found no relationship between industrial property and education expenditures for school "jointures," comprising districts which have agreed to make joint expenditure decisions. He regarded industrial property as representing wealth which could be taxed without regard to the preferences of its (absentee) owners. Davis' results in part support the prevailing hypothesis, though, like Bahl, he does not consider his results in that context; indeed, he appears to believe that industrial property constitutes solely a measure of fiscal capacity without generating any expenditure demands, in the manner of Scott and Feder's interpretation of per capita retail sales (Davis, 1965, p. 96).

The previous literature is far from conclusive. Williams et al. provide evidence against the prevailing hypothesis about business activity; Davis provides some evidence for it; Bahl provides evidence both ways.

The impact of suburbanization is also unclear from the literature. Brazer (1959) found that an increase in suburbanization raised education expenditures and lowered those for parks, using the 40 largest cities in 1950; Bahl (1969), found no significant relationship between suburbanization and parks expenditures.

14. The coefficients in equations (35) and (36) are rather unwieldy; it may be helpful to explain their components. For example, in the coefficient of C_1 in either equation a_{Ry} is the amount spent to provide the service to a rich resident, in the initial equilibrium; it is also the amount the city would spend if the tax base and expenditures changed in the same proportion as the result of an increase in rich residents. The term in parentheses measures the surplus revenue generated by an increase in the number of rich residents; it is positive if the rich residents are taxed to provide services to other groups, and negative if these others are taxed to provide services to rich residents. The parameters d_y and d_z represent marginal propensities to spend on the respective services out of this surplus revenue.

In equation (35), the coefficients of S_1, T_1, and M_1 contain only the surplus revenue and the marginal propensity to spend on the service Y; the service is not provided to suburban population or city businesses.

15. Sources of data for school systems include U.S. Department of Health, Education and Welfare, Office of Education, *Current Expenditures Per Pupil in Large Public School Systems* (Washington, Government Printing Office, 1962); National Education Association, Research Division, *Selected Statistics of Local School Districts* (Washington: National Education Association), entitled *Selected Statistics of Local School Systems* beginning in 1963–64; as well as the *Compendium of City Government Finances*. The usefulness of these sets of data over time is limited. The first two change in cities covered and data reported from year to year, while the last provides expenditure data without enrollment for cities in which the school systems are part of the municipal government, without separate taxing powers.

16. The interpretation of other coefficients, however, is affected. If Z is also disaggregated, then individual coefficients may be negative if surplus revenue is negative. For example, the coefficient of manufacturing activity, for a

particular service such as police protection, becomes: $g_{\text{police}} \neq d_z (t_0 \gamma - g)$. This *may* be negative, since g_{police} is less than g. This coefficient, however, does not test the prevailing hypothesis; g_{police} is still non-negative, and the entire coefficient may be positive even if the surplus revenue (the term in parentheses) is negative. A negative coefficient, however, is very strong refutation of the prevailing hypothesis, in regard to business.

The prevailing hypothesis in regard to suburbanization implies that surplus revenue is negative; a negative coefficient for suburbanization in a Z service regression would be strong support of the prevailing hypothesis, since the amount spent by the city to provide the service to suburbanites cannot be less than zero. A positive coefficient, in this case also, however, does not test the hypothesis.

Several studies have estimated "non-education" expenditures, which nearly corresponds to the entire Z category, although it is more inclusive (Kee, 1965; Kee, 1967; Campbell and Sacks, 1967). The results of these studies are useless for our purposes, as the model demonstrates. Other studies have looked at individual Z services (Brazer, 1959; Williams *et al.*, 1965; Bahl, 1969), usually finding positive or insignificant coefficients for suburbanization or business. These results would be useful as evidence on the prevailing hypotheses only if they were negative; as argued above, it is incorrect to infer from them that the prevailing hypotheses are true or false.

17. "Data in this report relate only to municipal corporations and their dependent agencies, and do not include amounts for other local governments overlying city areas. Therefore, expenditure figures here for 'education' do not include spending by the separate school districts which administer public schools within most municipal areas. Variations in the assignment of governmental responsibility for public assistance, health, hospitals, public housing, and other functions to a lesser degree, also have an important effect upon reported amounts of city expenditure, revenue, and debt." U.S. Bureau of the Census, *Compendium of City Government Finances in 1960* (Washington: 1961), p. 4.
18. Brazer (1959), p. 69. Even for other common functions there are very large differences between individual cities which are likely to be explainable only of the basis of local government structure. For example, Decatur, Illinois, spent nothing whatsoever on sewers and sanitation in 1960, but it is not (and was not then) noticeably filthier than Peoria or Springfield, which spent $3.49 and $5.28 per capita, respectively, in 1960. Data on expenditures is taken from U.S. Bureau of the Census (1961).
19. The disparities in intercity parks and recreation expenditures, apparently reflecting differences in assignment of governmental responsibility, suggest that Brazer's and Bahl's regression results for this service should not be given too great weight as evidence for or against the competing hypotheses. The argument, however, does not apply to Williams, *et al.*, since their study was confined to a single metroplitan area, where presumably all municipal governments have the same responsibilities.
20. Data on education expenditures are taken from U.S. Bureau of the Census, *Census of Governments 1962*, Vol. V (Washington: Government Printing

Office, 1964). Data on all independent variables except enrollment are taken from U.S. Bureau of the Census, *County and City Data Book 1962* (Washington: Government Printing Office, 1962). The measure of T_1 used is retail sales; the measure of M_1 is employment in manufacturing. Enrollment data are taken from U.S. Bureau of the Census (1964) for those cities whose school systems are legally independent governments, and from U.S. Office of Education (*1962-1963 Education Directory*, Washington: Government Printing Office, 1963), for school systems which are financially dependent on their municipal governments.

Central cities in SMA's having only one central city are included if they had at least 50,000 residents in 1960. In the case of SMA's having more than one central city, smaller central cities are included only if they are at least half as large as the largest central city (e.g., Gary and Hammond), or if their Urbanized Areas are geographically separate (Beaumont and Port Arthur). For 38 central cities which meet these qualifications, part or all of the public schools are organized on a county-wide basis. These, which are primarily in the South, are excluded. In addition, three other cities are omitted for lack of data on some of the independent variables, leaving 168 cities in the analysis.

21. Expenditures and retail sales are in units of dollars per capita; all other variables are per cent. Mean values for the variables are: Y_1/C_1, $77.80; C_{P1}/C_1, 17.9 (%); S_1/C_1, 131.2 (%); T_1/C_1, $1,588.70; M_1/C_1, 12.1 (%); E_1/C_1. 19.8 (%).

The high values for the coefficient of determination and the F-ratio occur because equation (37) is deflated by central city population, in order to compare it to other studies and later work in this paper. If expenditures are deflated by enrollment rather than population, the results are:

$$\frac{Y_1}{E_1} = 0.120 \frac{C_1}{(1.88)E_1} - 1.129 \frac{C_{P1}}{(7.25)E_1} + 0.332 \frac{S_1}{(4.20)E_1}$$

$$+ .00770 \frac{T_1}{(2.31)E_1} - 0.122 \frac{M_1}{(2.69)E_1} + 358.99 \atop (19.21)$$

$$R^2 = .386 \qquad\qquad F = 20.4 \qquad\qquad (37')$$

The only differences of note are that the constant in equation (37) becomes the coefficient of C_1/E_1 in equation (37'), and ceases to be statistically significant in the usual sense; while the coefficient of E_1/C_1 in equation (37) becomes the constant term in equation (37'). The result of these changes is to lower both the coefficient of determination and the F-ratio, but the signs and significance of the other coefficients are unchanged, and the results have exactly the same implications for the test of the prevailing hypotheses.

22. Brazer (1959), p. 3, found that the coefficients of variation for these three

functions were lower than for other common functions in 1951, suggesting, but not proving, that there was less variation in the assignment of government responsibility between states for these three functions. In the present study, the same is true: the coefficients of variation are: police, 40.3; fire, 32.6; highways, 39.1. These are higher than for education (20.6), suggesting more variation in assignment of responsibility for the three common functions, but the difference may also reflect greater variability in tastes for the common functions. By contrast, the coefficient of variation for general control, a common function not analyzed in this study, is 48.8.

23. The data for the dependent variables are from U.S. Bureau of the Census (1961).

24. While at variance with the model, the coefficient appears to be consistent with other empirical work. Bahl (1969) finds a positive insignificant coefficient for C_1/S_1 in his highways regression for both 1960 and 1950, the former even with 16 other independent variables included; his results of course have the same interpretation as that in Table 11-1. Brazer (1959) found an insignificant relationship for a similar variable for 1950 highway expenditures by 40 large cities; the sign was unreported. In contrast, he found negative coefficients in all other "common functions" regressions, including police and fire protection, which are analogous to the positive coefficients for S_1/C_1 in Table 11-1.

   These sets of results are particularly interesting in light of the fact that this service seems to be generally regarded as an obvious example of suburban exploitation of central cities. See for example Mayor Alioto's comment in footnote 2. The same opinion seems to be stated in at least two public finance texts: Eckstein (1967), p. 48, and Herber (1967), p. 491. Additional investigation of this service clearly is called for.

25. Muth (1967, pp. 291-292) has gone so far as to explain part of the observed pattern of population densities in metropolitan areas on the hypothesis that richer families realize that their taxes are used by central cities to finance expenditures for poorer persons, and that the rich therefore choose to move to suburbs rather than to neighborhoods within the city with similar quality housing.

26. The variable which has most commonly been used in expenditure studies is some measure of aid received from other levels of government. The use of the latter variable has been convincingly criticized by Morss (1966), who has shown that studies using it are in fact regressing expenditures against part of revenue, particularly when total expenditures are used as the dependent variable, or when expenditures on an individual category are regressed against aid earmarked for that category. Since this clearly applies to education expenditures, it is appropriate to exclude this variable from the present analysis. In addition, U.S. Bureau of the Census (1964) does not report intergovernmental aid to education for financially dependent school systems, although such information is available for a smaller number of systems in National Education Association (1961).

   Even using this variable, however, coefficients of determination are not particularly high. The most similar study of police, fire and highway expenditures is Brazer (1959); for 462 cities he obtained coefficients of .26, .27, and .16, respectively. However, Bahl (1969), using nine independent variables, reported coefficients of determination of .54, .41, and .19. Several studies have analyzed education expenditures for smaller groups of central cities (usually about 40); coefficients of determination in these studies include .41 by both Brazer (1959) and Kee (1967), and .53 by Campbell and Sacks (1967).

References

Bahl, Roy W., *Metropolitan City Expenditures*, University of Kentucky Press, Lexington (1969).

Baumol, William J., "Macroeconomics of Unbalanced Growth: The Anatomy of Urban Crisis", *A.E.R.*, Vol. LVII, 415–426 (June, 1967).

Bollens, John C., and Schmandt, Henry J., *The Metropolis*, Harper and Row, New York (1965).

Brazer, Harvey E., *City Expenditures in the United States*, National Bureau of Economic Research, New York (1959).

Brazer, Harvey E., "Some Fiscal Implications of Metropolitanism", in Benjamin Chinitz, ed., *City and Suburb*, Prentice-Hall, Englewood Cliffs (1964).

Campbell, Alan K., and Sacks, Seymour, *Metropolitan America*, The Free Press, New York (1967).

Davis, Otto A., "Empirical Evidence of Political Influences upon the Expenditure Policies of Public Schools", in Julius Margolis, ed., *The Public Economy of Urban Communities*, Resources for the Future, Washington (1965).

Due, John F., *Government Finance*, 4th ed., Richard D. Irwin, Homewood (1968).

Eckstein, Otto, *Public Finance*, 2nd ed., Prentice-Hall, Englewood Cliffs (1967).

Feinberg, Mordecai S., "The Implications of Core-City Decline for the Fiscal Structure of the Core-City", *National Tax Journal*, Vol. XVI, pp. 213–231 (December, 1965).

Fitch, Lyle C., "Metropolitan Fiscal Problems", in Benjamin Chinitz, *op. cit.*

Gramlich, Edward M., "State and Local Governments and Their Budget Constraint", *International Economic Review*, Vol. X, 163–182 (June, 1969).

Groves, Harold M., and Riew, John, "The Impact of Industry on Local Taxes – A Simple Model", *National Tax Journal*, Vol. XVI, 137–146 (June, 1963).

Hawley, Amos H., "Metropolitan Population and Municipal Government Expenditures in Central Cities," in Paul K. Hatt and Albert J. Reiss, Jr., eds., *Cities and Society*, The Free Press, Glencoe (1956).

Herber, Bernard P., *Modern Public Finance*, Richard D. Irwin, Homewood (1967).

Hirsch, Werner Z., "The Supply of Urban Public Services", in Harvey S. Perloff and Lowdon Wingo, Jr., eds., *Issues in Urban Economics,* Johns Hopkins, Baltimore (1968).

Isard, Walter, and Coughlin, Robert, *Municipal Costs and Revenues Resulting from Community Growth,* Chandler–Davis, Wellesley (1957).

Kee, Woo Sik, "Central City Expenditures and Metropolitan Areas", *National Tax Journal,* Vol. XVIII, pp. 183–189 (December, 1965).

Kee Woo Sik, "Suburban Population Growth and Its Implications for Core City Finance", *Land Economics,* Vol. XLIII, pp. 202–211 (May, 1967).

Lipsey, Richard G. and Steiner, Peter O., *Economics,* Harper and Row, New York (1966).

Loewenstein, Louis K., "The Impact of New Industry on the Fiscal Revenues and Expenditures of Suburban Communities", *National Tax Journal,* Vol. XVI, pp. 113–136 (June, 1963).

Margolis, Julius, "Municipal Fiscal Structure in a Metropolitan Region", *J.P.E.,* Vol. LXV, pp. 225–236 (June, 1957).

Morss, Elliott R., "Some Thoughts on the Determinants of State and Local Expenditures", *National Tax Journal,* Vol. XIX, 95–103 (March, 1966).

Muth, Richard F., "The Distribution of Population Within Urban Areas", in Robert Ferber, ed., *Determinants of Investment Behavior,* National Bureau of Economic Research, New York (1967).

National Education Association, Research Division, *Selected Statistics of Local School Districts,* National Education Association (annual), Washington.

Scott, Stanley, and Feder, Edward L., *Factors Associated with Variations in Municipal Expenditure Levels,* Bureau of Public Administration, University of California, Berkeley (1957).

de Torres, Juan, *Financing Local Government,* National Industrial Conference Board, New York (1967).

U.S. Bureau of the Census, *Census of Governments 1962,* Vol. V, Government Printing Office, Washington (1964).

U.S. Bureau of the Census, *Census of Governments 1967,* Vol. II, Government Printing Office, Washington (1968).

U.S. Bureau of the Census, *Compendium of City Government Finances 1960,* Government Printing Office, Washington (1961).

U.S. Bureau of the Census, *1962 County and City Data Book,* Government Printing Office, Washington (1962).

U.S. Office of Education, *Current Expenditures Per Pupil in Large Public School Systems.* Government Printing Office, Washington (1962)

U.S. Office of Education, *1962-1963 Education Directory,* Government Printing Office, Washington (1963).

Williams, Oliver P., Herman, Harold, Liebman, Charles S., and Dye, Thomas R., *Suburban Differences and Metropolitan Policies,* University of Pennsylvania, Philadelphia (1965).

The National Observer (April 1, 1968).

12 Computer Mapping of Urban Structure

Harold L. Goldstein

The other papers presented in this section focus upon the use of mathematical techniques in the development of specific quantitative models for the analysis of urban structures. This paper is not mathematical; it discusses a different type of tool that can be used in the development, testing, and evaluation of such models.

The scope of urban systems is such that it is difficult to readily comprehend and interpret verbal or quantitative descriptions in their totality. Thus the widespread usage of maps by urban analysts. But a map is only a picture and a picture can only be taken at a point in time. The dynamics of urban systems are such that a picture taken today will often be of limited utility tomorrow. In order to be of continued value, an urban description must have the capability of being readily updated. Computer-mapping systems provide for that capability, and for this and other reasons are becoming an accepted part of the urban analysts tool kit.

Caution is Needed

This acceptance of computer-mapping systems is not totally satisfactory. The introduction of any innovation should be thought of as part of a continuing educational process. The indiscriminant and often incorrect use of such a tool can create negative impressions and thus limit further applications of and improvements in the tool. In this regard, computer mapping is not unlike quantitative model development.

It is clear that the misapplication of a model can lead to inappropriate decision making. For example, if the assumptions behind the model output are not understood, it is probable that the output will be misinterpreted. Similarly, unfamiliarity with the mapping technique employed, the geographic identification methods used, or the area under consideration can cause a poor translation of the map message into the appropriate terms. In some situations computer mapping might allow the production and use of maps where none was used before. Unfamiliarity with maps in general, in these cases, makes improper usage highly probable unless the introduction of the mapping tool is accompanied by an orientation session or something comparable.

In some cases, a person misinterpreting a computer map will misinterpret any other map he is given; theoretically no additional harm is done. However, in some circles the computer is regarded as a mystical device, and conclusions based on "computer output" are often deferred to and can result in important decisions by themselves. It appears that it is difficult to talk of minor problems in the use of an urban analysis tool without getting into issues of extreme importance. It is clear that our decision making processes are faulty and misunderstood. Although this is not the place for a discussion of this issue, it should be recognized.

Returning to the topic at hand, the output of a computer-mapping program can be very different in appearance from traditionally prepared maps. Every individual using computer maps goes through at least a mental reorientation if he is to properly learn to use this new tool.

Thus there are dangers from incorrect application of computer-mapping techniques. There is a further indirect danger which might come when the public interacts with more computer maps. If the public does not understand the maps, or cannot see their relevance to the solution of immediate problems, hostility can be developed toward the method or the agency using the method. For example, a map showing ranges of housing quality may be produced. Since computer maps usually show averages or general trends, good housing may be included in an area depicted as having low quality housing. A person living in the good housing will generally react unfavorably to this seeming lowering of his status. The process might work in the opposite direction as well but, in any case, the agency displaying the maps cannot benefit from this situation.

Another danger, already referred to, is the unquestioned acceptance of computer output. The danger can be heightened by the release or publication of computer maps with such captions as: "A series of these maps [referring to a map of the percent of nonwhites in public schools] over a period of time indicates indicates how fast all Boston public schools are being socially balanced";[1] or "Housing developers used this map [depicting noise levels near a housing project] to help them decide where to put up additional buildings".[2] It is easy to see a person reading these captions and thinking "Well, we've just solved another problem."

Thus, computer maps, or any other maps for that matter, should only be presented with accompanying information that allows the intended audience to relate properly to them.

Criteria for Computer Mapping

To avoid the potential pitfalls of misuse, the users should consider the characteristics of the particular application at hand. The Harvard Laboratory for Computer Graphics has developed criteria to aid in determining the appropriateness of computer maps for particular cases:

"Computer mapping can be a significant asset when maps are being used as an *analytical tool during the conduct of a study* as well as a means to display and convey to others the end results of a study. The value of preparing maps on a computer is enhanced particularly to the extent that maps can be used to test and evaluate alternative hypotheses and assumptions during the course of a study. In this respect, computer mapping provides a means of using maps in an unconventional manner; the preparation of numerous maps to evaluate the intermediate as well as the end results of a given study.

"The mapping applications most likely to benefit from the use of computers have one or more of the following characteristics. A large number of maps is needed at one time or maps for a given area are needed on a recurring basis over a period of time; flexibility as to size, content, scale and data manipulation are important; uniformity of map appearance for many different types of data is desired; the time required to prepare a number of maps is to be minimized; and highly accurate (though not necessarily precise) maps are needed.

"The data should have some of the following characteristics. Large amounts of data are to be mapped; the data are in machine readable form or can be readily converted; the data contain geographic codes for the zones by which they are to be mapped or include basic record identifiers which can be used to aggregate the data into map zones; possible sources of human error in handling the data and preparing the maps are to be minimized; the data to be mapped measure a dynamic rather than a static phenomenon and will be updated to provide measures of change over time . . . "[3]

Sometimes it is not possible to consider characteristics of specific applications. For example, in designing a geographical coding system, one consideration would be whether or not a computer mapping capability is needed. But whereas specific applications might not be known, the type of data to be handled and the general areas of interest to which the coding system is to be applied can indicate the need for computer mapping.

Map Usage

The overall context of the application of a map is important in the development of particular mapping techniques. Unfortunately, the way maps are used in urban analysis and related areas is not well understood. The thought process involved in using a map within a nondeterministic framework (i.e., where instructions covering all possible occurrences do not exist) is not clear, and this makes it difficult to evaluate the appropriateness of a particular type of map — either as a preuse judgment or a postuse evaluation.

In general, however, it can be hypothesized that for urban related activities maps may be used:[4]

"(1) To effect a visual understanding of the physical character of the land. For example, topographical maps portray the configuration of an area by showing the relative elevations of its natural and man-made features. A street map is constructed so that one may determine the relationships between the arteries of a city in order that he might move easily from place to place.

"(2) To describe characteristics and qualities of the functional environment and learn how these interrelate. Such maps might deal with the residents of an area (their socio-economic character), the housing in the area (its quality or age), service levels available in the area (education facilities, police stations), etc.

"(3) To synthesize combinations of activities toward, perhaps, the development of a comprehensive plan or a statement of regional goals. A land-use map is the easiest way of describing proposed plans for a region."[4]

In themselves, these generalizations do not resolve anything. Until the nature of the "visual understanding" can be better specified and until there is some clarity as to what happens with the "visual understanding", we will have to proceed with the understanding that all is not right.

That this situation exists is unfortunate — especially so at this time in the development of a new mapping tool. Development should always proceed at a rate which allows comprehension of the effects of development on the eventual application of the new tool. When the user cannot communicate with the developer (i.e., the computer-map system designer), a misunderstanding by the developer can result as to what is desired by the user and as to how the eventual system is to satisfy this desire. Lack of communication in the other direction can cause user misunderstanding of computer mappings which in turn might result in its rejection.

A study of potential users of computer-drawn maps, conducted in conjunction with the New Haven Census Use Study, indicates that this rejection hypothesis is not farfetched. Persons tended, almost instinctively, to dichotomize when classifying maps. Whether the categories were "internal maps versus external maps", "maps for analysis versus maps for display", etc., the dichotomy involved the extremes of maps to be looked at and admired and those that were to be worked with and dirtied.

The distinction is important. Maps that are to be admired must be pleasing to the eye and easy to interpret. Thus the stress is on precision and clarity and on the immediate visual impact of the map — qualities lacking in most computer maps produced to date. But past maps used in urban studies have primarily been in this "to be admired" class — maps that are used in reports or public displays. In the few cases where analysis was aided by maps, the limitations of hand drawn maps placed too much of a constraint on the analysis for it to be of much use.

This situation is being changed, partly because the urban analyst is beginning to see himself as an interactive device in an urban system. He needs new tools — computer mapping being one — to aid him in functioning properly. But the change is slow; most analysts still use maps in the traditional ways and most react to computer drawn maps in terms of appropriateness as display devices.

"The planning fraternity is unable to appreciate the value of maps as research tools or as instruments to learn from rather than teach with."[5]

But systems analysis techniques, long thought to be of limited value for application outside the hard sciences, are beginning to be considered by the urban analyst. The nature of these techniques requires a more comprehensive planning with fuller consideration of alternatives and consequences. This requires much more evaluation at intermediate study points; it requires the testing of imaginative hypotheses of urban change; it requires real public interaction in the total process. It calls for acceptance of the fact that improvement of the urban system is a never ending cycle of implementation, evaluation, and revision. It calls for the use of the most advanced tools available in the most efficient manner.

Urban Information Systems

Great masses of data will be required to make computer mapping for urban planners possible. It is generally acknowledged that the most formidable hurdle in the development of a workable model is the gathering of the kind of data required to calibrate and operate the model. However, such data availability is not the only problem in this regard; oftentimes data exist, in some form, somewhere, waiting to be used. Knowledge of data accessibility is thus a large problem. The traditional approaches to data organization still in use today inherently result in an uncoordinated data base. Existing data sources have been compiled using different areal units, collected at different times for different time periods, and utilizing different measurement approaches for different levels of aggregation. And, because of a lack of interagency cooperation — or, for that matter, the existence of interagency hostility — data may be "unavailable" even when found.

The information environment of a city can be ordered. In fact this is what the urban information system concept is all about.[6] More and more cities are embarking on programs that could lead to a better organized and managed information environment. HUD has acknowledged the importance of these programs through the formation of Urban Systems Advisory Council (USAC) and the awarding of several research grants for the development of such systems.

Geographic Identification

One necessarily prominent feature in the development of such information systems is the creation of a logical means to manipulate data by geographic area. Most methods used to date may be classed as "name methods"; they merely serve to differentiate between areas without providing additional information. Recent research has spurred the creation of "locational methods" of geographic identification which can provide detail as to the specific location in space of each area, proximity to other areas, distances, etc.

The Bureau of the Census is responsible for much of this kind of work. The Nineteenth Decennial Census of Population and Housing, recently taken, was largely a mail census. To make it possible, an Address Coding Guide (ACG) was required for all metropolitan areas. Initially consisting of assignments of address locations to block faces, ACG could provide a base for a geocoding system. "However, several weaknesses in the ACG-based system led to the proposal of an experimental mapping data base."[7] The resultant DIME (Dual Independent Map Encoding) file developed by the New Haven Census Use Study, can provide, in its most extensive form, inputs to facilitate preparation of a geographic base file. The experiences of the study indicate that a DIME-based system satisfies the input requirements of most established computer-mapping routines.[8]

The development of a geographic base file, whether it be based on DIME or any other system,[9] is itself an aid in the visualization of urban structure. For example, the DIME file has been described as nothing more than a machine-readable map — a modernistic street guide, if you will. The availability of DIME and the increased use of computer terminals imply that someday, from a lonely street corner in a confusing metropolis, a stranger will be able to punch an address and be given visual instructions in the form of a map as to the best method of proceeding to it.

Computer Mapping Systems

A complete discussion of the state of the art of computer mapping is out of the question in the space allowed here. This section will attempt to provide a briefing on the characteristics of systems available for use today. With two exceptions, mapping systems known to the author utilize line printers, mechanical plotters, or electronic plotters as output devices.

The Line Printer. The great majority of computer maps have been, thus far, produced on the line printer. Basically, the printer prints "typewriter-like characters on standard 11 × 15-inch computer output paper."[10] The device is convenient; if a computer is available a line printer invariably will be available. Maps can be produced on the line printer, in quantity, very inexpensively and the printing process is rather quick. However, the line printer was not designed to produce map output and consequently there are inconveniences to be circumvented. Continuous lines cannot be drawn — printed characters must be used to approximate line drawings. Lines other than horizontal or vertical must be made in a step-like fashion. It is, therefore, impossible to display boundaries or specific locations with any degree of precision. Fortunately most urban analytic applications do not require precision and this drawback is not critical.

SYMAP. The best known and most widely used line-printer computer-mapping package — SYMAP, for *S*ynagraphic *MAP*ping *P*rogram — was developed in 1963 by Howard Fisher at Northwestern University. Fisher later established the Laboratory for Computer Graphics at Harvard. The Laboratory devotes much of its energies to the maintenance and improvement of SYMAP.

The latest revision of SYMAP offers three basic formats for output, with some 35 options available (i.e. map scale, data levels, external information to be printed, etc.). Up to ten levels of shading can be provided by superimposing two or more characters. The three output options are described below.

Contour. "The contour (or isoline) map consists of closed curves . . . which connect all points havint the same numeric value . . . Contour lines emerge . . . at selected levels . . . determined from the scale of the map and the range of the data . . . Between . . . lines a continuous variation is assumed. Therefore the use of contour lines should be restricted to the representation of continuous information . . . "[11] (See Figure 12-1.)

Conformant. "The conformant (or choropleth) map is best suited for data, either qualitative or quantitative, whose areal limits are of significance and whose representation as a continuous surface is inappropriate. Each data zone is enclosed by a boundary "conformant" to some predefined spatial unit. The entire spatial unit is. . . (assigned) the same value and symbolism is assigned according to its numeric class. Local variation of data within the boundary will not be apparent. . . "[12] (See Figure 12-2.)

Proximal. On a proximal map "the spatial units are defined by nearest neighbor methods from *point* information. Each character location on the output map is assigned the value of the data point nearest to it. Boundaries are assumed along the line where the values change and the conformant mapping is applied."[13] (See Figure 12-3.)

Interpretation of SYMAP output should be cautious. The map output can only show overall patterns, and the constraints imposed by the areal set and by character printer may actually distort these patterns. Thus the maps must not be viewed as precise representations of the data. The output itself may not be readily interpreted by persons unfamiliar with SYMAP or with the areas mapped. This is especially true for the contour option since this type of map has rarely been used in urban analysis. The maps are also unsuitable for display purposes unless additional cosmetics provide clear details of what has been mapped. However, even with these constraints, SYMAP output is very useful for analysis.

There are innumerable mapping programs with output very similar to SYMAP and some, indeed, are direct outgrowths.[14] These have been written to satisfy the requirements of specific applications, to conform to the availability

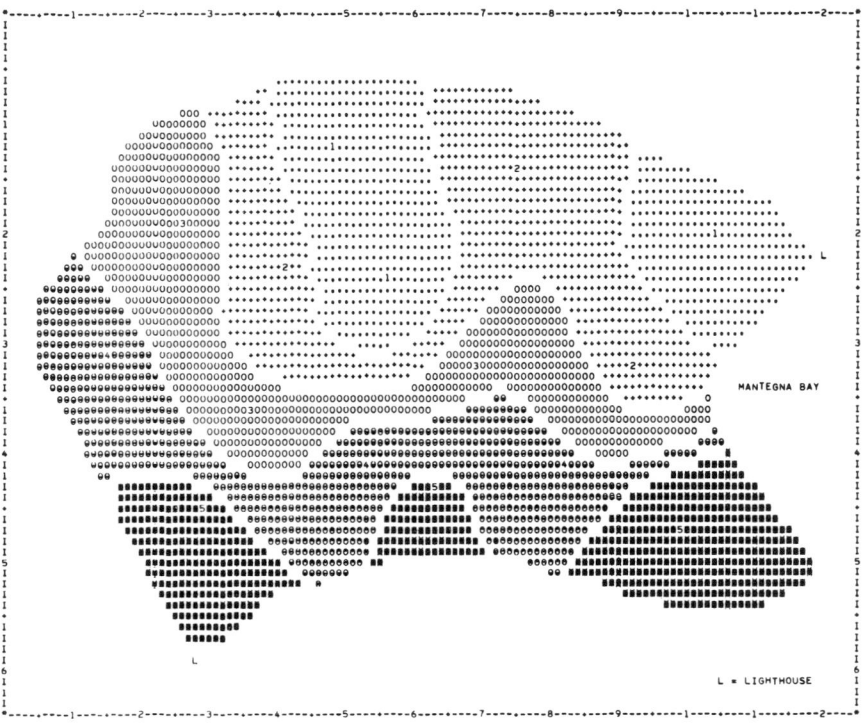

Figure 12-1. Map Generated Using SYMAP (Contour Option) on a Line Printer Using a CDC 6400 Computer. Source: Battelle-Columbus

of computer hardware (SYMAP was written for the IBM 7090 and has been made operational on the CDC 6400 and the IBM 360 series — many groups do not have access to large machines as these), and to satisfy individual egos. Since SYMAP is fairly representative of the outputs of these systems, they will not be described here. (See Figure 12-4.)

MAP 01. Developed by the Subdivision of Transportation Planning and Programming of the New York State Department of Public Works, MAP 01 was intended to be a poor man's mapping system. It originally ran on the IBM 1401 and appears to be the most inexpensive producer of maps. An updated version, MAP 360, is being developed by the Census Use Study for operation on the IBM 360/30.

"The program assigns data to a ½ inch × ½ inch grid on the printed output. Two basic output format options are available: value maps which print numeric values within the ½ inch-square grid cells and density maps which print from

COMPUTER MAPPING

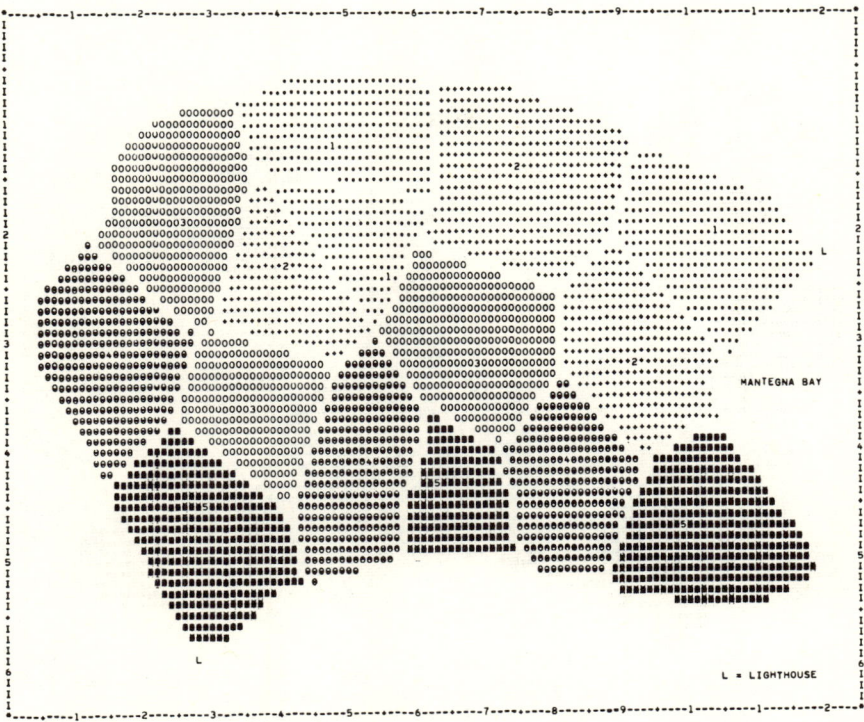

Figure 12-2. Map Generated Using SYMAP (Conformant Option) on a Line Printer Using a CDC 6400 Computer. Source: Battelle-Columbus

0 to 20 characters within the cells based on data values."[15] (See Figures 12-5 and 12-6.)

As with SYMAP, caution is required when presenting the output. The placement of the numbers or characters are dictated by the artificial grid rather than an actual areal unit. And the maps definitely require added information for legibility. At a minimum, a transparant overlay with important boundaries is required to provide the user with a frame of reference.

Use of the Typesetter to Produce Color Maps. The Urban Planning Directorate of the Ministry of Housing and Local Government in Britain has developed LINMAP (LINeprinter MAPping) which produces maps on the lineprinter. Although the output differs somewhat from SYMAP output the basics involved are similar and, as indicated previously, LINMAP will not be described here.

However, to satisfy complaints of planners concerning the poor quality of

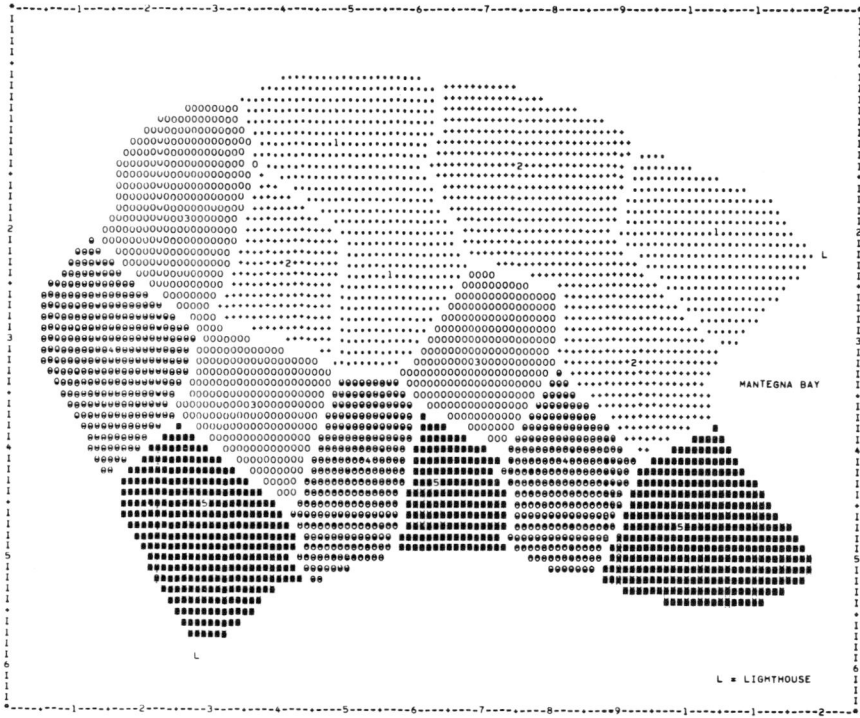

Figure 12-3. Map Generated Using SYMAP (Proximal Option) on a Line Printer Using a CDC 6400 Computer. Source: Battelle-Columbus

the black and white output of the lineprinter, the developers designed COLMAP (COLour MAPping), a "system which employs fast photo-electronic typesetting equipment to produce color separated masters of the thematic map for multicolor printing on conventional presses".[16] The program produces either a paper or magnetic tape read by the typesetter which writes the required character on photo-sensitive film paper. This is then developed and used to obtain lithoplates for final map printing.

Mechanical Plotters. Mechanical plotters are relatively slow map producers, but they are inexpensive if the hardware is available. There are two types — flatbed and drum. Flatbed plotters can produce maps in a variety of sizes ranging to 5 × 24 feet. A pen can be moved, usually in two directions, over a flat sheet of paper to produce the map. Lines in other directions can be produced in a stepwise manner by drawing very small lines alternating in the X and Y directions.

COMPUTER MAPPING

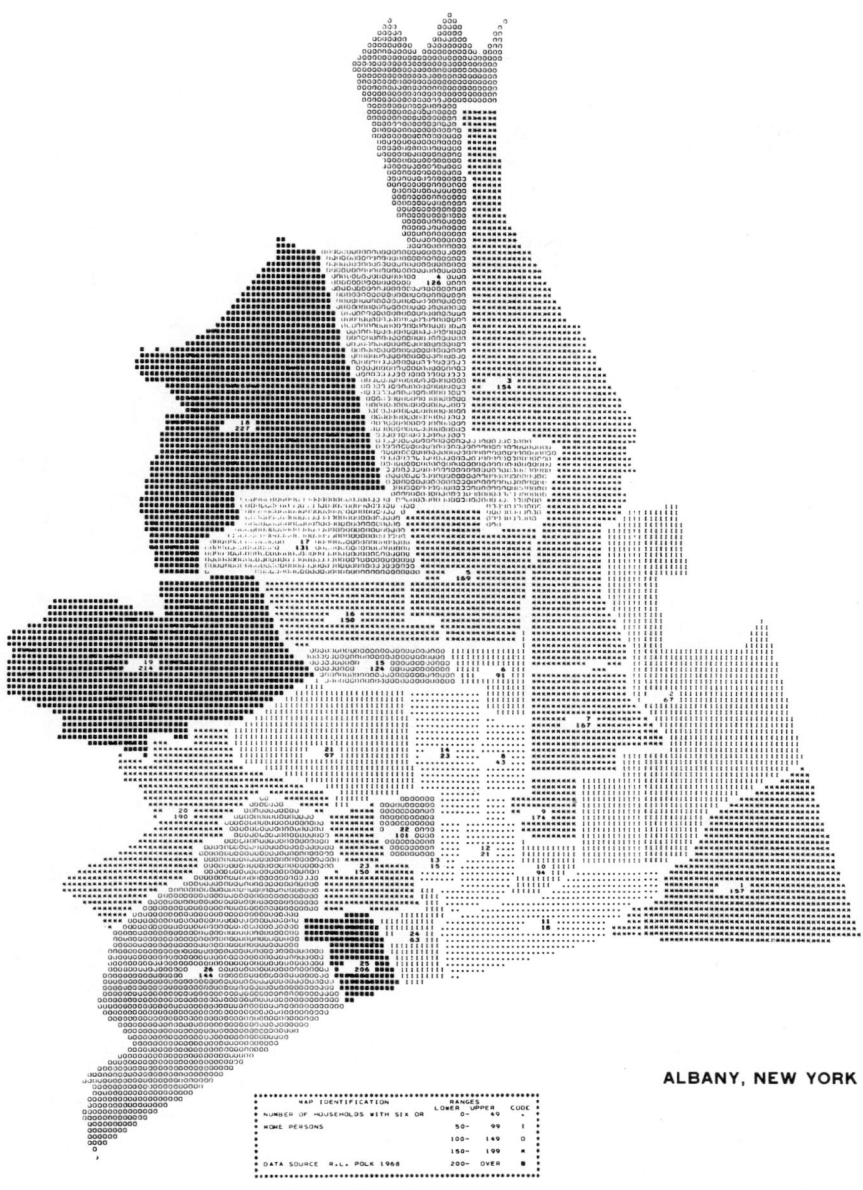

Figure 12-4. Map Generated by Special Polk Program on a Line Printer Using an IBM 360-30 Computer. Source: *Urban Information System*, R. L. Polk and Co.

Figure 12-5. Map Generated Using Map 01 (Numberical Display) on a Line Printer Using an IBM 1401 Computer. Source: New Haven Census Use Study.

On drum plotters the paper is rotated in a direction perpendicular to the motion of the pen. Plots can be of infinite dimension in one direction (actually limited to the length of a roll of paper) and are from 11 to 30 inches wide. Only a portion of the plot can be viewed at one time and in some cases a complete map can only be produced after a number of runs on the same sheet. (See Figure 12-7.)

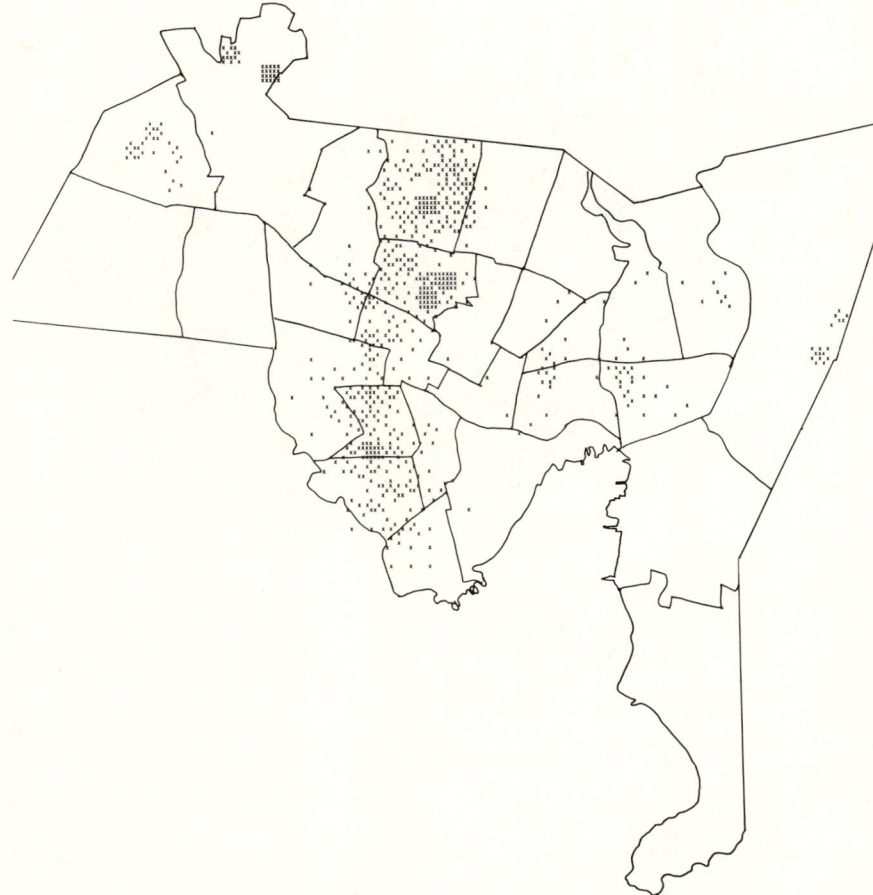

Figure 12-6. Map Generated Using Map 01 (Single Character Shading) — with Overlay — on a Line Printer Using an IBM 1401 Computer. Source: New Haven Census Use Study.

Plotter output is more appropriate for display than the output of the line printer. Plotters can produce better cosmetics, can be more precise and, in general, can provide a more polished map. But their slow speed is a distinct handicap for analysis maps. This would be especially apparent if they were required to produce shaded maps.

Electronic Plotters. Electronic plotters utilize cathode-ray tubes (CRT) for image generation, and the image may be photographed to produce hard copy.[17] CRT plotters are quite expensive but, if available, the cost to print maps is small.

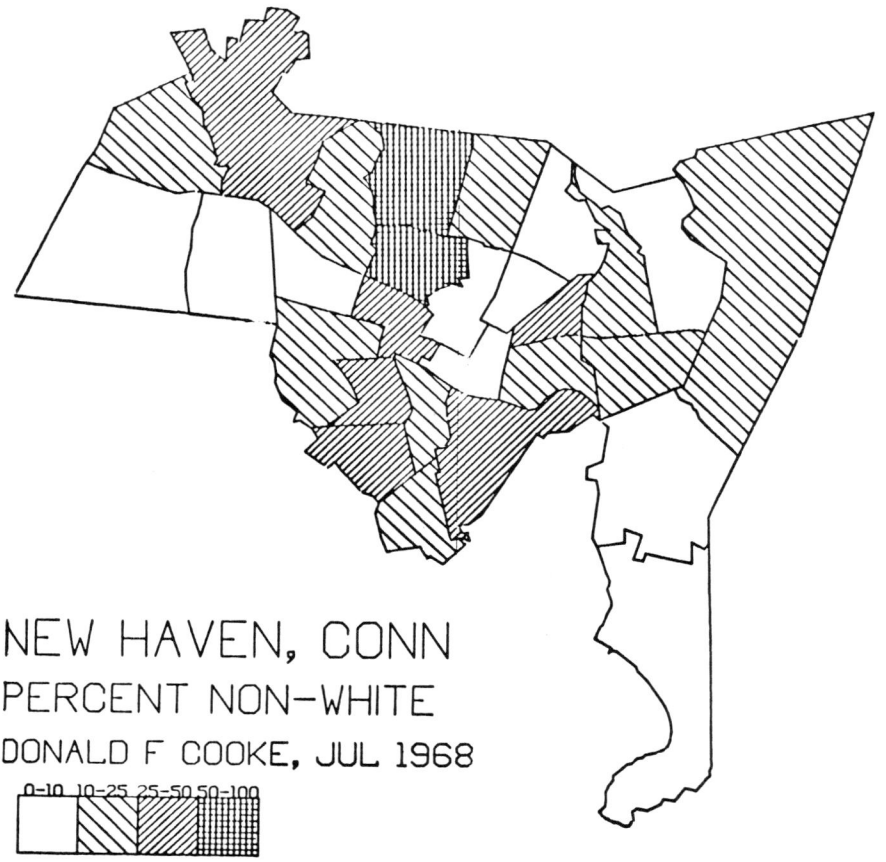

Figure 12-7. Map Generated on a Calcomp Plotter. Source: New Haven Census Use Study.

Maps may be produced quite rapidly on CRT's but the surface area available for drawing is small. The Census Use Study did find that, on a good CRT, fine line work is possible. However, if extreme detail or large size is required then CRT's are, with one exception, unsuitable. (See Figures 12-8 and 12-9.)

Geo Space Plotter. The exception – the plotter produced by Geo Space Corporation of Houston – consists of a camera device moving on a track perpendicular to the surface of a drum. The recording medium, either film or photosensitive paper, is wrapped around the drum and a lens system projects the image from the CRT onto the drum. The action of the camera is synchronized

COMPUTER MAPPING 219

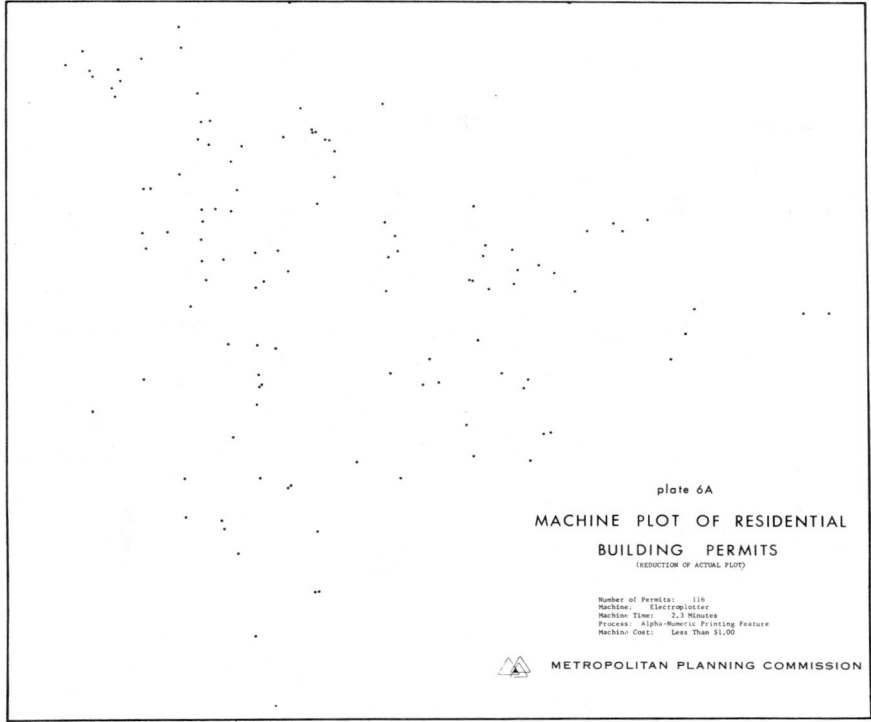

Figure 12-8. Plot Generated on a Benson-Lehner Electroplotter. Source: *Progress Towards a Metropolitan Databank*, Metropolitan Planning Commission, Portland, Oregon.

with the drum rotation and one strip of the map is plotted with each rotation.[18] (See Figures 12-10 and 12-11.)

The Geo Space plotter is versatile. It can draw anything a cartographer can draw. The final output is, as with mechanical plotters, in reasonably polished form, quite suitable for display, and relatively easy to read and interpret. In addition, the size constraint of most CRT plotters has been removed. However Geo Space maps are more expensive to produce than other computer drawn maps, even assuming the plotter is available (however, they do compete with hand drawn maps in terms of cost and quality). Furthermore there are ways to reduce the cost which are being investigated.

One of the present problems with the Geo Space plotters is the long delay time between image generation and the development of the film. The Census Use Study has found, though, that the use of a dry-copy device would shorten the delay to a few minutes and significantly reduce the cost per map.

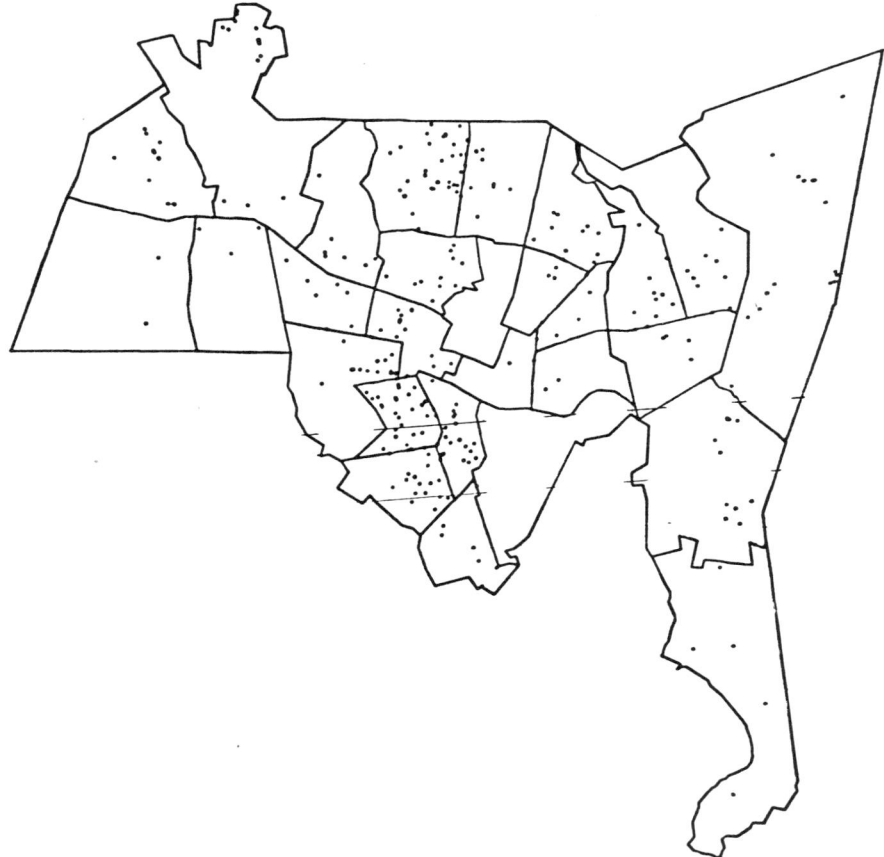

Figure 12-9. Map Generated on a Stromberg Carlson SC-4020 CRT Plotter. Source: New Haven Census Use Study.

Three-Dimensional Maps. There is no doubt that maps in three dimensions can be of greater value then maps in two dimensions. The Tri-State Transportation Commission in New York City even went to the trouble of preparing three-dimensional wooden models of much of their data. These models were extremely costly and were of limited utility for other than pedagogical purposes, especially since they were outdated soon after they were built. Computer mapping techniques provide more flexibility in the preparation of "3-D" maps.

SYMVU, developed by the Laboratory for Computer Graphics at Harvard, uses outputs available from SYMAP to provide oblique views of three dimensions printed on plotters (in two dimensional space, of course). Other programs have

COMPUTER MAPPING   221

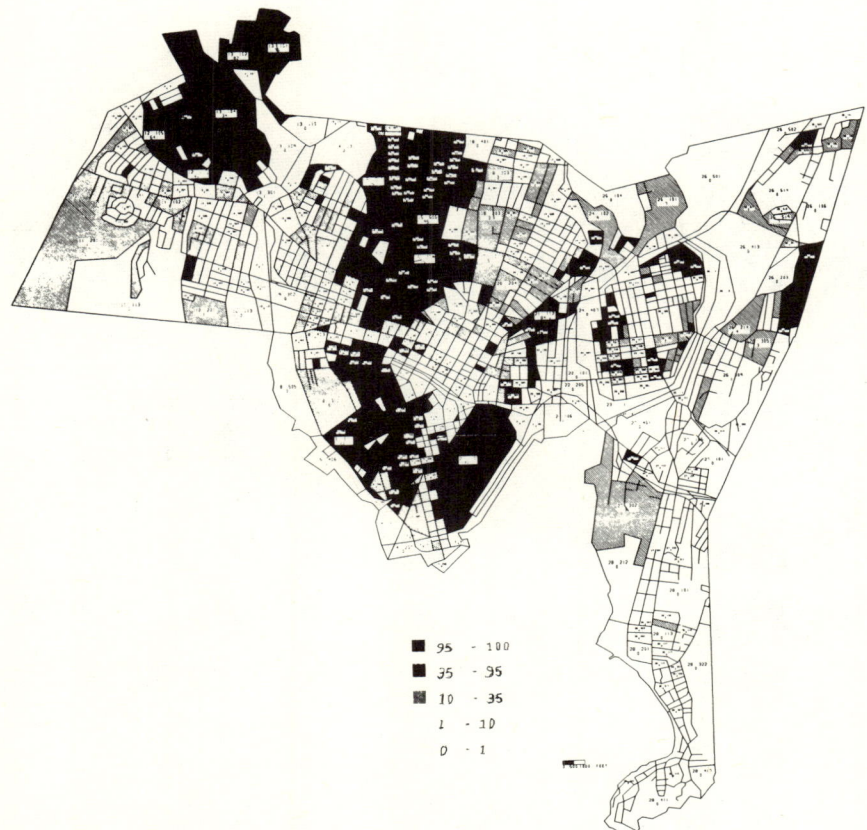

Figure 12-10. Map Generated on a Geo Space Plotter, First Type. Source: New Haven Census Use Study (prepared by IBM New York Scientific Center).

produced oblique views of block type maps on CRT PLOTTERS. The major problem in developing these representations has been solved and almost any data can be depicted three dimensionally as an oblique view.

A unique three-dimensional plotter, developed by Spatial Data Systems, actually produces plots in three dimensions. Steel wire is fed to a plotting head which is automatically positioned by an X-Y mechanism under tape control. The wire is driven through a plotting board in the Z dimension and cut off when it reaches the proper height. Large numbers of wires can produce very well defined surface areas. Output is expensive in comparison with two dimensional output.

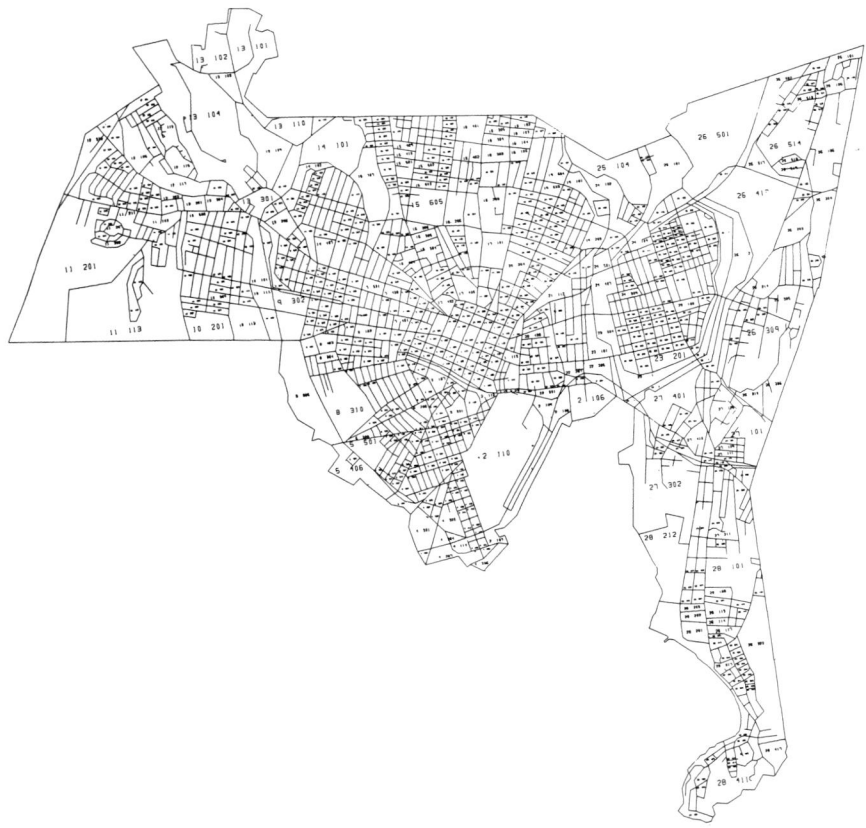

Figure 12-11. Map Generated on a Geo Space Plotter, Second Type. Source: New Haven Census Use Study (prepared by IBM New York Scientific Center).

Real-Time Potential. The already proven capability of on-line interaction provided by computer-operated CRT's presents a number of exciting alternatives to the urban analyst. This capability has already been used on numerous occasions to create interactive man-machine design situations.[19] However maps have not been used in this manner; the content of maps produced by the already described systems have been specified beforehand. This neglect is puzzling because of the obvious benefits offered by such interactive systems using maps. With the given availability of proven interactive languages and the experimentation with map output using CRT's it seems certain that this oversight will be corrected in time.

Example of Use of Advanced Computer-Mapping Systems. It is appropriate to provide here an example of the potential use of advanced computer-mapping systems. Consider the problem of creating a series of "neighborhood units" (or, for that matter, any other areal units) within a city. Research into urban behavior has not been structured in the framework of scientific information. There are numerous manifestations of this fact, one of which is the general inability to duplicate studies in an effort to check their reliability or to extend their results. One reason for this, among many, is the apparent randomness in choosing areal units for a study. But, for our research to provide meaningful results, "the geographic area used as the frame for study or as the specific subject of the study approximates in its spacial extensions some functional . . . entity . . ."[20] Further, for practical planning purposes, we find that grandiose city master plans have little or no relevance, and that planning must proceed at the neighborhood level. The Model Cities Program, in its undiluted form, indicated Federal Government awareness of this fact. So now the methodology of forming such units must be considered.

Much work on the subject has been done, with varying approaches. Some approaches have tried to form homogeneous social areas based on predetermined or otherwise developed criteria. Others have tried to develop methods to visually determine neighborhood areas. Still others have tried to determine what is perceived to be a neighborhood unit. These approaches have involved the use of many statistical techniques ranging from principal-components analysis to numerical taxonomy.

Results of these efforts might best be communicated and compared visually. The cited criteria for computer mapping indicate that the technique is appropriate for use here. It is probable that a large number of maps for given areas would be involved; that accuracy, but not precision, is important; that uniform map appearance is desirable; that large amounts of data will be mapped; etc.

Comparisons of the different results would indicate major discrepancies and, perhaps, how these might be overcome. Or they might show which areas could not, in any sense, be part of functional neighborhoods. Similarly, those areas which consistently stand out can be inferred to be the most cohesive and meaningful neighborhood areas. In any case, the functional differences in the various approaches are more likely to stand out. This application seems ideal for computer mapping; it will be "used as an analytical tool during the conduct of the study."[21]

The on-line capability of the computer-operated CRT could be an aid in the formation of areal units. A priori notions, either of the researchers or of someone else (i.e., census tracts) can be tested to get an initial set of areas. These may be quantitatively described with parameters developed for the study. Means and variances of the individual parameters and the functions derived from them may be used as measures of the relative homogeneity within areas and of the level of difference between areas. The visual implications of spatial patterns of variance might be clearer than any meaning the figures themselves could transmit.

Results obtained by this process can be used to make immediate map changes, and their effects may be examined. This iterative process may be repeated until satisfactory areas are obtained. It is realized that, if criteria can be predeveloped, this process can be worked out without man-machine interaction. However this would not allow the researcher to alter criteria if he sees fit; it would not allow him to view the process of getting to the final areas; and it would not allow him to see the spatial implications of the data and its attributes.

There are many parallel examples where an analysis can be completed without graphic assistance but where maps would be of assistance and could increase the value of the results, and where interaction with the mapping-analysis process could further add to an understanding of the basic interactions involved.

In the real world, the operations of various organizations lend themselves to on-line map assistance. Police departments, for example, would like to know the location of all members of the force, patrol cars, etc., at all times. A periodic check-in — or punch-in, if you will — could enable a CRT plotter to keep track of and display such imformation for immediate reference. Periodic crime reports could be mapped and used to spot the spatial patterns (or the lack thereof) of crime, and through comparison with patterns of surveillance (i.e., location of personnel) determine areas with insufficient coverage.

Summary

The tools needed to make computer mapping a valuable device in the analysis of urban systems are readily available. And, in fact, the computer-mapping systems already operable do provide useful inputs to the study of urban structure. However, they do not live up their full potential primarily because there is relatively little communication between the developers of the tool and the potential users of it. This is most unfortunate as there are cases which show that relatively minor changes in computer map output can markedly increase output value for particular uses and the prospects for acceptance by the user community. This is especially true for maps that are primarily display-type maps. There is definitely a lack of ordered knowledge on how persons relate to spatial patterns, and, consequently, how individual perception processes can be used to provide more understandable maps. There is a need for emphasis in this direction; a map of urban structure is worthless if no one understands what it means.

It is impossible to discuss computer mapping per se without moving into some very broad and fundamental systems issues. Computer mapping can be viewed as a subsystem of a geographic identification system which, in turn, is a subsystem of a total urban information system. Discussion of the smaller subsystem cannot be meaningful if it is not placed in its proper context within these systems of systems. Urban structure itself can be placed further up in this hierarchy. Realization of the existence of this hierarchy will aid in the ordering of knowledge within and between levels of the hierarchy and will aid in an understanding of the computer mapping of urban structure.

Notes

1. McManus, Richard W., "Maps a la Computer", *The Christian Science Monitor,* p. 13 (March 11, 1970).
2. *Ibid.*
3. "A Report on the Feasibility of Using Computer Mapping Techniques as an Aid in the Processing of Mortgage Insurance Applications", Laboratory For Computer Graphics, Graduate School of Design, Harvard University, Cambridge, pp. 1–2.
4. Goldstein, Harold, Wertz, James, and Sweet, David, "Computer Mapping – A Tool For Urban Planners", Battelle Memorial Institute Urban Studies Working Paper, Columbus, pp. 1–2 (March 1969).
5. Letter from Caby C. Smith, U.S. Bureau of the Census, to Harold Goldstein, November 19, 1968.
6. Goldstein, Harold, "The Urban Information System: Some Concepts, Issues and Experiences", Battelle Memorial Institute Urban Studies Working Paper, Columbus (May 1968).
7. Cooke, Donald E., and Maxfield, William H., "The Development of a Geographic Base File and Its Uses For Mapping", in *Urban and Regional Systems For Social Programs,* papers from the Fifth Annual Conference of the Urban and Regional Information Systems Association, Garden City, p. 207 (Sept. 1967).
8. The experiences of the Census Use Study are documented. See especially Census Use Study Report No. 2, "Computer Mapping", August 1969 and Census Use Study Report No. 9, "Data Uses in Urban Planning," February 1970, U.S. Bureau of the Census, Washington, D.C.
9. Other geographic base systems lend themselves to computer mapping applications. For example, the Street Address Conversion System developed at the University of Washington's Urban Data Center was one of the first such systems. See Dial, Robert B., "Street Address Conversion System", *Planning 1965,* joint planning conference of the American Society of Planning Officials and the Planning Association of Canada, Toronto (April, 1965).
10. Census Use Study Report No. 9, "Data Uses in Urban Planning", *op. cit.,* p. 15.
11. Fisher, H.T., et al., "Reference Manual for Synagraphic Computer Mapping (SYMAP). Version V", Laboratory for Computer Graphics, Harvard University, Cambridge (June, 1968).
12. *Ibid.*
13. *Ibid.*

14. For example, R.L. Polk and Company of Detroit, Barton–Aschman and Associates of Chicago, The Hudson River Valley Authority, CONSAD Research Corporation of Pittsburgh, The Ministry of Housing and Local Government of Britain, and others have developed programs with outputs similar to those of SYMAP.
15. Census Use Study Report No. 2, "Computer Mapping," *op. cit.,* p. 6.
16. Gaits, G. M., "Thematic Mapping by Computer", reprinted from the Journal of the British Cartographic Society, p. 9 (June, 1969).
17. "Hard" copy refers to permanent output, as opposed to "soft" output.
18. For further reference to the Geo Space plotter see Loomis, R.G. and Lorenzo, J.J., "Experiments in Mapping With a Geo Space Plotter", in *Urban and Regional Information Systems for Social Programs,* op. cit., pp. 219–223.
19. For example see Negroponte, Nicholes, "Urban Five: An On–Line Urban Design Partner", presented at the First Annual International Conference of the Design Methods Group, Cambridge, Massachusetts (June, 1968), and Cameron, Scott H., Ewing, Duncan, and Liveright, Michael, "DIALOG: A Conversational Programming System With a Graphical Orientation, IIT Research Institute, Technical Note No. 109 (September 1966).
20. Rosenberg, Harry M., "An Approach to the Functional Aggregation of Blacks For Social Area Analysis", mimeo paper (December, 1968).
21. "A Report on the Feasibility of Using Computer Mapping Techniques as an Aid in the Processing of Mortgage Insurance Applications", *op. cit.,* p. 1.

Appendix A

Models of Urban Structure —
Annotated Bibliography

Alonso, W., *Location and Land-Use Towards a General Theory of Land Rent*, Harvard University Press, Cambridge, Massachusetts (1964). One of the few basic theoretical statements of the urban land-use mechanisms with respect to households and businesses. The trade-off between accessibility and commuting and business costs is emphasized. The concept of "bid-rent" functions is developed.

Alonso, W., "The Quality of Data and the Choice and Design of Predictive Models," Highway Research Board Special Report, No. 97, Highway Research Board, Washington, D.C., pp. 178-192 (1968). One of the few discussions of data quality and measurement error as they affect urban development predictions. Concludes that urban models should avoid intercorrelated variables, should *add* where possible and if this is not possible multiply or divide, should avoid taking differences and powers, and should avoid chain structures.

Berry, Brian J. L., "The Retail Component of the Urban Model," *Journal of the American Institute of Planners,* Vol. 31, No. 2, pp. 150-155 (May, 1965). A discussion of some approaches to modeling retail systems. A series of regression equations are used to relate the number of retail establishments and changes in retail and service establishments to population and income variables. Discusses a factor analysis of variables relating to business centers and their market areas. Some relationships to central place theory are discussed.

Boyce, D. E., "Communication in the Field of Urban Development Models," Highway Research Board Special Report, No. 97, Highway Research Board, Washington, D.C., pp. 239-250 (1968). A discussion of the problems of communication among researchers and users with particular emphasis on the publications that serve these audiences.

Boyce, D. E. and R. W. Cote, "Verification of Land-Use Forecasting Models: Procedures and Data Requirements," *Highway Research Record*, No. 126, pp. 60-65 (1966). Emphasizes the limitations of existing land-use models in that confidence statements as the forecast variables are not available. Suggests use of Monte Carlo methods to obtain sampling distributions for non-statistical forecast variates; for statistical models standard confidence intervals can be derived. Bayesian procedures are suggested as being relevant also in the second context. Questions of data requirements for model verification are noted.

Boyce, D. E. and N. D. Day, *Metropolitan Plan Evaluation Methodology* (Inst. for Environmental Studies, University of Pennsylvania, 1969).

Brand, D., B. Barber, and J. Jacobs, "Techniques for Relating Transportation Improvements and Urban Development Patterns," *Highway Research Record*, No. 207, pp. 53-57 (1967). An overview of four main phases of the Boston EMPIRIC study. First, the formulations of the simultaneous linear regression equations of the model are discussed. The distinction between *policy* and *non-policy* variables is noted. Second, estimation of the equations is discussed with emphasis on the results obtained for the most disaggregated version (626 traffic zones). Third, some generalized land-use forecasting equations reflecting knowledge already gained from use of the model are reviewed. Finally, some results of forecasting with the model are given.

Carlson, E. D., "Operational Aspects of a Probabilistic Model for Residential Growth," Environmental Policies and Urban Development Thesis Series, No. 10, Center for Urban and Regional Studies, University of North Carolina, Chapel Hill, 89 pp. (1968). A basic review of the nature of the UNC simulation model and a report on the results of a questionnaire survey of U. S. planning agencies concerning their potential use of the model. Problems of computer program adaptation and data availability are discussed and useful guidelines are presented.

Chapin, F. S., "Activity Systems as a Source of Inputs for Land-Use Models," Highway Research Board Special Report, No. 97, Highway Research Board, Washington, D.C., pp. 77-101 (1968). A review of the North Carolina work on the analysis of daily routines of land-users, of policies of firms or institutions, and of preferences of individuals or households which govern location behavior. Specific emphasis is placed on household activity systems.

Chapin, F. Stuart, Jr., "A Model for Simulating Residential Development," *Journal of the American Institute of Planners*, Vol. 31, No. 2, pp. 120-125 (May, 1965). This article describes the development of a simulation model of the "residential development process." The emphasis is upon the effects of consumer activity patterns in influencing household locational decisions. This model was developed at the Center for Urban and Regional Studies at the University of North Carolina.

Chapin, F. Stuart, Jr. and Shirley F. Weiss, "Some Input Refinements for a Residential Model," Urban Studies Monograph, Institute for Research in Social Science, University of North Carolina, Chapel Hill (1965). This monograph is a companion publication to the two discussed in Lieser's review, No. 23, although this was published about a year later. This discusses refinements which were made to input data for a second series of tests using the residential model described in review No. 23.

Crecine, J. P., "TOMM (Time Oriented Metropolitan Model)," CRP Technical Bulletin, No. 6, Community Renewal Program, Pittsburgh Department of City Planning, 18 pp. (1964). A modification of Lowry's model to allow for (1) a marginal allocation model that allows only a portion of the establishments and households to move in a certain time period, (2) differentiation of households by income, housing characteristics, and social attributes, and (3) the desire to limit the simulation study to locational characteristics within the City's boundaries. Simulation is used to obtain solutions to difference equations.

Deutschman, H. D. and N. L. Jaschik, "Income and Related Transportation and Land-Use Planning Implications," *Highway Research Record*, No. 240, pp. 52–65 (1968). Discusses relationship of household income to housing market, auto ownership, auto and transit trip generation and time and distance separation of residence and worksite.

Donnelly, Thomas G., F. Stuart Chapin, Jr., and Shirley F. Weiss, "A Probabilistic Model for Residential Growth," *Urban Studies Monograph*, Center for Urban and Regional Studies, University of North Carolina, Chapel Hill (1964). Also, see the monograph *Factors Influencing Land Development*, by Chapin and Weiss, same publisher, in 1962. The two monographs combined describe a five-year research effort to develop a logical mathematical structure for predicting the future pattern of residential development in urban areas. Highly aggregative, stressing only "urban development" *per se*. Cells have attractiveness measures computed for them; Monte Carlo simulation.

Duke, R. D., Gaming-Simulation in Urban Research, East Lansing: Institute for Community Development and Services, MSU, 72 pp. (1964). A detailed discussion of the first metropolis game-simulation, a land simulation. At each cycle, simultaneous decisions are required on two-levels – the first is private and involves personal gain on the part of the developer; the second is public and focuses on a capital improvement program. This work superceded by M.E.T.R.O. project (Duke, 1966).

Duke, R. D., "The M.E.T.R.O. Urban Game-Simulation: An Experiment in In-Service Training," *Proceedings Fourth Annual Conference on Urban Planning Information Systems and Programs*, Berkeley: Department of City and Regional Planning, pp. 142–154 (1966). Discusses the metro game-simulation model, a pedagogic device for decision makers concerned with aspects of the growth of the city. Involves teams of *governmental units* and *professional associations groups* and decisions have to be made on budgets, issues and policies.

Ellis, R. H., *A Behavioral Residential Location Model*, Research Report, The Transportation Center, Northwestern University 159 pp. (1966). A M.Sc. thesis which includes a good review of existing land-use models. Develops a simulation model of urban residential development which assumes that the choice of location is a basically rational decision related to the socio-economic characteristics of the household. The model involves two steps. First, the environment selected by a household with given socio-economic characteristics is selected. Then a search process is utilized to select one such site as the new home for the family. Multivariate analysis of Tucson data are used to establish environmental and household vectors and to achieve discriminations.

Ellis, Raymond H., "Modeling of Household Location: A Statistical Approach," *Highway Research Record*, No. 207, pp. 42-52 (1967). Goal is to simulate the behavior of households in choosing their homes. A two-phase model is proposed. In the first phase, the housing preferences of the locating family are determined. In the second phase, the search process by which the family picks a location having these characteristics is simulated. Multivariate statistical techniques are employed in the partial calibration of the model with respect to data for Tucson, Arizona.

Feldt, A. G., "The Cornell Land-Use Game," *Miscellaneous Papers*, No. 3, Cornell University: Center for Housing and Environmental Studies (1965).

Feldt, A. G., "Current Developments in Heuristic Gaming at Cornell University," *Proceedings Fourth Annual Conference on Urban Planning and Information Systems and Programs*, pp. 160-167 (1966). An overview of the Cornell Land-Use Game with emphasis on experience in running the game to date. Application to Syracuse situation discussed and related problems reviewed.

Fidler, J., "Commercial Activity Location Model," *Highway Research Record*, No. 207, pp. 68-84 (1967). Paper describes simulation model based on Niagara Frontier Transportation Study. A gravity model assigns person-trip origins (for commercial demand) to commercial destinations. Commercial centers are then located in accord with this assignment, forecasting of future demand for commercial goods allows for prediction of new center locations.

Fleet, C. R. and S. R. Robertson, "Trip Generation in the Transportation Planning Process," *Highway Research Record*, No. 240, pp. 11-31 (1968). Includes a provocative discussion of the effects of areal aggregation of data on estimation of trip generation. Problems of ecological correlation and fallacies related to behavioral inferences are recognized. The desirability of analysis at the household level is noted. Questions of sampling variations and related confidence levels are discussed.

Forrester, J. W., *Urban Dynamics*, The M.I.T. Press, Cambridge, Massachusetts, 285 pp. (1969). A complex simulation of an urban complex drawing upon the author's studies of industrial dynamics. There are two parts to the study; the first simulated the growth of an area over 250 years up to a state of stagnation and decay; the second considers the effects of different policies on this depressed complex. The first simulation involves 9 system levels (new enterprise, mature business, declining industry, premium housing, worker housing, underemployed housing, managerial-professional, labor, underemployed) and 22 flow rates (e.g., labor arrivals, construction). The second considers 11 urban management programs (e.g., underemployed job program) and 17 different systems variables (e.g., labor, housing). The systems simulation uses the MIT Dynamic II compiler.

Garin, R. A. (Comment by A. Rogers), "A Matrix Formulation of the Lowry Model for Intrametropolitan Activity Allocation," *Journal of the American Institute of Planners*, Vol. 32, pp. 361-366 (November, 1966). In two notes, the first by Garin and the second by A. Rogers, a matrix algebra formulation of Lowry's model is presented. Rogers suggests a dynamic formulation of the model.

Garrison, W. L., "Difficult Decisions in Land Use Model Construction," *Highway Research Record*, No. 126, pp. 17-23 (1966). Elaborates on issues related to decisions about the inclusion of behavioral notions in models, and decisions concerning the formal structure of models (questions of aggregation and types of relationships).

Gruen, C., "The Role of Models in Setting Values," *Proceedings Fourth Annual Conference on Urban Planning Information Systems and Programs*, pp. 111-118 (1966). Essay on role of urban models in setting the values which determine decision makers' judgments. Stresses dangers of "dictators" using models to impose their values on society and need to educate public on role of models. Notes also that plans should be evaluated by several and not just one model.

Hadfield, S. M. and J. D. Orzeske, "A Sampling Technique for Updating a Quantitative Land Use Inventory," *Highway Research Record*, No. 126, pp. 79-87 (1966). Discusses use of stratified, systematic unaligned point sampling on aerial photographs to estimate proportions of various land-uses within an area. Accuracy tests supported the use of the technique.

Hamburg, J. R., R. L. Creighton, and R. S. Scott, "Evaluation of Land Use Patterns," Highway Research Board Special Report, No. 97, Highway Research Board, Washington, D.C., pp. 231-238 (1968). A general discussion of some issues related to plan evaluation. The authors suggest ten possible goals for urban living and review some strategies for plan evaluation.

Hansen, W. G., "How Accessibility Shapes Land Use," *Journal of the American Institute of Planners*, Vol. 25, No. 2, pp. 73-76 (1959). Hypothetical accessibility model distributes future residential development to metropolitan zones. Accessibility is defined and discussed and empirical tests are outlined. Equations, parameters and an illustration are given.

Hansen, W. G., "Land Use Forecasting for Transportation Planning," *Highway Research Bulletin*, No. 253, pp. 145-151 (1960).

Harris, B., "Computers and Urban Planning," *Journal of Socio-Economic Planning* (1967).

Harris, B., "Conference Summary and Recommendations," Highway Research Board Special Report, No. 97, Highway Research Board, Washington, D.C., pp. 3-17 (1968). An overview of the Dartmouth conference with emphasis on the problems of building and operationalizing models. There is a summary of the conference themes and the presentation of the conference recommendations. These fall into four categories — those concerned with the institutional setting for model building and analysis, those on questions of data availability, those on broad scale emphases in model building which appear feasible now, and finally, those on longer term, more general issues.

Harris, B., *et al.*, "Construction of Models" (Panel discussion), Highway Research Board Special Report, No. 97, Highway Research Board, Washington, D.C., pp. 193-216 (1968). A broad discussion of problems related to urban models development. Includes discussions of philosophical objects, design considerations, data requirements, and nonresidential models.

Harris, Britton, "How to Succeed With Computers Without Really Trying," *Journal of the American Institute of Planners*, Vol. 33, No. 1, American Institute of Planners, pp. 11-17 (June, 1967). Harris discusses ways of easing the inevitable (his word) transition to the use of computer methods in local planning offices. This is a very general, nontechnical discussion.

Harris, Britton, "Inventing the Future Metropolis," *Shaping an Urban Future: Essays in Memory of Catherine Bauer Wurster*, M.I.T. Press Cambridge, Massachusetts, pp. 179-203 (1969). An essay discussing some critical issues confronting the planning process. Focuses on problems of the time scale of planning, the appropriate vehicles for invention, configurational planning, and the resolution of the conflict between humanism and science in planning.

Harris, Britton, "The Limits of Science and Humanism in Planning," *Journal of the American Institute of Planners*, Vol. 33, No. 5, pp. 324-335 (September, 1967). This is a somewhat rambling and philosophical article, part of which consists of a very general discussion of the capabilities and limitations of the use of computers in planning. Technically, this is of marginal relevance, but it might make a good source of introductory comments.

Harris, Britton, "New Tools for Planning," *Journal of the American Institute of Planners*, Vol. 31, No. 2, pp. 90-94 (May, 1965). An introduction to the collection of papers on urban development models contained in this issue. There is given a general discussion of the use of computers both for data processing and for simulation analysis of urban interrelated models. A preliminary discussion of the dimensions of models is outlined.

Harris, B., "Quantitative Models of Urban Development: Their Role in Metropolitan Policy Making," *Issues in Urban Economics*, H. S. Perloff and L. Wingo (eds.), Baltimore: The Johns Hopkins Press, pp. 363-412 (1968). An excellent overview of the dimensions of urban land-use modeling and specific models. Six basic dimensions are discussed, specifically "descriptive versus analytic", "holistic versus partial", "macro versus micro," "static versus dynamic," "deterministic versus probabilistic," and "simultaneous versus sequential." Then follows a review of models of retail trade, residential, manufacturing and other land-uses locations.

Harris, B., "Regional Growth Model Activity Distribution Sub-Model," P. J. Paper, No. 7, Philadelphia: Penn-Jersey Transportation Study, 12 pp. (1961). A discussion of the early P. J. thinking on the inputs required for the activities allocation sub-model.

Harris, B., "The Uses of Theory in the Simulation of Urban Phenomena," *Highway Research Record*, No. 126, Highway Research Board, Washington, D.C., pp. 1-16 (1966). A philosophical discussion of issues related to the role of theory and its relation to practice. Three criteria for useful theories are discussed: capacity for manipulation, fruitfulness, and economy. Other criteria such as realism and comprehensiveness are also discussed. Conclusions are drawn regarding future directions of research and some of the desirable characteristics of research establishments.

Harris, C. C., Jr., "A Stochastic Process Model of Residential Development," *Journal of Regional Science*, Vol. 8, No. 1, pp. 29-39 (1968). Attempt to handle the uncertainty of direction and timing of suburban growth in a model. The model developed is a semi-Markov process; there are units of land which move from undeveloped to developed states with certain transition probabilities, and there is a distribution function of the "wait" in one state before the transition to the other. An application to growth in the rural-urban fringe of Sacramento is outlined.

Hemmens, George C., "Experiments in Urban Form and Structure," *Highway Research Record*, No. 207, pp. 32-41 (1967). Proposes a simple model for examining the impact of changes in components of urban form (physical arrangement of residences, work places, etc.) on urban spatial structure (patterns formed by connection of these elements in daily activities of population). A linear programming model provides the allocation rule for evaluating urban form alternatives by two criteria: (1) efficiency of the alternatives in terms of minimal travel requirements (2) the equity of the alternatives in terms of locational advantage of residence locations.

Hemmens, G. C., "The Structure of Urban Activity Linkages," Urban Studies Research Monograph, Chapel Hill, North Carolina: Center for Urban and Regional Studies, U.N.C., 54 pp. (1966). A discussion which emphasizes the linkage patterns formed among urban activities by travel of persons. The third chapter considers land-use linkages.

Hemmens, G. C., "Survey of Planning Agency Experience With Urban Development Models, Data Processing, and Computers," Highway Research Board Special Report, No. 97, Highway Research Board, Washington, D.C. pp. 219-230 (1968). A report on a questionnaire survey of 34 major planning agencies. Emphasizes two major problems facing agencies — the lack of computer systems personnel, and the difficulties of communication between planners and programmers.

Hemmens, G. C. (ed.), "Urban Development Models," Highway Research Board Special Report, No. 97, Highway Research Board, Washington, D.C., 266 pp. (1968). The proceedings of the Dartmouth conference held from June 26-30, 1967. There are four major sections to the report. The first includes introductory statements, then follows a section on "Planning, Decision-Making and the Urban Development Process"; the third section is on "Design and Construction of Models," the final section is on the "Use of Models". Papers and discussions are included. See references by Harris, Zwick, Steger, Chapin, Leven, Lowry, Schneider, Alonso, Hemmens, Hamburg *et al.*, and Boyce.

Herbert, John D. and Benjamin H. Stevens, "A Model for the Distribution of Residential Activity in Urban Areas," *Journal of Regional Science*, Vol. 2, No. 2, Wharton School, University of Pennsylvania, pp. 21-36 (1960). This model was constructed as part of the Penn-Jersey Transportation Study. It was designed to distribute households to residential land in an optimal configuration. It is a linear programming solution, which maximizes aggregate rent-paying ability, subject to land availability and number of households constraints.

Hill, Donald M., "A Growth Allocation Model for the Boston Region," *Journal of the American Institute of Planners*, Vol. 31, No. 2, pp. 111-120 (May, 1965). A discussion of the EMPIRIC growth allocation model. The simultaneous multiple regression equations involving the changes in the subregional slaves of the located and locator variables are discussed. Calibration results are given the sensitivity of the model to variations in the length of the forecast periods and the size and number of subregions is discussed.

Hill, D. M. and D. Brand, "Methodology for Developing Activity Distribution Models by Linear Regression Analysis," *Highway Research Record*, No. 126, pp. 66-78 (1966). A good semi-technical discussion of several questions concerning linear regression analyses. Model design by linear equations involves consideration of the additive influences of independent variables and the linear influences of all variables. Identification of equation systems is discussed as are tests of model design. Several types of regression processes and factor analyses are reviewed.

Hill, D. M., D. Brand, and W. B. Hansen, "Prototype Development of Statistical Land-Use Prediction Model for Greater Boston Region," *Highway Research Record*, No. 114, pp. 51-70 (1965). Discusses the initial formulation of, and the different problems of calibration and sensitivity analysis performed with the EMPIRIC model for Boston.

Irwin, N. A. and D. Brand, "Planning and Forecasting Metropolitan Development," *Traffic Quarterly*, pp. 520-540 (October, 1965). A good review of the formulations and sensitivity analyses of the *EMPIRIC* and *POLIMETRIC* models developed for Boston. The first involves a set of simultaneous linear equations which predict changes in the subregional shapes of *located* variables. There were seven (including white collar population, blue collar population, retail and wholesale employment, manufacturing employment, other employment, total resident population, and total employment) on the basis of (1) changes in subregional shapes of all other located variables in subregions, (2) changes in subregional shares of selected locator variables in subregions, and (3) absolute value of subregional shares of other locator variables. The POLIMETRIC model involves a series of nonlinear differential equations which relate changes in the level of subregional activity to the existing level and the in-migrations and out-migrations of activities.

Isler, Morton L., "Selecting Data for Community Renewal Programming," *Journal of the American Institute of Planners*, Vol. 33, No. 2, pp. 66-77

(March, 1967). Isler is talking about "programming" in general rather than programming for computer analysis. He presents a "strategy for data selection", consisting of four key steps:
  (1) Anticipating the nature of key decisions
  (2) Identifying the underlying issues
  (3) Evolving an analytic capability
  (4) Developing a comprehensive program.

Jeffries, W. R. and E. C. Carter, "Simplified Techniques for Developing Transportation Plans," *Highway Research Record*, No. 240, pp. 66-87 (1968). A study of the socio-economic and land-use characteristics of small urban areas (under 200,000) that influence work trip generation with aim of forecasting future work trip generation. Empirical analysis of data on Lancaster, York, and Reading (Pa.), Hutchinson (Ks), Rock Hill (S.C.), and Sheboygan (Wisc.). Regression analyses of relationships between trip generation and land-use activity and intensity, employment and financial status, family size and other variables. Best single predictor is vehicle ownership.

Kaiser, E. J., "A Producer Model for Residential Growth", Urban Studies Monograph, Institute for Social Science Research, University of North Carolina, 77 pp. (1968). An attempt to model the decision making processes involved in the purchase, development and promotion of urban land projects.

Kilbridge, M. D., R. P. O'Block, and P. V. Teplitz, "A Conceptual Framework for Urban Planning Models," *Management Science*, Vol. 15, No. 6, pp. B-246-B-266 (1969). Reviews urban planning models with respect to four basic characteristics — subject, function, theory, and method. The subjects may be land use, transportation, population, and economic activity. Functions include projection, allocation, and derivation. As regards theory, models are classified into behavior or choice models, and macro-analytic growth forces or index models. The methods considered include econometric forms, mathematical programming, and simulation.

Lakshmanan, T. R. and Walter G. Hansen, "A Retail Market Potential Model," *Journal of the American Institute of Planners*, Vol. 31, No. 2, pp. 134-143 (May, 1965). This computerized model was designed to test possible equilibrium distributions for large retail trade centers included in the Metrotown Plan for Baltimore. Possible sites for centers are selected on "general planning grounds" and tested for feasibility and "balance," where balance is defined in terms of the volume of business attracted to each center in relation to its size. A gravity model is used to compute volume of business. Both authors were with Voorhees at the time this was published.

Lamb, D. B., "Research of Existing Land Use Models," Report No. 1045, Pittsburgh: South West Pennsylvania Regional Planning Commission (1967).

Lathrop, George T. and John R. Hamburg, "An Opportunity-Accessibility Model for Allocating Regional Growth," *Journal of the American Institute of Planners*, Vol. 31, No. 2, American Institute of Planners, 97 pp. (May,

1965). This article describes the inputs, operation, and results of a working computerized model for projecting land and transportation requirements for a metropolitan region. The model is a variation on the intervening opportunities model; the spatial distribution of an activity is seen as the successive evaluation of alternative opportunities for sites which are rank ordered in travel time from an urban center. Applications to Niagara Frontier area are given.

Lee, D. B., "Models and Techniques for Urban Planning," *CAL Rep. No. VY-2474-G.1*, Cornell Aeronautical Lab., Inc. (1969). An excellent comprehensive review of models in urban planning. The report discusses the conceptual frameworks, the techniques, the model construction and applications of urban land use models.

Leven, C., "Towards a Theory of the City," Highway Research Board Special Report, No. 97, Highway Research Board, Washington, D.C., pp. 102-115 (1968). A general discussion of the structure of a theory of the urban spatial form. The critical determinants of city form are suggested and research needs in connection with these are identified.

Little, Arthur D., Inc., "Model of San Francisco Housing Market," TP #8, San Francisco Community Renewal Program (1966). This is one part of ADL's big effort for the San Francisco Community Renewal Program (CRP). This model was constructed to simulate those factors that influence availability, price, type, and quality of San Francisco's residential space. Model matches households and housing supply. Includes a mark or model for housing deterioration; also, location characteristics, neighborhood classification, "fracts", space pressure, and housing types. Requires 2-1/2 hrs. IBM 7094 time.

Lowry, Ira S., "A Model of Metropolis," RM-4035-RC, Rand Corporation, Santa Monica (1964). Lowry's model starts with predetermined total population, location of "basic" employment, and constraints imposed on the use of land by physical and legal circumstances. His basic economy consists of industrial, commercial, and administrative establishments in which employment is externally conditioned. Allocation rules are applied to these to generate the number of households and retail employees to be assigned to each square mile of the metropolis.

Lowry, Ira S., "Seven Models of Urban Development: A Structural Comparison," Highway Research Board Special Report, No. 97, Highway Research Board, Washington, D.C., pp. 121-163 (1968), appeared earlier as P-3673, Rand Corporation — Santa Monica (1967). A review of the seven models against the backdrop of a discussion of the urban land market mechanism models are classified according to whether they deal mainly with land-use patterns, or location patterns, or land-use succession, or migration. The models discussed, and their major focus, are as follows:

(1) *Land Use*: The Chicago Area Transportation Study (CATS) Model
(2) *Land Use Succession:* The University of North Carolina Model

(3) *Location*: The EMPIRIC Model (used in Boston Regional Planning Project)

(4) *Migration*: The POLIMETRIC Model (also used in Boston project, but was abandoned in favor of EMPIRIC)

(5) *Hybrid*: The Pittsburgh Model

(6) *Market Demand*: The Penn-Jersey Model

(7) *Market Supply*: The San Francisco Model.

Lowry, Ira S., "A Short Course in Model Design," *Journal of the American Institute of Planners*, Vol. 31, No. 2, pp. 158-166 (May, 1965). This is a succinct, layman-oriented discussion of different types of models used in urban analysis. Lowry is somewhat pessimistic about the efficacy of computer models, but cautiously recommends their use as being better than doing nothing. There is an excellent review of the uses of models (description, prediction, planning), of the strategy of model design, and of the fitting of a model.

Meier, Richard L. and Richard D. Duke, "Gaming Simulation for Urban Planning," *Journal of the American Institute of Planners*, Vol. 32, No. 1, American Institute of Planners, pp. 3-16 (January, 1966). This is a general discussion of the uses of heuristic gaming in urban planning. The authors describe conditions which warrant the use of computers:

(1) Data are numerous

(2) Optimization of the balance between standard services is desired.

Mitchell, R. B. and C. Rapkin, *Urban Traffic: A Function of Land Use*, Columbia University Press, New York (1954). Recognized as one of the earliest authoritative systematic studies of the interdependence of land use, location, activity and travel interaction.

Putman, S. H., "Industrial Location Model," CRP Technical Bulletin, No. 5, Pittsburgh: Community Renewal Program, Consad Research Corporation, 21 pp. (1963). The model involves submodels which project intra-city movement of industrial activity, allocate projected employment changes by SIC to census tracts and predict birth or death of firms in the city, and do sensitivity analyses for different urban renewal plans.

Robinson, Ira M., Harry B. Wolfe, and Robert L. Barringer, "A Simulation Model for Renewal Programming," *Journal of the American Institute of Planners*, Vol. 31, No. 2, pp. 126-134 (May, 1965). This article describes another phase in the Arthur D. Little CRP simulation model for San Francisco. Discussion covers the uses (for renewal planning and programming), structure, and operations of the model. The mathematical simulation model focuses on the location decisions of different users (especially residential users) of space, the investment behavior of private investors, and public policies, programs, and actions. Transportation and accessibility not considered.

Schlager, Kenneth J., "A Land-Use Plan Design Model," *Journal of the American Institute of Planners*, Vol. 31, No. 2, American Institute of Planners, pp. 103-111 (May, 1965). Schlager describes the use of linear and dynamic programming techniques in computer models for the design of land-use plans in multi-zoned regions. Basic approach involves minimizing total public and private investment costs subject to a number of design restraints which can be manipulated.

Schlager, K. J., "A Recursive Programming Theory of the Residential Land Development Process," *Highway Research Record*, No. 126, pp. 24-32 (1966). A discussion of recursive programming as a decision framework for residential land development theory model allows for minimization of land development costs at each period, subject to constraints that land developed must equal forecast of land requirements (which is based on demand in previous period) and a level determined by a certain development rate from the previous period. The roles of the household and government are also discussed. Questions of model implementation, especially in the definition of variables and relationships, in parameter estimation, and in plan design are outlined.

Schlager, K. J., "Simulation Models in Urban and Regional Planning," *Technical Record*, Southeastern Wisconsin Regional Planning Commission, Vol 2, No. 1, 36 pp. (1964). Discussion of regional economic simulation model. Three primary classes of relationships are considered: external relationships referring to the input-output flow relationships, short-term internal relationships, and long-term internal relationships. The land-use model is subsumed by this regional model and involves five primary sectors (residential, industrial, services, special, and agricultural). Linear programming is used in allocating aggregate land demand for different lot types in each period to the model zones and also in allocating different industry types.

Schneider, M., "Access and Land Development," Highway Research Board Special Report, No. 97, Highway Research Board, Washington, D.C., pp. 164-177 (1968). A discussion of trip generation and the relationships with access, modes of travel, and the geography of places. The variable measuring those characteristics of an area which attract people to it is defined in terms of land area and floor area.

Seidman, D. R., "The Construction of an Urban Growth Model," *DVRPC Plan Report*, No. 1, DVRPC, Philadelphia, 229 pp. (1969). A detailed discussion, often technical, of the seven models developed by the Delaware Valley Regional Planning Commission for Philadelphia.

Seidman, D. R., "The Present and Futures of Urban Land-Use Models," *Proceedings Fourth Annual Conference on Urban Planning Information Systems and Programs*, pp. 119-128 (1966). Begins with review of Delaware Valley RPC activities allocation model which involves seven submodels for 192 districts in Philadelphia. Models are solved in sequence for series of five-year recursive steps, 1960-1985. Discusses calibration results and forecasting runs. Reviews other land-use models especially with respect to problems of areal aggregation and calibration, and long-range versus short-range forecasting.

Seidman, D. R., "Report on the Activities Allocation Model," P. J. Paper, No. 22, Philadelphia: Penn-Jersey Transportation Study, 27 pp. (1964). A discussion of the seven submodels which together yield projected land-uses for 1985. The projections are obtained recursively over five-year periods. The models are run in the following sequence (1) RESLOC – residential location (2) SPACEC I – residential space consumption (3) LINTA – manufacturing location (4) SPACEC-II – manufacturing space consumption (5) BALFLO – nonmanufacturing location model (6) SPACEC III – street area model.

Southeastern Wisconsin Regional Planning Commission, "A Land Use Plan Design Model, Vol. I. Model Development," Technical Report, No. 8, p. 120 (1968). Presents the first published phase of the work on the land-use design model. The linear programming model discussed in earlier reports is replaced by linear graph theory.

Southeastern Wisconsin Regional Planning Commission, "A Mathematical Approach to Urban Design," Technical Report, No. 3, 54 pp. (1966). A detailed discussion of the land-use simulation model and the related land-use plan design model. The land-use model is to provide a means of testing regional land-use plans for feasibility of implementation and is not intended primarily for forecasting. The residential sector involves the use of recursive programming to handle land development decision-making. Reports on tests of the models with regard to the 1950–1962 period of land development in Waukesha and environs.

Steger, Wilbur A., "The Pittsburgh Urban Renewal Simulation Model," *Journal of the American Institute of Planners*, Vol. 31, No. 2, American Institute of Planners, pp. 144–150 (May, 1965). This model is a modification of the (Ira S.) Lowry model for the Pittsburgh Region Economic Study. It differs in several important ways from its precursor:

(1) It predicts the location of basic industry

(2) The prediction of residential locational choice on the basis of job location, and of the location of commercial activity on the basis of residential location is made incremental and thus dependent on previous development. The second modification identifies the TOMM model.

Steger, W. A. and T. R. Lakshmanan, "Plan Evaluation Methodologies: Some Aspects of Decision Requirements and Analytical Response," Highway Research Board Special Report, No. 97, Highway Research Board, Washington, D.C., pp. 33–76 (1968). A lengthy discussion of issues related to the evaluation of plans. Specifically, the paper attempts to locate the evaluation phase in the planning process, to derive requirements for evaluation, to identify gaps between these requirements and capabilities, and to suggest appropriate long-run and short-run analytical devices addressed to these gaps.

Steger, Wilbur A., "Review of Analytic Techniques for the CRP," *Journal of the American Institute of Publishers*, Vol. 31, No. 2, 166–172 (May, 1965). Steger discusses several kinds of models which have been used in CRP studies:

(1) Controlled variation of independent variables (e.g., Baltimore, Boston, and Penn-Jersey)

(2) Simulation forecasting models (e.g., Pittsburgh and San Francisco)

(3) Mathematical optimizing models (e.g., submodels of the Penn-Jersey, Pittsburgh, and Southeastern Wisconsin Regional Planning Model).

This article seems to tie a lot of loose ends together.

Swerdloff, Carl N., "Residential Density Structure: An Analysis and Forecast With Evaluation," *Highway Research Record*, No. 207, pp. 1–21 (1967). Empirical analysis of the residential density structure of Greensboro, North Carolina. Two major lines of inquiry are pursued:

(1) Analysis of 1948 residential density structure with emphasis on mathematical forms of distance-gradients. Negative expoential forms are stressed.

(2) Comparative analysis of several attempts at forecasting the 1960 density structure by way of multiple regression analysis.

Swerdloff, C. N. and J. R. Stowers, "A Test of Some First Generation Residential Land Use Models," *Highway Research Record*, No. 126, pp. 38–59 (1966). A comparative evaluation of five operational land-use forecasting techniques, specifically the density-saturation gradient method, accessibility model, multiple regression. Stouffer's opportunity, and Schneider's opportunity formulation. Data for Greensboro, North Carolina, was used in comparing the performances of the models. Nine major conclusions: (1) the models, which did not discriminate between household types, were sufficiently accurate, (2) the models worked best when areal units contained about 2,000 persons each, (3) differences in forecasting accuracy slight, (4) simple accessibility model was the most accurate, (5) multiple regressions no better than two-variable models, (6) multiple regressions involved particular technical problems, (7) multiple nuclei seemed relevant to computation of the two opportunities models, (8) the density saturation method (used in CATS) not amenable to computerization, and (9) models are nonbehavioral and will be superceded by later forms.

Voorhees, A. M., "The Nature and Uses of Models in City Planning," *Journal of the American Institute of Planners*, Vol. 25, No. 2, pp. 57–60 (1959).

Wendt, P. F., et al., *Jobs, People and Land. Bay Area Simulation Study (BASS)*, Special Report No. 6, Center for Real Estate and Urban Economics, University of California, Berkeley, 447 pp. (1968). This simulation model for the San Francisco Bay Area involves two major components. The first is a set of employment and population submodels which take inputs of state and national economic forecasts and population parameters and generate employment forecasts for 21 industries in 13 counties for the year 2020 and also population forecasts for the same counties. These outputs are the inputs for the second component of the BASS model, the employment and residential location models. These provide for 777 subareas for the year 2020 forecasts of employment, housing units, population, and seven land uses. Simulation is used to obtain solutions to the many equations. Computer requirements IBM 7094, and more recently CDC 6400. Required 20 minutes of 7094 time per iteration.

Wilson, A. G., "Models in Urban Planning: A Synoptic Review of Recent Literature," *Urban Studies*, Vol. 5, No. 3, Oliver and Boyd: Edinburgh, pp. 249-276 (1968). Outlines a simple conceptual framework for planning within which the use of models can be studied. The framework is based on the use of an hierarchial relevance tree (highest level is *policy*, then *design*, then *understanding*). Paper delineates urban systems which can be modeled, gives rules for model design, and discusses technique problems in model construction. It is argued that models are developed at lower levels in such a hierarchy to represent understanding of the systems being planned. Recent literature is reviewed on model development for spatially aggregated population and economic systems, urban structure (land use), transport, and social systems. The possible applications of models in the design process and higher levels of the planning process is discussed.

Wolfe, Harry B., "Models for Condition Aging of Residential Structures," *Journal of the American Institute of Planners*, Vol. 33, No. 3, American Institute of Planners, pp. 192-196 (May, 1967). Wolfe is in charge of ADL's O.R. activity in San Francisco. This article describes one part of ADL's CRP simulation model of San Francisco, a method for forecasting the condition state of various types of structures as a function of time. The model is a Markov chain analysis.

Zwick, C. J., "Agency Expectations From Predictive Models," Highway Research Board Special Report, No. 97, Highway Research Board, Washington, D.C., pp. 24-30 (1968). Begins with a review of certain questions on model building, specifically (1) What models are we talking about? (2) Models for what purpose? (3) Models are useful for making what kinds of decisions? (4) Models are amoral. The author then considers what kinds of decisions must be made in the area of urban development and the time-frame for decision making with reference to the Bureau of the Budget's position and the probable future decisions in urban transportation.

Appendix B

**Computer Utilization
and Model Development
in Urban Planning Programs**[a]

To develop a better information base on the use of models in urban planning programs a survey was undertaken to provide information on the state of the art of urban model development and computer utilization by metropolitan planning agencies. This survey was intended to supplement information developed at the "Models of Urban Structure Conference". Questionnaires were sent to 226 regional and metropolitan planning commissions in an effort to obtain a complete survey. The source listing of agencies was the *1969 Directory of Regional Councils,* published by the National Service to Regional Councils, and the *Directory of Urbanized Area Transportation Planning Programs,* prepared by the U.S. Department of Transportation. Each agency selected is responsible for the development of a comprehensive land use and/or transportation plan for the region or metropolitan area. The results of the survey are hopefully representative of not only those agencies which responded, but of all regional planning agencies.

Responses were received from 91 of the 226 agencies surveyed (40 percent). Twenty-seven agencies indicated that no models or computer facilities are being used at present; furthermore, no model or computer utilization is planned in the future. Thirteen agencies have no computer usage planned for the future, but may use hand-computed models, while 25 agencies are not using computers now, but expect to be utilizing them in the future. Twenty-six agencies reported they are currently using computers for model development, data storage and processing. The questionnaire analysis, therefore, is based on the replies of those 64 agencies which are presently utilizing, or plan to utilize in the future, land-use models and/or computer facilities.

Table B-1 indicates four population size classes representing the total population served by each of the 64 agencies. It is evident that the Battelle survey has received responses from a wide range of metropolitan and regional planning agencies, in terms of the population size of the areas being served. We hope, then, that the results of our analysis may be regarded as representative of the entire urban planning profession.

---

[a]Prepared and analyzed by Robert W. Cobb and David C. Sweet.

Table B-1
Population Served by Responding Agencies

Population	Number of Agencies
0 – 100,000	11
100,000 – 250,000	25
250,000 – 500,000	15
500,000 or more	13

Source: Battelle-Columbus Computer Utilization Survey

Computer Usage in Urban Planning

Facilities, Staffing, and Time

Since only 51 of the 91 agencies surveyed are presently using or planning to use computers, one might assume computer utilization is not always associated with the planning process. Only in large metropolitan areas with sizable planning operations is there a tendency for the widespread use of computers. Most of the agencies reporting computer usage utilize small computers for data storage and data processing (less than 32K storage) and larger computers for model forecasting and testing and evaluation procedures (greater than 64K storage).

Only four agencies reported in-house computer facilities — most use small computers located in other public agencies and rent time on larger computers from a service bureau or local agency. Just over one-third of the agencies had staff members who are responsible for developing and maintaining their data files; most have been developed by outside consultants. Only nine agencies reported they employ full-time systems men. Average usage of computers varied widely. Smaller agencies reported less than five hours use per week, while large agencies actively engaged in model development reported usage in excess of 20 hours per week. Most agencies expect an increase in future usage as information systems are developed.

Data Storage and Retrieval

Most agencies do not have a fully developed data bank, but there are varying levels of sophistication in data collection and storage techniques. Table B-2 shows those variables which are most commonly collected by planning agencies.

The variables most often found in data files are land use, population, employment, housing, transportation network, traffic volume, school enumeration, and origin-destination. Only land use is found in the data files of all 26 planning agencies which report computer utilization. It is expected that

Table B-2
Data Collected by Planning Agencies

Type of Data	Number of Agencies
Agriculture	6
Assessment	9
Employment	20
Health	2
Housing	19
Land Use	26
Land Value	10
Migration	6
Origin Destination	15
Personal Income	10
Population	23
Production and Other Economic Data (Input/Output)	2
Retail Sales	7
School	16
Shopping Trip Behavior	10
Transportation Network	18
Traffic Volume	17
Welfare	1
Zoning	9

Source: Battelle-Columbus Computer Utilization Survey

extensive use of census data in the future will give more standardization to data files. A number of reporting agencies indicated that they would be acquiring the DIME file for storage and retrieval of census and other data. The DIME file should speed up the development of well integrated information systems.

Computer Mapping

Several agencies reported the use of computer graphics to display results of data collection and manipulation. The most common used device is the line printer, and lesser use is reported with the pen plotter and cathode-ray-tube plotter. Computer mapping programs in use include SYMAP and Map 01, both of which are adapted for the line printer.

Additional Data

When asked what additional data would be most beneficial to the planning process, the agencies reported the following:

1. collection of socio-economic and land-use data which affect modal split would add to trip generation and trip distribution models;
2. better utility and local governmental administration data; and
3. more reliable data need to be collected concerning household income and consumer expenditures.

Land-Use and Transportation Models

Development and Operation

Twenty-six agencies reported the use of urban development models, 17 involving transportation models, and 9 employing existing land-use models. Only 8 of the above agencies have originally developed either a land-use or transportation model.

The majority of agencies chose to contract with a consultant for the utilization of an existing model package which could be used without making any significant program modifications. Most often mentioned was the Bureau of Public Roads (BPR) transportation package which has been operationalized by a number of state highway departments, service bureaus, and consulting agencies. A number of land-use models have been used, most of which are merely allocation models for population, occupation, and employment. The most commonly used data collection methods involved special surveys such as origin-destination and land-use surveys. These are often very costly, as evidenced by their infrequency of collection, usually at 5- or 10-year intervals. The traffic analysis zone is the areal unit which is most often used for data collection purposes, followed by census tracts and origin destination zones.

Only five agencies reported data collection by parcel in their land-use models. Most agencies responding to the questionnaire felt that additional data are either essentially necessary or are desirable but not critical. Only one-third felt that additional data would not add to the model; most of these comments, however, were concerned with the data requirements for the BPR transportation package.

A significant finding was that the development and operationalization of land-use and transportation models require many man-months of agency time, therefore restricting model development to those agencies with large operations, large specialized staff, and budgets which will allow for model development and calibration. A typical example of model development indicates that 2 to 3 years are required to develop and operationalize an urban land-use model. In addition, data collection requirements for the model are often time consuming and therefore quite costly. An additional drawback to model development for many agencies is that a model developed for one urban area may not be suitable for another urban area. According to the results of the questionnaire, it appears that recalibration may involve nearly as much time as the original model development.

Techniques most often used in land-use models are linear regression, factor analysis, and recursive programming. In the transportation packages a basic Fratar model or gravity model may be found. Only six agencies reported the use of sensitivity analysis of output given certain changes in inputs and parameters.

Reliability of Models

When asked if they felt that existing models were useful in terms of policy formation, most agencies replied they had only average confidence in actions taken as a result of predictions of a model; yet the results of the model had high influence in policy formation. In addition, nearly all respondents indicated that they would be using the model in the future.

The comparative role of land-use vs. transportation models is by no means distinct. Respondents were divided when asked to give the relative importance of land-use and transportation studies. It appears they are of equal value when planning decisions are made.

Future Needs and Model Development

Respondents were asked to indicate whether each of a series of statements is of vital concern, desirable but not vital, or of little relevance to future needs of planning agencies. Most often mentioned as vital to the urban decision-making process is the need for better information systems. Associated with this general feeling is the plea for "good, reliable small-area data", better data updating techniques, and the development of census tapes as they become available.

Regarding model development, most agencies would like to obtain a model to quantify impacts of proposed land-use changes. Of secondary importance here is the need for better forecast and allocation models, which tends to point out the dissatisfaction with existing forecast and allocation models.

Desirable model characteristics are commensurate with overall future needs of planning agencies, namely the capability of being updated annually. Also desirable is that the model be more sensitive to basic data such as employment, income, trip generations, etc.

A summary of the statements regarding future needs, model development, and model characteristics may be found in the questionnaire analysis at the end of this appendix.

APPENDIX B

Battelle-Columbus
Computer Utilization Questionnaire

Please indicate the names of the persons responding to this questionnaire:

   Name_____
   Position_____

   Name_____
   Position_____

   Agency_____
   Address_____
   _____
   _____
   _____

   Date_____

Would you be interested in receiving a copy of the results of this questionnaire?

   Yes_____   No_____

Directions: Please answer the following questions as accurately and concisely as possible. If additional space is needed, use last page and indicate question number.

I. Computer Use

   1. Are computer facilities presently being used by your agency? Yes 26   No 38

       If No, is the use of computers planned for in the future? Yes 25   No_____ (Skip to Section II)
       If Yes, what system is used for the following:

	Manufacturer	Model	Core
Data storage and retrieval			
Data processing			
Forecasting models			
Testing and evaluation procedures			

   2. Of the above facilities, which are located in-house? _____
       _____

   3. Who is responsible for developing and maintaining your data files?
       Staff members   12
       Outside consultants   2
       Combination of the above   14
       Do you have a full-time systems man? Yes 9   No_____

QUESTIONNAIRE

4. What is the estimated average usage of computer facilities (hr/wk)?

Machine	Hr/wk	Will usage increase in future?

What proportion of your agency's total budget is allocated to computer usage? _____

5. What types of data are presently in your data files, and are you able to update these data?

	In Data File		Able to Update	
Type of Data	Yes	No	Yes	No
Agriculture	6		5	
Assessment	9		7	
Employment	20		12	
Health	2		1	
Housing	19		13	
Land Use	26		18	
Land Value	10		8	
Migration	6		2	
Origin Destination	15		6	
Personal Income	10		5	
Population	23		14	
Production and Other Economic Data (Input/Output)	2		0	
Retail Sales	7		4	
School	16		10	
Shopping Trip Behavior	10		4	
Transportation Network	18		12	
Traffic Volume	17		11	
Welfare	1		0	
Zoning	9		6	
Other _____				
Other _____				

6. What methods of graphic display are computerized by your agency, i.e., point plotters, computer mapping, scattergrams, etc.?

250   APPENDIX B

II. Land-Use and Transportation Models
     Complete the following questions for each land-use model and for each transportation model being used by your agency.

   1. What is the model name? _____

   2. What is the origin of the model?
         __8__ The model was originally developed by this agency.
         __7__ The model was originally developed by a consultant for this agency. (Name of consultant _____ consultant _____)
         __6__ The model was developed, operationalized, and run, and the results were analyzed, by a consultant. (Name of consultant _____)
         __10__ The model is a canned program obtained from another planning agency or consultant (please specify source _____) and is used without making significant program modifications.
         __3__ The model was originally developed by another agency, but significant modifications have been made by this agency (please specify source _____).

   3. Give a brief description of the purpose and objectives of the model.

   4. What methods of data collection were used to obtain input data and calibration data for the model?
         __25__ Census
         __22__ Other published data
         __35__ Special survey

   5. What areal units have been used for data collection?
         __14__ Census tracts
         __8__ Census blocks
         __5__ Parcels
         __7__ Square grid units
         __23__ Traffic zones
         __11__ Origin-destination zones
         _____ Other (specify _____)

   6. What would be the incremental value of additional data to the model?
         __4__ Additional data are essentially necessary.
         __14__ Additional data are desirable but not critical.
         __9__ Additional data would not add to the model.
      What additional data would be most useful?

QUESTIONNAIRE

251

13. Assuming that you are forecasting the state of a system, what level of confidence do you have in actions taken as a result of the predictions of the model?
    - ___8___ A high degree of confidence
    - ___14___ Average confidence
    - ___0___ A low degree of confidence
    - ___0___ No confidence

14. List any observed practical limitations of the model.

15. Evaluate the usefulness of the model in terms of policy formation for your agency.
    - ___1___ Very high influence
    - ___17___ High influence
    - ___12___ Medium influence
    - ___4___ Low influence
    - ___0___ No influence

16. Will you be using this model in the future? Yes ___32___ No _____

17. If applicable, to what extent does the transportation model dictate the output of the land-use model?
    - ___0___ Almost entirely
    - ___6___ To a large extent
    - ___6___ To a moderate extent
    - ___5___ Somewhat
    - ___3___ Not at all

18. In your agency, land-use studies:
    - ___7___ Are more important than transportation studies in planning decisions.
    - ___10___ Have equal value with transportation studies in planning decisions.
    - ___6___ Reinforce decisions made as the result of transportation studies.
    - _____ Have little influence on planning decisions.

Future Needs and Model Development:

Directions: Indicate the degree to which you think each of the statements in this section needs more emphasis in the future of urban decision making. Assign a value of 1 if the statement is of vital concern, 2 if the statement is desirable but not vital, or 3 if the statement is of little relevance to future needs.

1. Future Needs:

1	2	3		
29	21	4	1.	More effective use of the relationship between aggregate forecasts and allocation to small areas is needed.
23	27	5	2.	Planners and computer programmers need to work more closely together.
20	17	13	3.	A coordinate grid system, instead of census tracts, census blocks or traffic zones, is needed to identify the specific location of all urban activities.
19	17	13	4.	Sensitivity analysis should be included in all model evaluation.
39	3	13	5.	Land-use and transportation models need to incorporate, to a greater extent, planning policy.
40	14	1	6.	More effort toward data updating is required.
10	28	15	7.	Planning agencies need more full-time computer-systems men.
42	9	1	8.	Planners need good, reliable small-area data.
30	23	2	9.	New policy-oriented land-use and transportation models need to be developed.
50	7	-	10.	Planning agencies need better information systems.
35	19	2	11.	Newly developed census tapes should be utilized as they become available.

2. Model Development: What kinds of models need to be developed to satisfy the expected needs of your agency?

30	13	4	1.	Better forecast and allocation models.
28	15	6	2.	Agencies must obtain data at the parcel, block face, or census block level and then aggregate to tracts, traffic zones, etc.
9	19	13	3.	Behavioral models – macro level.
10	15	19	4.	Behavioral models – micro level.
31	11	4	5.	Simpler models which are cheaper to run and therefore may be updated more frequently.
20	20	8	6.	A standardized package of land-use models similar to the Bureau of Public Roads transportation package.
39	12	1	7.	A model to quantify impacts of proposed land-use changes.
1	2	26	8.	No new models need be developed to satisfy the needs of this agency.

3. Model Characteristics: What would be the operating characteristics of these future models?

39	10	1	1.	Capability of updating annually.
25	11	12	2.	Capability of being run by a single employee of this agency.
32	16	-	3.	More sensitive to basic data such as employment, income, trip generations, etc.
24	18	4	4.	Better adapted to utilize existing data files.